Texts and Monographs in Computer Science

Texts and Monographs in Computer Science

(continued after index)

A Practical Theory of Programming

Eric C.R. Hehner

Springer Science+Business Media, LLC

Eric C.R. Hehner
Department of Computer Science
University of Toronto
Toronto, Ontario M5S 1A4
Canada

Series Editors:

David Gries
Department of Computer Science
Cornell University
Upson Hall
Ithaca, NY 14853-7501
USA

Fred B. Schneider
Department of Computer Science
Cornell University
Upson Hall
Ithaca, NY 14853-7501
USA

With ten illustrations.

Library of Congress Cataloging-in-Publication Data
Hehner, Eric C. R.
    A practical theory of programming / Eric C.R. Hehner.
        p.   cm. — (Texts and monographs in computer science)
    Includes bibliographical references and index.
    ISBN 978-0-387-94106-6   ISBN 978-1-4419-8596-5 (eBook)
    DOI 10.1007/978-1-4419-8596-5
    1. Programming (Electronic computers).   I. Title.   II. Series.
QA76.6.H428   1993
005.1—dc20   93-5269

Printed on acid-free paper.

© 1993 Springer Science+Business Media New York
Originally published by Springer-Verlag New York, Inc. in 1993

Camera-ready copy prepared from the author's PostScript files using MacWrite.

9 8 7 6 5 4 3 2 1

ISBN 978-0-387-94106-6

Contents

0 Preface

Introduction

What good is a theory of programming? Who wants one? Thousands of programmers program every day without any theory. Why should they bother to learn one? The answer is the same as for any other theory. For example, why should anyone learn a theory of motion? You can move around perfectly well without one. You can throw a ball without one. Yet we think it important enough to teach a theory of motion in high school.

One answer is that a mathematical theory gives a much greater degree of precision by providing a method of calculation. It is unlikely that we could send a rocket to Jupiter without a mathematical theory of motion. And even baseball pitchers are finding that their pitch can be improved by hiring an expert who knows some theory. Similarly a lot of mundane programming can be done without the aid of a theory, but the more difficult programming is very unlikely to be done correctly without a good theory. The software industry has an overwhelming experience of buggy programs to support that statement. And even mundane programming can be improved by the use of a theory.

Another answer is that a theory provides a kind of understanding. Our ability to control and predict motion changes from an art to a science when we learn a mathematical theory. Similarly programming changes from an art to a science when we learn to understand programs in the same way we understand mathematical theorems. With a scientific outlook, we change our view of the world. We attribute less to spirits or chance, and increase our understanding of what is possible and what is not. It is a valuable part of education for anyone.

Professional engineering maintains its high reputation in our society by insisting that, to be a professional engineer, one must know and apply the relevant theories. A civil engineer must know and apply the theories of geometry and material stress. An electrical engineer must know and apply electromagnetic theory. Software engineers, to be worthy of the name, must know and apply a theory of programming.

The subject of this book sometimes goes by the name "programming methodology", sometimes "science of programming", "logic of programming", "theory of programming", "formal methods of program development", or "verification". It concerns those aspects of programming that are amenable to mathematical proof. A good theory helps us to write precise specifications, and to design programs whose executions provably satisfy the specifications. We will be considering the state of a computation, the time of a computation, and the interactions with a computation. There are other important aspects of software design and production that are not touched by this book: the management of people, the user interface, documentation, and testing.

There are several theories of programming. The first usable theory, often called "Hoare's Logic", is still probably the most widely known. In it, a specification is a pair of predicates: a precondition and postcondition (these and all technical terms will be defined in due course). Another popular and closely related theory by Dijkstra uses the weakest precondition predicate transformer, which is a function from programs and postconditions to preconditions. Jones's Vienna Development Method has been used to advantage in some industries; in it, a specification is a pair of predicates (as in Hoare's Logic), but the second predicate is a relation. Temporal Logic is yet another formalism that introduces some special operators and quantifiers to describe some aspects of computation.

The theory in this book is simpler than any of those just mentioned. In it, a specification is just a boolean expression. Refinement is just ordinary implication. This theory is also more general than those just mentioned, applying to both terminating and nonterminating computation, to both sequential and parallel computation, to both stand-alone and interactive computation. And it includes time bounds, both for algorithm classification and for tightly constrained real-time applications.

———End of Introduction

Quick Tour

All technical terms used in this book are explained in this book. Each new term that you should learn is underlined. As much as possible, the terminology is descriptive rather than honorary (notable exception: "boolean"). There are no abbreviations, acronyms, or other obscurities of language to annoy you. No specific previous mathematical knowledge or programming experience is assumed. However, the preparatory material on booleans, numbers, lists, and functions in Chapters 1, 2, and 3 is brief, and previous exposure might be helpful.

The following chart shows the dependence of each chapter on previous chapters.

$$1 \longrightarrow 2 \longrightarrow 3 \longrightarrow 4 \begin{array}{c} \nearrow 5 \\ \longrightarrow 6 \longrightarrow 7 \\ \searrow \\ 8 \longrightarrow 9 \end{array}$$

Chapter 4, Program Theory, is the heart of the book. After that, chapters may be selected or omitted according to interest and the chart. The only deviations from the chart are that Chapter 9 uses variable declaration (**var**) presented in the first section of Chapter 5, and a small optional section within Chapter 9 depends on Chapter 6.

Chapter 10 consists entirely of exercises grouped according to the chapter in which the necessary theory is presented. All the exercises in the section "Program Theory" can be done according to the methods presented in Chapter 4; however, as new notations and methods are presented in later chapters, those same exercises can be redone taking advantage of the later material.

At the back of the book, Chapter 11 contains reference material. The first section, "Justifications", answers questions about earlier chapters, such as: why was this presented that way? why was this presented at all? why wasn't something else presented instead? It may be of interest to teachers and researchers who already know enough theory of programming to ask such questions. It is probably not of interest to students who are meeting formal methods for the first time. If you find yourself asking such questions, don't hesitate to consult the Justifications.

Chapter 11 also contains an index of terminology and a complete list of all laws used in the book. To a serious student of programming, these laws should become friends, on a first name basis. The final pages list all the notations used in the book. You are not expected to know these notations before reading the book; they are all explained as we come to them. You are welcome to invent new notations if you explain their use. Sometimes the choice of notation makes all the difference in our ability to solve a problem.

Transparency masters and solutions to exercises are available to course instructors from the author.

————————————————————————————————————End of Quick Tour

Acknowledgments

For inspiration and guidance I thank Working Group 2.3 (Programming Methodology) of the International Federation for Information Processing, particularly Edsger Dijkstra, David Gries, John Guttag, Tony Hoare, Jim Horning, Cliff Jones, Bill McKeeman, Carroll Morgan, Greg Nelson, John Reynolds, Wlad Turski. I thank my graduate students and teaching assistants from whom I have learned so much, especially Ray Blaak, Lorene Gupta, Chris Lengauer, Andrew Malton, Theo Norvell, Alan Rosenthal. For their critical and helpful reading of the first draft I am most grateful to Wim Hesselink, Jim Horning, Jan van de Snepscheut. For good ideas I thank Ralph Back, Eike Best, Jo Ebergen, Wim Feijen, Netty van Gasteren, Nicolas Halbwachs, Gilles Kahn, Alain Martin, Martin Rem, Pierre-Yves Schobbens, Mary Shaw, Bob Tennent, Jan Tijmen Udding. For reading the draft and suggesting improvements I thank Jules Desharnais, Andy Gravell, Peter Lauer, Ali Mili, Bernhard Möller, Helmut Partsch, Jørgen Steensgaard-Madsen, Norbert Völker. I thank my class for finding errors.

————————————————————————————————————End of Acknowledgments

This book is dedicated to my daughter, Amanda Susan, who at age 3 already shows signs of the organization and attention to detail of a good programmer.

————————————————————————————————————End of Preface

1   Basic Theories

Boolean Theory

Boolean Theory, also known as logic, was designed as an aid to reasoning, and we will use it to reason about computation. The expressions of Boolean Theory are called <u>boolean</u> expressions. We divide boolean expressions into two classes; those in one class are called <u>theorem</u>s, and those in the other are called <u>antitheorems</u>.

The expressions of Boolean Theory can be used to represent statements about the world; the theorems represent true statements, and the antitheorems represent false statements. That is the original application of the theory, the one it was designed for, and the one that supplies most of the terminology. Another application for which Boolean Theory is perfectly suited is digital circuit design. In that application, boolean expressions represent circuits; theorems represent circuits with high voltage output, and antitheorems represent circuits with low voltage output.

The two simplest boolean expressions are $\top$ and $\bot$. The first one, $\top$, is a theorem, and the second one, $\bot$, is an antitheorem. When Boolean Theory is being used for its original purpose, we pronounce $\top$ as "true" and $\bot$ as "false" because the former represents an arbitrary true statement and the latter represents an arbitrary false statement. When Boolean Theory is being used for digital circuit design, we pronounce $\top$ and $\bot$ as "high voltage" and "low voltage", or as "power" and "ground". They are sometimes called the "boolean values"; they may also be called the "nullary boolean operators", meaning that they have no operands.

There are four unary (one operand) boolean operators, of which only one is interesting. Its symbol is $\neg$, pronounced "not". It is a prefix operator (placed before its operand). An expression of the form $\neg x$ is called a <u>negation</u>. If we negate a theorem we obtain an antitheorem; if we negate an antitheorem we obtain a theorem. This is depicted by the following <u>truth table</u>.

$$
\begin{array}{c|cc}
 & \top & \bot \\
\hline
\neg & \bot & \top
\end{array}
$$

Above the horizontal line, $\top$ means that the operand is a theorem, and $\bot$ means that the operand is an antitheorem. Below the horizontal line, $\top$ means that the result is a theorem, and $\bot$ means that the result is an antitheorem.

There are sixteen binary (two operand) boolean operators. Mainly due to tradition, we will use only six of them, though they are not the only interesting ones. These operators are infix (placed between their operands). Here are the symbols and some pronunciations; for each symbol, the first pronunciation is the preferred one.

∧	"and"
∨	"or"
⇒	"implies", "is as strong as", "is equal to or stronger than"
⇐	"follows from", "is implied by", "is as weak as", "is weaker than or equal to"
=	"equals", "if and only if"
⧧	"differs from", "is unequal to", "exclusive or", "boolean plus"

An expression of the form $x \wedge y$ is called a <u>conjunction</u>, and the operands x and y are called <u>conjunct</u>s. An expression of the form $x \vee y$ is called a <u>disjunction</u>, and the operands are called <u>disjunct</u>s. An expression of the form $x \Rightarrow y$ is called an <u>implication</u>, x is called the <u>antecedent</u>, and y is called the <u>consequent</u>. An expression of the form $x \Leftarrow y$ is also called an implication, but now x is the consequent and y is the antecedent. An expression of the form $x = y$ is called an <u>equation</u>, and the operands are called the <u>left side</u> and the <u>right side</u>. An expression of the form $x \neq y$ is called an <u>unequation</u>, and again the operands are called the left side and the right side.

The following truth table shows how the classification of boolean expressions formed with binary operators can be obtained from the classification of the operands. Above the horizontal line, the pair $\top\top$ means that both operands are theorems; the pair $\top\perp$ means that the left operand is a theorem and the right operand is an antitheorem; and so on. Below the horizontal line, $\top$ means that the result is a theorem, and $\perp$ means that the result is an antitheorem.

	$\top\top$	$\top\perp$	$\perp\top$	$\perp\perp$
∧	$\top$	$\perp$	$\perp$	$\perp$
∨	$\top$	$\top$	$\top$	$\perp$
⇒	$\top$	$\perp$	$\top$	$\top$
⇐	$\top$	$\top$	$\perp$	$\top$
=	$\top$	$\perp$	$\perp$	$\top$
⧧	$\perp$	$\top$	$\top$	$\perp$

Infix operators make some expressions ambiguous. For example, $\perp \wedge \top \vee \top$ might be read as the conjunction $\perp \wedge \top$, which is an antitheorem, disjoined with $\top$, resulting in a theorem. Or it might be read as $\perp$ conjoined with the disjunction $\top \vee \top$, resulting in an antitheorem. To say which is meant, we can use parentheses: either $(\perp \wedge \top) \vee \top$ or $\perp \wedge (\top \vee \top)$. To prevent a clutter of parentheses, we employ a table of precedence levels, listed on the final page of the book. In the table, $\wedge$ can be found on level 9, and $\vee$ on level 10; that means, in the absence of parentheses, apply $\wedge$ before $\vee$. The example $\perp \wedge \top \vee \top$ is therefore a theorem.

Each of the operators $=$ $\Rightarrow$ $\Leftarrow$ appears twice in the precedence table. The large versions $=$ $\Rightarrow$ $\Leftarrow$ on level 14 are applied after all other operators. Except for precedence, the small versions and large versions of these operators are identical. Used with restraint, these duplicate operators can sometimes improve readability by reducing the parenthesis clutter still further. But a word of caution: a few well-chosen parentheses, even if they are unnecessary according to precedence, can help us see structure. Judgment is required.

There are 256 ternary (three operand) operators, of which we show only one. It is called <u>conditional composition</u>, and written **if** x **then** y **else** z . Here is its truth table.

	$\top\top\top$	$\top\top\bot$	$\top\bot\top$	$\top\bot\bot$	$\bot\top\top$	$\bot\top\bot$	$\bot\bot\top$	$\bot\bot\bot$
if then else	$\top$	$\top$	$\bot$	$\bot$	$\top$	$\bot$	$\top$	$\bot$

For every natural number n , there are 2^{2^n} operators of n operands, but we now have quite enough.

When we stated earlier that a conjunction is an expression of the form $x\wedge y$, we were using $x\wedge y$ to stand for all expressions obtained by replacing the <u>variable</u>s x and y with arbitrary boolean expressions. For example, we might replace x with $(\bot \Rightarrow \neg(\bot \vee \top))$ and replace y with $(\bot \vee \top)$ to obtain the conjunction

$$(\bot \Rightarrow \neg(\bot \vee \top)) \wedge (\bot \vee \top)$$

Replacing a variable with an expression is called <u>substitution</u> or <u>instantiation</u>. With the understanding that variables are there to be replaced, we admit variables into our expressions, being careful of the following three points.

• We sometimes have to insert parentheses around expressions that are replacing variables in order to maintain the precedence of operators. In the example of the preceding paragraph, we replaced a conjunct x with an implication $\bot \Rightarrow \neg(\bot \vee \top)$; since conjunction comes before implication in the precedence table, we had to enclose the implication in parentheses. We also replaced a conjunct y with a disjunction $\bot \vee \top$, so we had to enclose the disjunction in parentheses.

• When the same variable occurs more than once in an expression, it must be replaced by the same expression at each occurrence. From $x \wedge x$ we can obtain $\top \wedge \top$, but not $\top \wedge \bot$.

• We are free to replace different variables by the same expression. From $x\wedge y$ we can obtain $\top \wedge \top$.

As we present other theories, we will introduce new boolean expressions that make use of the expressions of those theories, and classify the new boolean expressions. For example, when we present Number Theory we will introduce the number expressions 1+1 and 2 , and the boolean expression 1+1=2 , and we will classify it as a theorem. We never intend to classify a boolean expression as both a theorem and an antitheorem. A statement about the world cannot be both true and (in the same sense) false; a circuit's output cannot be both high and low voltage. If, by accident, we do classify a boolean expression both ways, we have made a serious error. But it is perfectly legitimate to leave a boolean expression unclassified. For example, $0/0=5$ will be neither a theorem nor an antitheorem. An unclassified boolean expression may correspond to a statement whose truth or falsity we do not know or do not care about, or to a circuit whose output we cannot predict. A theory is called <u>consistent</u> if no boolean expression is both a theorem and an antitheorem, and <u>inconsistent</u> if some boolean expression is both a theorem and an antitheorem. A theory is called <u>complete</u> if every fully instantiated boolean expression is either a theorem or an antitheorem, and <u>incomplete</u> if some fully instantiated boolean expression is neither a theorem nor an antitheorem.

Axioms and Proof Rules

To prove that a boolean expression is a theorem, or to prove that it is an antitheorem, we must follow the five rules of proof. We state them first, then discuss them after.

<u>Axiom Rule</u>   If a boolean expression is an axiom, then it is a theorem. If a boolean expression is an antiaxiom, then it is an antitheorem.

<u>Evaluation Rule</u>   If all the boolean subexpressions of a boolean expression are classified, then it is classified according to the truth tables.

<u>Completion Rule</u>   If a boolean expression contains unclassified boolean subexpressions, and all ways of classifying them place it in the same class, then it is in that class.

<u>Consistency Rule</u>   If a classified boolean expression contains boolean subexpressions, and at most one way of classifying them is consistent, then they are classified that way.

<u>Instance Rule</u>   If a boolean expression is classified, then all its instances have that same classification.

We present a theory by saying what its expressions are, and what its theorems and antitheorems are. An <u>axiom</u> is a boolean expression that is stated to be a theorem. An <u>antiaxiom</u> is similarly a boolean expression stated to be an antitheorem. The only axiom of Boolean Theory is $\top$ and the only antiaxiom is $\bot$. So, by the Axiom Rule, $\top$ is a theorem and $\bot$ is an antitheorem.

Before the invention of formal logic, the word "axiom" was used for a statement whose truth was supposed to be obvious. In modern mathematics, an axiom is part of the design and presentation of a theory. Different axioms may yield different theories, and different theories may have different applications. When we design a theory, we can choose any axioms we like, but a bad choice can result in a useless theory.

The first entry in the truth table for the binary operators does not say $\top \wedge \top = \top$. It says that the conjunction of any two theorems is a theorem. To prove that $\top \wedge \top = \top$ is a theorem requires the boolean axiom (to prove that $\top$ is a theorem), the first entry in the truth table (to prove that $\top \wedge \top$ is a theorem), and the first entry on the $=$ row of the truth table (to prove that $\top \wedge \top = \top$ is a theorem).

The boolean expression

$\quad\quad \top \vee x$

contains an unclassified boolean subexpression, so we cannot use the Evaluation Rule to tell us which class it is in. If x were a theorem, the Evaluation Rule would say that the whole expression is a theorem. If x were an antitheorem, the Evaluation Rule would again say that the whole expression is a theorem. We can therefore conclude by the Completion Rule that the whole expression is indeed a theorem. The Completion Rule also says that

$\quad\quad x \vee \neg x$

is a theorem, and when we come to Number Theory, that

$\quad\quad 0/0 = 5 \vee \neg\, 0/0 = 5$

is a theorem. We do not need to know that a subexpression is unclassified to use the Completion Rule. If we are ignorant of the classification of a subexpression, and we suppose it to be unclassified, any conclusion we come to by the use of the Completion Rule will still be correct.

In a classified boolean expression, if it would be inconsistent to place a boolean subexpression in one class, then the Consistency Rule says it is in the other class. For example, suppose we know that *expression0* is a theorem, and that *expression0* $\Rightarrow$ *expression1* is also a theorem. Can we determine what class *expression1* is in? If *expression1* were an antitheorem, then by the Evaluation Rule *expression0* $\Rightarrow$ *expression1* would be an antitheorem, and that would be inconsistent. So, by the Consistency Rule, *expression1* is a theorem. This use of the Consistency Rule is traditionally called "detachment" or "modus ponens". As another example, if $\neg$*expression* is a theorem, then the Consistency Rule says that *expression* is an antitheorem.

Thanks to the negation operator and the Consistency Rule, we never need to talk about antitheorems. Instead of saying that *expression* is an antitheorem, we can say that $\neg$*expression* is a theorem. But a word of caution: if a theory is incomplete, it is possible that neither *expression* nor $\neg$*expression* is a theorem. Thus "antitheorem" is not the same as "not a theorem". Our preference for theorems over antitheorems encourages some shortcuts of speech. We sometimes state a boolean expression, such as $1+1=2$, without saying anything about it; when we do so, we mean that it is a theorem. We sometimes say we will prove something, meaning we will prove it is a theorem.

───End of Axioms and Proof Rules

With our two axioms ($\top$ and $\neg\bot$) and five proof rules we can now prove theorems. Some theorems are useful enough to be given a name and be memorized, or at least be kept in a handy list. Such a theorem is called a <u>law</u>. Some laws of Boolean Theory are listed at the back of the book. Laws concerning $\Leftarrow$ have not been included, but any law that uses $\Rightarrow$ can be easily rearranged into one using $\Leftarrow$. All of them can be proven using the Completion Rule, classifying the variables in all possible ways, and evaluating each way. When the number of variables is more than about 2, this kind of proof is quite inefficient. It is much better to prove new laws by making use of already proven old laws. In the next subsection we see how.

Expression and Proof Format

The precedence table on the final page of this book tells how to parse an expression in the absence of parentheses. To help the eye group the symbols properly, it is a good idea to leave space for absent parentheses. Consider the following two ways of spacing the same expression.

$a{\wedge}b \vee c$

$a \wedge b{\vee}c$

According to our rules of precedence, the parentheses belong around $a{\wedge}b$, so the first spacing is helpful and the second misleading.

An expression that is too long to fit on one line must be broken into parts. There are several reasonable ways to do it; here is one suggestion. A long expression in parentheses can be broken at its main connective, which is placed under the opening parenthesis. For example,

$(\quad$ *first part*

$\wedge\quad$ *second part* $\quad)$

A long expression without parentheses can be broken at its main connective, which is placed under where the opening parenthesis belongs. For example,

first part

$=\quad$ *second part*

Attention to format makes a big difference in our ability to understand a complex expression.

A proof may be written in the following format.

	expression0	short hint 0
$=$	*expression1*	short hint 1
$=$	*expression2*	short hint 2
$=$	*expression3*	short hint 3

On the left side of the page is a continuing equation. If we did not use equations in this continuing fashion, we would have to write

expression0 = expression1

$\wedge\quad$ *expression1 = expression2*

$\wedge\quad$ *expression2 = expression3*

We intend it to be clear that this continuing equation is a theorem. The hints on the right side of the page are used, when necessary, to help make it clear. The "short hint 0" is supposed to make it clear that *expression0 = expression1* is a theorem. The "short hint 1" is supposed to make it clear that *expression1 = expression2* is a theorem. And so on. If the theorem to be proven is *expression0 = expression3* , then there is no "short hint 3", and the theorem to be proven follows from the transitivity of = . If the theorem to be proven is *expression0* , then "short hint 3" is supposed to make it clear that *expression3* is a theorem, and the theorem to be proven follows from the transitivity of = and the Consistency Rule.

Here is an example. Suppose we want to prove the first Law of Portation

$$a \wedge b \Rightarrow c \;=\; a \Rightarrow (b \Rightarrow c)$$

Here is a proof.

	$a \wedge b \Rightarrow c$	Material Implication
$=$	$\neg(a \wedge b) \vee c$	Duality
$=$	$\neg a \vee \neg b \vee c$	Material Implication
$=$	$a \Rightarrow \neg b \vee c$	Material Implication
$=$	$a \Rightarrow (b \Rightarrow c)$	

From the first line of the proof, we are told to use "Material Implication", which is the first of the Laws of Inclusion. This law says that an implication can be changed to a disjunction if we also negate the antecedent. Doing so, we obtain the second line of the proof. The hint now is "Duality", and we see that the third line is obtained by replacing $\neg(a \wedge b)$ with $\neg a \vee \neg b$ in accordance with the first of the Duality Laws. By not using parentheses on the third line, we silently use the Associative Law of disjunction, in preparation for the next step. The next hint is again "Material Implication"; this time it is used in the opposite direction, to replace the first disjunction with an implication. And once more, "Material Implication" is used to replace the remaining disjunction with an implication. Therefore, by transitivity of = , we conclude that the first Law of Portation is a theorem.

Here is the same proof again, but using the proof format the other way.

	$(a \wedge b \Rightarrow c \;=\; a \Rightarrow (b \Rightarrow c))$	Material Implication, 3 times
$=$	$(\neg(a \wedge b) \vee c \;=\; \neg a \vee (\neg b \vee c))$	Duality
$=$	$(\neg a \vee \neg b \vee c \;=\; \neg a \vee \neg b \vee c)$	Reflexivity of =

The final hint tells us that the final line is a theorem, hence each of the other lines is a theorem, and in particular, the first line is a theorem. It may be tempting to write one more line in this proof:

$=$	$\top$

so that every hint takes us from one line to the next. But once we see that we have a theorem, it is superfluous to write more. Indeed, it is always superfluous to equate a boolean expression to $\top$ just as it is to add 0 to a number expression. On the other hand, it doesn't hurt, and it makes proof the same as simplification, with the last line being the simplest expression that's equal to the first line. So we leave it as a matter of taste whether to add this line.

Sometimes it is clear enough how to get from one line to the next without a hint, and in that case no hint will be given. Hints are optional, to be used whenever they are helpful.

Sometimes a hint is too long to fit on the remainder of a line. When that is the case, the hint may be written in normal text form, between the lines of the proof. We may have

$\qquad$ *expression0* $\qquad\qquad\qquad\qquad\qquad\qquad$ short hint

$\quad=\quad$ *expression1*

and now a very long hint, written just as this is written, on as many lines as necessary, followed by

$\quad=\quad$ *expression2*

We cannot excuse an inadequate hint by the limited space on one line.

Our proof of the first Law of Portation was a continuing equation. A proof can also be a continuing implication, or a continuing mixture of these and other operators. As an example, here is a proof of the first Law of Confutation, which says

$$(a \Rightarrow b) \wedge (c \Rightarrow d) \;\Longrightarrow\; a \wedge c \Rightarrow b \wedge d$$

The proof goes this way:

$\qquad a \wedge c \Rightarrow b \wedge d \qquad\qquad\qquad\qquad\qquad$ distribute $\Rightarrow$ over second $\wedge$

$\quad=\quad (a \wedge c \Rightarrow b) \wedge (a \wedge c \Rightarrow d) \qquad\qquad$ antidistribution twice

$\quad=\quad ((a{\Rightarrow}b) \vee (c{\Rightarrow}b)) \wedge ((a{\Rightarrow}d) \vee (c{\Rightarrow}d)) \qquad$ distribute $\wedge$ over $\vee$ twice

$\quad=\quad (a{\Rightarrow}b){\wedge}(a{\Rightarrow}d) \vee (a{\Rightarrow}b){\wedge}(c{\Rightarrow}d) \vee (c{\Rightarrow}b){\wedge}(a{\Rightarrow}d) \vee (c{\Rightarrow}b){\wedge}(c{\Rightarrow}d)$ generalization

$\quad\Leftarrow\quad (a{\Rightarrow}b) \wedge (c{\Rightarrow}d)$

From the mutual transitivity of $=$ and $\Leftarrow$, we have proven

$$a \wedge c \Rightarrow b \wedge d \;\Leftarrow\; (a{\Rightarrow}b) \wedge (c{\Rightarrow}d)$$

which can easily be rearranged to give the desired theorem.

A proof, or part of a proof, can make use of local assumptions. A proof may have the format

$\qquad$ *assumption* $\Rightarrow$ (*expression0*

$\qquad\qquad\qquad = $ *expression1*

$\qquad\qquad\qquad = $ *expression2*

$\qquad\qquad\qquad = $ *expression3*)

for example. The step *expression0 = expression1* can make use of the *assumption* just as though it were an axiom. So can the step *expression1 = expression2* , and so on. Within the parentheses we have a proof; it can be any kind of proof including one that makes further local assumptions. We thus can have proofs within proofs, indenting appropriately. If the subproof is proving *expression0 = expression3* , then the whole proof is proving

$\qquad$ *assumption* $\Rightarrow$ (*expression0 = expression3*)

If the subproof is proving *expression0* , then the whole proof is proving

$\qquad$ *assumption* $\Rightarrow$ *expression0*

If the subproof is proving $\perp$, then the whole proof is proving

$\qquad assumption \Rightarrow \perp$

which is equal to $\neg assumption$. This is called "proof by contradiction".

We can also use **if then else** as a proof, or part of a proof, in a similar manner. The format is

$\qquad$ **if** *possibility*

$\qquad$ **then** (first subproof

$\qquad\qquad$ assuming *possibility*

$\qquad\qquad$ as a local axiom)

$\qquad$ **else** (second subproof

$\qquad\qquad$ assuming $\neg possibility$

$\qquad\qquad$ as a local axiom)

If the first subproof proves *something* and the second proves *something else* , the whole proof proves

$\qquad$ **if** *possibility* **then** *something* **else** *something else*

If both subproofs prove the same thing, then by the Case Idempotent Law, so does the whole proof, and that is its most frequent use.

In this book, a proof is just a theorem, written with enough detail so that it is easily seen to be a theorem.

$\rule{6cm}{0.4pt}$ End of Expression and Proof Format

Formalization

We use computers to solve problems, or to provide services, or just for fun. The desired computer behavior is usually described at first informally, in a natural language (like English), perhaps with some diagrams, perhaps with some hand gestures, rather than formally, using mathematical formulas (notations). In the end, the desired computer behavior is described formally as a program. A programmer must be able to translate informal descriptions to formal ones.

A statement in a natural language can be vague, ambiguous, or subtle, and can rely on a great deal of cultural context. This makes formalization difficult, but also necessary. We cannot possibly say how to formalize, in general; it requires a thorough knowledge of the natural language, and is always subject to argument. In this subsection we just point out a few pitfalls in the translation from English to boolean expressions.

The best translation may not be a one-for-one substitution of symbols for words. Also, the same word in different places may be translated to different symbols. And conversely, different words may be translated to the same symbol. The words "and", "also", "but", "yet", "however", and "moreover" might all be translated as $\wedge$. Just putting things next to each other sometimes means $\wedge$. For example, "They're red, ripe, and juicy, but not sweet." becomes $red \wedge ripe \wedge juicy \wedge \neg sweet$.

The word "or" in English is sometimes best translated as $\vee$, and sometimes as $\neq$. For example, "They're either small or rotten." probably includes the possibility that they're both small and rotten, and should be translated as $small \vee rotten$. But "Either we eat them or we preserve them." probably excludes doing both, and is best translated as $eat \neq preserve$.

The word "if" in English is sometimes best translated as $\Rightarrow$, and sometimes as $=$. For example, "If it rains, I'll get wet." probably leaves open the possibility that I might get wet for some other reason, and should be translated as $rain \Rightarrow wet$. But "If I get wet, I'll blame you for it." probably means "if and only if", and is best translated as $wet = blame$.

———End of Formalization
———End of Boolean Theory

Number Theory

Number Theory, also known as arithmetic, was designed to represent quantity. In the version we present, a <u>number</u> expression is formed in the following ways.

a sequence of one or more decimal digits

∞	"infinity"
$+x$	"plus x"
$-x$	"minus x"
$x + y$	"x plus y"
$x - y$	"x minus y"
$x \times y$	"x times y" (when unambiguous, $\times$ may be omitted)
x / y	"x divided by y"
x^y	"x to the power y"

if a **then** x **else** y

where x and y are any number expressions, and a is any boolean expression. The infinite number expression ∞ will be essential when we talk about the execution time of programs. We also introduce several new ways of forming boolean expressions:

$x < y$	"x is less than y", "x is smaller than y"
$x \leq y$	"x is less than or equal to y", "x is as small as y"
$x > y$	"x is greater than y", "x is bigger than y"
$x \geq y$	"x is greater than or equal to y", "x is as big as y"
$x = y$	"x equals y", "x is equal to y"
$x \neq y$	"x differs from y", "x is unequal to y"

The axioms of Number Theory are listed at the back of the book. It's a long list, but most of them should be familiar to you already. Notice particularly the two axioms

$$-\infty \le x \le \infty \qquad\qquad \text{extremes}$$
$$\infty + 1 = \infty \qquad\qquad \text{additive absorption}$$

Number Theory is incomplete. For example, the boolean expressions $0/0 = 5$ and $0 < (-1)^{1/2}$ can neither be proven nor disproven.

———End of Number Theory

All our theories use the operators $=$ $\ne$ **if then else** , so their laws are listed at the back of the book under the heading "Generic", meaning that they are part of every theory. These laws are not needed as axioms of Boolean Theory; for example, $x=x$ can be proven using the Completion and Evaluation rules. But in Number Theory and other theories, they are axioms; without them we cannot even prove $5=5$.

The operators $< \le > \ge$ apply to some, but not all, types of expression. Whenever they do apply, their axioms, as listed under the heading "Generic" at the back of the book, go with them.

Character Theory

The simplest <u>character</u> expressions are written as a prequote followed by a graphical shape. For example, `A is the "capital A" character, `1 is the "one" character, ` is the "space" character, and `` is the "prequote" character. Character Theory is trivial. It has operators *succ* (successor), *pred* (predecessor), and $=$ $\ne$ $< \le > \ge$ **if then else** . We leave the details of this theory to the reader's inclination.

———End of Character Theory

In this chapter, we have talked about boolean expressions, number expressions, and character expressions. In the following chapters, we will talk about bunch expressions, set expressions, string expressions, list expressions, function expressions, predicate expressions, relation expressions, specification expressions, and program expressions; so many expressions. For brevity in the following chapters, we will often omit the word "expression", just saying boolean, number, character, bunch, set, string, list, function, predicate, relation, specification, and program, meaning in each case a type of expression. If this bothers you, please mentally insert the word "expression" wherever you would like it to be.

———End of Basic Theories

2   Basic Data Structures

A data structure is a collection, or aggregate, of data. The data may be booleans, numbers, characters, or data structures. The basic kinds of structuring we consider are packaging and indexing. These two kinds of structure give us four basic data structures.

unpackaged, unindexed:	<u>bunch</u>
packaged, unindexed:	<u>set</u>
unpackaged, indexed:	<u>string</u>
packaged, indexed:	<u>list</u>

Bunch Theory

A bunch represents a collection of objects. For contrast, a set represents a collection of objects in a package or container. A bunch is the contents of a set. These vague descriptions are made precise as follows.

Any number, character, or boolean (and later also set) is an <u>elementary bunch</u>, or <u>element</u>. For example, the number 2 is an elementary bunch, or synonymously, an element. Indeed, every expression is a bunch expression, though not all are elementary.

If A and B are bunches, then

$$A , B \qquad \text{“ } A \text{ union } B \text{ ”}$$
$$A \text{ ‘ } B \qquad \text{“ } A \text{ intersection } B \text{ ”}$$

are bunches,

$$\text{¢}A \qquad \text{“size of } A \text{ ”, “cardinality of } A \text{ ”}$$

is a number, and

$$A : B \qquad \text{“ } A \text{ is in } B \text{ ”, “ } A \text{ is included in } B \text{ ”}$$

is a boolean.

The size of a bunch is the number of elements it includes. Elements are bunches of size 1 .

$$\text{¢}2 = 1$$
$$\text{¢}(0, 2, 5, 9) = 4$$

Here are three quick examples of bunch <u>inclusion</u>.

$$2 : 0, 2, 5, 9$$
$$2 : 2$$
$$2, 9 : 0, 2, 5, 9$$

The first says that 2 is in the bunch consisting of 0, 2, 5, 9 . The second says that 2 is in the bunch consisting of only 2 . Note that we do not say "a bunch contains its elements", but rather "a bunch consists of its elements". The third example says that both 2 and 9 are in 0, 2, 5, 9 , or in other words, the bunch 2, 9 is included in the bunch 0, 2, 5, 9 .

Here are the axioms of Bunch Theory. In these axioms, x and y are elements (elementary bunches), and A, B, and C are arbitrary bunches.

$$x{:}\,y \;=\; x{=}y \qquad\qquad \text{elementary axiom}$$

$x{:}\,A,B \;=\; x{:}\,A \;\vee\; x{:}\,B$	compound axiom
$A,A = A$	idempotence
$A,B = B,A$	symmetry
$A,(B,C) = (A,B),C$	associativity
$A'A = A$	idempotence
$A'B = B'A$	symmetry
$A'(B'C) = (A'B)'C$	associativity
$A,B{:}\,C \;=\; A{:}\,C \;\wedge\; B{:}\,C$	
$A{:}\,B'C \;=\; A{:}\,B \;\wedge\; A{:}\,C$	
$A{:}\,A,B$	generalization
$A'B{:}\,A$	specialization
$A{:}\,A$	reflexivity
$A{:}\,B \;\wedge\; B{:}\,A \;=\; A{=}B$	antisymmetry
$A{:}\,B \;\wedge\; B{:}\,C \;\Rightarrow\; A{:}\,C$	transitivity
$\mathcal{\mathrm{¢}}x = 1$	
$\mathrm{¢}(A,\,B) + \mathrm{¢}(A'B) = \mathrm{¢}A + \mathrm{¢}B$	
$\neg\,x{:}\,A \;\Rightarrow\; \mathrm{¢}(A'x) = 0$	
$A{:}\,B \;\Rightarrow\; \mathrm{¢}A \le \mathrm{¢}B$	

From these axioms, many laws can be proven. Among them:

$A,(A'B) \;=\; A$	absorption
$A'(A,B) \;=\; A$	absorption
$A{:}\,B \;\Rightarrow\; C,A{:}\,C,B$	monotonicity
$A{:}\,B \;\Rightarrow\; C'A{:}\,C'B$	monotonicity
$A{:}\,B \;=\; A,B = B \;=\; A = A'B$	inclusion
$A,(B,C) \;=\; (A,B),(A,C)$	distributivity
$A,(B'C) \;=\; (A,B)'(A,C)$	distributivity
$A'(B,C) \;=\; (A'B),\,(A'C)$	distributivity
$A'(B'C) \;=\; (A'B)'(A'C)$	distributivity
$A{:}\,B \;\wedge\; C{:}\,D \;\Rightarrow\; A,C{:}\,B,D$	confutation
$A{:}\,B \;\wedge\; C{:}\,D \;\Rightarrow\; A'C{:}\,B'D$	confutation

Here are several bunches that we will find useful:

null	the empty bunch
bool $=$ T, $\bot$	the booleans
nat $=$ 0, 1, 2, ...	the natural numbers
int $=$ ..., –2, –1, 0, 1, 2, ...	the integer numbers

rat	=	0, −1, 2/3, ...	the rational numbers
xnat	=	*nat*, ∞	the extended naturals
xint	=	−∞, *int*, ∞	the extended integers
xrat	=	−∞, *rat*, ∞	the extended rationals
char	=	..., `a, `A, ...	the characters

We define the empty bunch, *null* , with the axioms

¢*null*: *A*

¢*A* = 0 ⇒ *A* = *null*

This gives us three more laws:

A, *null* = *A*   identity

A ' *null* = *null*   base

¢ *null* = 0

The bunch *bool* is defined by the axiom *bool* = T, ⊥ . The next six of these bunches (the number bunches) are infinite, and we have not yet defined them formally; the three dots are saying "guess what goes here". We define them formally in the chapter "Recursive Definition"; until then, we rely on your experience. In some books, particularly older ones, the natural numbers start at 1 ; we will use the term with its current and more useful meaning, starting at 0 . The bunch *char* may or may not be infinite; we do not care to define it.

We also use the notation

x, . . *y*   " *x* to *y* " (not " *x* through *y* ")

where *x* and *y* are extended integers and *x*≤*y* . Its axiom is

i: *x*, . . *y* = *x*≤*i*<*y*

The notation ,.. is asymmetric as a reminder that the left end of the interval is included and the right end is excluded. For example,

0, . . ∞ = *nat*

5, . . 5 = *null*

¢(*x*, . . *y*) = *y*−*x*

The operators , ' ¢ : = ‡ **if then else** apply to bunch operands according to the axioms already presented. Other operators can be applied to bunches with the understanding that they apply to the elements of the bunch. In other words, they distribute over bunch union. For example,

−*null* = *null*

−(*A*, *B*) = −*A*, −*B*

(*A*, *B*)+*null* = *null*

(*A*, *B*)+*C* = *A*+*C*, *B*+*C*

(*A*, *B*)+(*C*, *D*) = *A*+*C*, *A*+*D*, *B*+*C*, *B*+*D*

This makes it easy to express the positive naturals (*nat*+1) , the even naturals (*nat*×2) , the squares (*nat*^{2}) , the powers of two (2^{nat}) , and many other things. We will make great use of this distribution. (The operators that distribute over bunch union are listed on the final page.)

——————————————————————————————————End of Bunch Theory

Except for a few brief mentions, we do not use sets in this book. After bunches, it is only a small step to define sets, and since they are so well-known, they may help to place the other theories in this chapter in perspective.

Set Theory

Let A be any bunch (anything). Then

$\qquad$ $\{A\}$ $\qquad\qquad\qquad\qquad\qquad\qquad$ "set containing A "

is a set. Thus $\{null\}$ is the empty set, and the set containing the first three natural numbers is expressed as $\{0, 1, 2\}$ or as $\{0,..3\}$. All sets are elements; not all bunches are elements; that is the difference between sets and bunches. We can form the bunch $1, \{3, 7\}$ consisting of two elements, and from it the set $\{1, \{3, 7\}\}$ containing two elements, and in that way we build a structure of nested sets.

The powerset operator $_2$ is a unary prefix operator that takes a set as operand and yields a set of sets as result. Here is an example.

$\qquad$ $_2\{0, 1\} \ = \ \{\{null\}, \{0\}, \{1\}, \{0, 1\}\}$

The inverse of set formation is also useful. If S is any set, then

$\qquad$ $\sim\!S$ $\qquad\qquad\qquad\qquad\qquad\qquad$ "contents of S "

is its contents. For example,

$\qquad$ $\sim\!\{0, 1\} \ = \ 0, 1$

We "promote" the bunch operators to obtain the set operators $\$ \in \subseteq \cup \cap =$. Here are the axioms.

$\qquad$ $\{A\} \ne A$
$\qquad$ $\sim\!\{A\} = A$ $\qquad\qquad\qquad\qquad\qquad$ "contents"
$\qquad$ $\$\{A\} = \cent A$ $\qquad\qquad\qquad\qquad\qquad$ "size", "cardinality"
$\qquad$ $A \in \{B\} \ = \ A\!:\!B$ $\qquad\qquad\qquad\quad$ "elements"
$\qquad$ $\{A\} \subseteq \{B\} \ = \ A\!:\!B$ $\qquad\qquad\qquad$ "subset"
$\qquad$ $\{A\} \in \ _2\{B\} \ = \ A\!:\!B$ $\qquad\qquad\quad$ "powerset"
$\qquad$ $\{A\} \cup \{B\} = \{A, B\}$ $\qquad\qquad\quad$ "union"
$\qquad$ $\{A\} \cap \{B\} = \{A \text{ '} B\}$ $\qquad\qquad\quad$ "intersection"
$\qquad$ $\{A\} = \{B\} \ = \ A = B$ $\qquad\qquad\quad$ "equation"

$\text{————————————————————————————————}$ End of Set Theory

Just as bunches and sets are, respectively, unpackaged and packaged collections, so strings and lists are, respectively, unpackaged and packaged sequences. There are sets of sets, and lists of lists, but there are neither bunches of bunches nor strings of strings.

String Theory

The simplest string is

    nil   the empty string

Any number, character, boolean, set (and later also list and function) is a one-item string, or <u>item</u>. For example, the number 2 is a one-item string, or item. Strings are <u>catenated</u> (joined) together by semicolons to make longer strings. For example,

    $4; 2; 4; 6$

is a four-item string. The length of a string is the number of items, and is obtained by the $\#$ operator.

    $\#(4; 2; 4; 6) = 4$

We can measure a string by placing it along a string-measuring ruler, as in the following picture.

Each of the numbers under the ruler is called an <u>index</u>. When we are considering the items in a string from beginning to end, and we say we are at index n , it is clear which items have been considered and which remain because we draw the items between the indexes. (If we were to draw an item at an index, saying we are at index n would leave doubt as to whether the item at that index has been considered.)

The picture saves one confusion, but causes another: we must refer to the items by index, and two indexes are equally near each item. We adopt the convention that most often avoids the need for a "+1" or "−1" in our expressions: the index of an item is the number of items that precede it. In other words, indexing is from 0 . Your life begins at year 0 , a highway begins at mile 0 , and so on. An index is not an arbitrary label, but a measure of how much has gone before. We refer to the items in a string as "item 0", "item 1", "item 2", and so on; we never say "the third item" due to the possible confusion between item 2 and item 3. When we are at index n , then n items have been considered, and item n will be considered next.

We obtain an item of a string by subscripting. For example,

    $(3; 5; 7; 9)_2 = 7$

In general, S_n is item n of string S . We can even pick out a whole string of items, as in the following example.

    $(3; 5; 7; 9)_{2; 1; 2} = 7; 5; 7$

If n is a natural and S is a string, then $n*S$ means n copies of S catenated together.

  $3 * (0; 1) = 0; 1; 0; 1; 0; 1$

Without any left operand, $*S$ means all strings formed by catenating any number of copies of S .

  $*(0; 1) = nil$, $0;1$, $0;1;0;1$, ...

Strings can be compared for equality and order. To be equal, strings must be of equal length, and have equal items at each index. The order of two strings is determined by the items at the first index where they differ. For example,

  $3; 6; 4; 7 < 3; 7; 2$

If there is no index where they differ, the shorter string comes before the longer one.

  $3; 6; 4 < 3; 6; 4; 7$

This ordering is known as <u>lexicographic order</u>; it is the ordering used in dictionaries.

Here is the syntax of strings. If i is an item, S and T are strings, and n is a natural number, then

nil	the empty string
i	an item
$S;T$	" S catenate T "
S_T	" S sub T "
$n*S$	" n copies of S "

are strings,

  $*S$ "copies of S "

is a bunch of strings, and

  $\#S$ "length of S "

is a natural number. The order operators $< \le > \ge$ apply to strings.

Here are the axioms of String Theory. In these axioms, S , T , and U are strings, i and j are items, and n is a natural number.

  $nil; S = S; nil = S$ identity

  $S; (T; U) = (S; T); U$ associativity

  $\#nil = 0$

  $\#i = 1$

  $\#(S; T) = \#S + \#T$

  $S_{nil} = nil$

  $(S; i; T)_{\#S} = i$

  $S_{T; U} = S_T; S_U$

  $S_{(T_U)} = (S_T)_U$

$0*S = nil$

$(n+1)*S = n*S; S$

$i=j \;=\; S; i; T = S; j; T$

$i<j \;\Rightarrow\; S; i; T < S; j; U$

$nil \leq S < S; i; T$

We also use the notation

$x; ..y$ "x to y" (same pronunciation as $x, ..y$)

where x and y are integers and $x \leq y$. As in the similar bunch notation, x is included and y excluded, so that

$\#(x; ..y) = y - x$

Here are the axioms.

$x; ..x = nil$

$x; ..x+1 = x$

$(x; ..y) ; (y; ..z) = x; ..z$

We allow string catenation to distribute over bunch union:

$A; null; B = null$

$(A, B); (C, D) = A; C, A; D, B; C, B; D$

So a string of bunches is equal to a bunch of strings. Thus, for example,

$0; 1; 2: \; nat; 1; (0, ..10)$

because $0: nat$ and $1: 1$ and $2: 0, ..10$. The * operator distributes over bunch union, but in its left operand only.

$null*a = null$

$(A, B) * C = A*C, B*C$

Using this left-distributivity, we define the unary star by the axiom

$*A = nat*A$

The strings we have just defined may be called "natural strings" because their lengths and indexes are natural numbers. With only a small change to a few axioms, we can have "extended natural strings", including strings of infinite length. By adding a new operator, the inverse of catenation, we obtain "negative strings"; natural strings and negative strings together are "integer strings". We leave these developments as Exercise 37.

———End of String Theory

Our main purpose in presenting String Theory is as a stepping stone to the presentation of List Theory.

List Theory

A list is a packaged string. For example,

[0; 1; 2]

is a list of three items. List brackets [ ] distribute over bunch union.

[*null*] = *null*

[*A*, *B*] = [*A*], [*B*]

Because of the distribution we can say

[0; 1; 2]: [*nat*; 1; (0,..10)]

On the left of the colon we have a list of integers; on the right we have a list of bunches, or equivalently, a bunch of lists. Progressing to larger bunches,

[0; 1; 2]: [*nat*; 1; (0,..10)]: [3**nat*]: [**nat*]

Here is the syntax of lists. Let *S* be a string, *L* and *M* be lists, *n* be a natural number, and *i* be an item. Then

[*S*]	"list containing *S* "
L M	" *L M* " or " *L* composed with *M* "
L+*M*	" *L* catenate *M* "
n→*i* | *L*	" *n* maps to *i* otherwise *L* "

are lists,

#*L*   "length of *L* "

is a natural number, and

L n   " *L n* " or " *L* index *n* "

is an item. Of course, parentheses may be used around any expression, so we may write *L*(*n*) if we want. If the index is not simple, we will have to enclose it in parentheses. When there is no danger of confusion, we may write *Ln* without a space between, but when we use multicharacter names, we must put a space between.

The length of a list is the number of items it contains.

#[3; 5; 7; 4] = 4

List indexes, like string indexes, start at 0 . An item can be selected from a list by juxtaposing (sitting next to each other) a list and an index.

[3; 5; 7; 4] 2 = 7

A list of indexes gives a list of selected items. For example,

[3; 5; 7; 4] [2; 1; 2] = [7; 5; 7]

This is called <u>list composition</u>. List catenation is written with a small raised plus sign + .

[3; 5; 7; 4]+[2; 1; 2] = [3; 5; 7; 4; 2; 1; 2]

The notation *n*→*i* \| *L* gives us a list just like *L* except that item *n* is *i* .

2→22 \| [10;..15] = [10; 11; 22; 13; 14]

2→22 \| 3→33 \| [10;..15] = [10; 11; 22; 33; 14]

Let $L = [10;..15]$. Then

$$2{\to}L3 \mid 3{\to}L2 \mid L = [10; 11; 13; 12; 14]$$

The order operators $< \le > \ge$ apply to lists; the order is lexicographic, just like string order.

Here are the axioms. Let S and T be strings, let n be a natural number, and let i and j be items.

$$\#[S] = \#S \qquad\qquad\qquad \text{length}$$
$$[S]^+[T] = [S; T] \qquad\qquad \text{catenation}$$
$$[S]\,n = S_n \qquad\qquad\qquad \text{indexing}$$
$$[S]\,[T] = [S_T] \qquad\qquad \text{composition}$$
$$(\#S) \to i \mid [S; j; T] = [S; i; T] \qquad \text{modification}$$
$$[S] = [T] \;\equiv\; S = T \qquad\qquad \text{equation}$$
$$[S] < [T] \;\equiv\; S < T \qquad\qquad \text{order}$$
$$[S; T]\colon [S] \qquad\qquad\qquad \text{inclusion}$$

We can now prove a variety of theorems, such as for lists L , M , N , and natural n that

$$(L\,M)\,n = L\,(M\,n)$$
$$(L\,M)\,N = L\,(M\,N) \qquad \text{associativity}$$
$$L\,(M^+N) = L\,M + L\,N \qquad \text{distributivity}$$

(The proofs assume that each list has the form $[S]$.)

When a list is indexed by a list, we get a list of results. More generally, the index can be any structure, and the result will have the same structure.

$$L\,null = null$$
$$L\,(A, B) = L\,A, L\,B$$
$$L\,\{A\} = \{L\,A\}$$
$$L\,nil = nil$$
$$L\,(S; T) = L\,S; L\,T$$
$$L\,[S] = [L\,S]$$

Here is a fancy example. Let $L = [10; 11; 12]$. Then

$$L\,[0, \{1, [2; 1]; 0\}] = [L\,0, \{L\,1, [L\,2; L\,1]; L\,0\}] = [10, \{11, [12; 11]; 10\}]$$

The <u>text</u> notation is an alternative way of writing a list of characters. A text begins with a double-quote, continues with any natural number of characters (but a double-quote must be repeated), and concludes with a double-quote. Here is a text of length 15 .

"Don't say ""no""." = [`D; `o; `n; `'; `t; ` ; `s; `a; `y; ` ; `"; `n; `o; `"; `.]

Composing a text with a list of indexes we obtain a subtext. For example,

"abcdefghij" [3;..6] = "def"

Here is a self-describing expression (self-reproducing automaton).

"""[0;0;2*(0;..17)]"[0;0;2*(0;..17)]

Multidimensional Structures

Lists can be items in a list. For example, let

$$A = [[6; 3; 7; 0] ;$$
$$[4; 9; 2; 5] ;$$
$$[1; 5; 8; 3]]$$

Then A is a 2-dimensional <u>array</u>, or more particularly, a 3×4 array. Formally, $A: [3*[4*nat]]$.
Indexing A with one index gives a list

$$A\ 1 = [4; 9; 2; 5]$$

which can then be indexed again to give a number.

$$A\ 1\ 2 = 2$$

Warning: The notations $A(1,2)$ and $A[1,2]$ are used in several programming languages to index
a 2-dimensional array. But in this book,

$$A\ (1, 2) = A\ 1, A\ 2 = [4; 9; 2; 5], [1; 5; 8; 3]$$
$$A\ [1, 2] = [A\ 1, A\ 2] = [[4; 9; 2; 5], [1; 5; 8; 3]]$$

We have just seen a rectangular array, a very regular structure, which requires two indexes to give
a number. Lists of lists can also be quite irregular in shape, not just by containing lists of different
lengths, but in dimensionality. For example, let

$$B = [[2; 3]; 4; [5; [6; 7]]]$$

Now $B\ 0\ 0 = 2$ and $B\ 1 = 4$, and $B\ 1\ 1$ is undefined. The number of indexes needed to obtain
a number varies. We can regain some regularity in the following way. Let L be a list, let n be an
index, and let S and T be strings of indexes. Then

$$L@nil = L$$
$$L@n = L\ n$$
$$L@(S; T) = L@S@T$$

Now we can always "index" with a single string, called a <u>pointer</u>, obtaining the same result as
indexing by the sequence of items in the string. In the example list,

$$B@(2; 1; 0) = B\ 2\ 1\ 0 = 6$$

We generalize the notation $S{\rightarrow}i\,|\,L$ to allow S to be a string of indexes. The axioms are

$$nil{\rightarrow}i\,|\,L = i$$
$$(S;T) \rightarrow i\,|\,L = S{\rightarrow}(T{\rightarrow}i\,|\,L@S)\,|\,L$$

Thus $S{\rightarrow}i\,|\,L$ is a list like L except that S points to item i . For example,

$$(0;1) \rightarrow 6\,|\,[[0; 1; 2] ;$$
$$[3; 4; 5]] = [[0; 6; 2] ;$$
$$[3; 4; 5]]$$

───End of Multidimensional Structures
──End of List Theory
───End of Basic Data Structures

3 Function Theory

We are always allowed to invent new syntax if we explain the rules for its use. A ready source of new syntax is names (identifiers), and the rules for their use are most easily given by some axioms. We might say something like "let $pi = 3.14$ ", meaning that we introduce the name pi and the axiom $pi = 3.14$. A similar example is "let x be an element such that $x: nat$ ", or more briefly, "let $x: nat$ ". We call pi a <u>constant</u> because the axiom constrains it to one value, and we call x a <u>variable</u> because the axiom allows it many possible values.

Here is an intermediate example: let p and q be numbers such that

$$p, q: nat$$
$$p{\times}q = p{+}q$$

From the axioms of Number Theory, plus nat induction (Chapter 6), plus these two axioms, we can prove $p{=}q{=}0 \lor p{=}q{=}2$. What are p and q ? They are not very variable, yet they are not completely constant. A theory is defined when we know what expressions we can write and how to prove theorems. Beyond that, it does not matter what we call anything. It no more matters whether p and q are called variables or constants than whether $<$ is called "less than" or "smaller than".

Usually when we introduce names and axioms we want them for some local purpose; we do not want to shout them to the world. The reader is supposed to understand their <u>scope</u>, the region where they apply, and not use them beyond it. Though the names and axioms are formal (expressions in our formalism), they were introduced informally in our examples (by an English sentence beginning with "let"), and the scope of informally introduced names and axioms is not always clear. In this chapter we present a formal notation for introducing a local name together with a local axiom to say what its possible values are.

Functions

Let v be a name, let D be a bunch of items (possibly using previously introduced names but not using v), and let b be any expression (possibly using previously introduced names and possibly using v). Then

$$\lambda v: D \cdot b \qquad \text{"map } v \text{ in } D \text{ to } b \text{", "local } v \text{ in } D \text{ maps to } b \text{"}$$

is a <u>function</u> of <u>variable</u> v with <u>domain</u> D and <u>body</u> b. The inclusion $v: D$ is a local axiom within the body b. For example,

$$\lambda n: nat \cdot n{+}1$$

is the successor function on the natural numbers. Here is a picture of it.

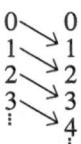

If f is a function, then

    Δf "domain of f"

is its domain. The <u>Domain Axiom</u> is

    $\Delta\, \lambda v\colon D\cdot\ b\ =\ D$

We say both that D is the domain of function $\lambda v\colon D\cdot\ b$ and that within the body b , D is the domain of variable v . The <u>range</u> of a function consists of the elements obtained by substituting each element of the domain for the variable in the body. The range of our successor function is $nat+1$.

The name introduced by a function is called a variable, or synonymously, a <u>parameter</u>. The purpose of the name is to help express the mapping from domain elements to range elements. The choice of name is irrelevant as long as it is fresh, not already in use for another purpose. The <u>Renaming Axiom</u> says that if v and w are names, and neither v nor w appears in D , and w does not appear in b , then

    $\lambda v\colon D\cdot\ b\ =\ \lambda w\colon D\cdot$ (substitute w for v in b)

The substitution must replace every occurrence of v with w .

If f is a function and x is an element of its domain, then

    $f x$ "f applied to x" or "f of x"

is the corresponding element of the range. This is function <u>application</u>, and x is the <u>argument</u>. Of course, parentheses may be used around any expression, so we may write $f(x)$ if we want. If the argument is not simple, we will have to enclose it in parentheses. When there is no danger of confusion, we may write $f x$ without a space between, but when we use multicharacter names, we must put a space between. As an example of application, if $suc = \lambda n\colon nat\cdot\ n+1$, then

    $suc\ 3\ =\ (\lambda n\colon nat\cdot\ n+1)\ 3\ =\ 3+1\ =\ 4$

Here is the <u>Application Axiom</u>. If element $x\colon D$, then

    $(\lambda v\colon D\cdot\ b)\,x\ =\ $ (substitute x for v in b)

We have already seen functions applied to arguments in previous chapters, but we called them operators applied to their operands. For example, $\neg\bot$ is the function $\neg$ applied to argument $\bot$, and -3 is the function $-$ applied to argument 3 .

A function of more than one variable is a function whose body is a function. Here are two examples.

$$max \;=\; \lambda x: rat \cdot \; \lambda y: rat \cdot \; \textbf{if } x \geq y \textbf{ then } x \textbf{ else } y$$
$$min \;=\; \lambda x: rat \cdot \; \lambda y: rat \cdot \; \textbf{if } x \leq y \textbf{ then } x \textbf{ else } y$$

If we apply *max* to an argument we obtain a function of one variable,

$$max\; 3 \;=\; \lambda y: rat \cdot \; \textbf{if } 3 \geq y \textbf{ then } 3 \textbf{ else } y$$

which can be applied to an argument to obtain a number.

$$max\; 3\; 5 \;=\; 5$$

We have already seen many binary functions (operators) such as $+$, but we have written them infix (between their arguments (operands)) rather than prefix (before their arguments (operands)). We have already seen one ternary function (operator), written **if** a **then** b **else** c instead of *if a b c* .

A <u>predicate</u> is a function whose body is a boolean expression. Two examples are

$$even \;=\; \lambda i: int \cdot \; i/2: int$$
$$odd \;=\; \lambda i: int \cdot \; \neg \; i/2: int$$

A <u>relation</u> is a function whose body is a predicate. Here is an example:

$$divides \;=\; \lambda n: nat{+}1 \cdot \; \lambda i: int \cdot \; i/n: int$$

Applying *divides* to 2 we obtain *even* . Applying *even* to 3 we obtain $\perp$.

One more operation on functions is <u>selective union</u>. If f and g are functions, then

$$f \,|\, g \qquad\qquad\qquad\qquad\qquad \text{``} f \text{ otherwise } g \text{''}, \text{``the selective union of } f \text{ and } g \text{''}$$

is a function that behaves like f when applied to an argument in the domain of f , and otherwise behaves like g . The axioms are

$$\Delta(f \,|\, g) \;=\; \Delta f, \Delta g$$
$$(f \,|\, g)\, x \;=\; \textbf{if } x: \Delta f \textbf{ then } f\, x \textbf{ else } g\, x$$

All the rules of proof apply to the body of a function with the additional local axiom that the new variable is included in its domain.

Abbreviated Function Notations

We allow some variations in the notation for functions partly for the sake of convenience and partly for the sake of tradition. The first variation is to group the introduction of variables. For example,

$$\lambda x, y: rat \cdot \; \textbf{if } x \geq y \textbf{ then } x \textbf{ else } y$$

is an abbreviation for the *max* function seen earlier.

We may omit the domain of a function if the surrounding explanation supplies it. For example, the successor function may be written $\lambda n \cdot \; n{+}1$ in a context where it is understood that the domain is *nat* .

We may omit the variable when the body of a function does not use it. In this case, we also omit the λ and we change the dot (·) to an arrow (→). For example, 2→3 is a function that maps 2 to 3 , which we could have written λn: 2· 3 with an unused variable.

Our final abbreviation is to omit both the variable and domain (and associated λ : ·), supplying them informally. For example, the function

> λx: *int*· λy: *int*· x+3

which introduces two variables, is often more conveniently written

> x+3

But we must say somewhere in the surrounding explanation that the variables are x and y , and that their domain is *int* . The example illustrates that the variables and their domains must be stated; they cannot be seen from the body. According to this abbreviation, arbitrary expressions can always be considered as functions whose variables were introduced informally. It also means that the variables we used in earlier chapters are the same as the variables we introduce ourselves in functions. However, informal variable introduction is not sufficiently precise (what exactly is the scope? in what order are the variables introduced?) to allow us to apply such an abbreviated function to an argument.

——End of Abbreviated Function Notations

Scope and Substitution

A variable is <u>global</u> to an expression if its introduction is outside the expression (whether formal or informal), and a variable is <u>local</u> to an expression if its introduction is inside the expression (and therefore formal). The words "global" and "local" are used relative to a particular expression or subexpression.

If we always use fresh names for our local variables, then a substitution replaces all occurrences of a variable. But if we reuse a name, we need to be more careful. Here is an example in which the gaps represent uninteresting parts.

> (λx· x (λx· x) x) 3

Variable x is introduced twice: it is reintroduced in the inner scope even though it was already introduced in the outer scope. Inside the inner scope, the x is the one introduced in the inner scope. The outer scope is a function, which is being applied to argument 3 . Assuming 3 is in its domain, the Application Axiom says that this expression is equal to one obtained by substituting 3 for x . The intention is to substitute 3 for the x introduced by this function, the outer scope, not the one introduced in the inner scope. The result is

> = (3   (λx· x)   3   )

Here is a worse example. Suppose x is a global variable, and we reintroduce it in an inner scope.

$$(\lambda y \cdot\ x\quad y\quad (\lambda x \cdot\ x\quad y\quad)\quad x\quad y\quad)\, x$$

The Application Axiom tells us to substitute x for all occurrences of y. All three uses of y are the variable introduced by the outer scope, so all three must be replaced by the global x used as argument. But that will place a global x inside a scope that reintroduces x, making it look local. Before we substitute, we must use the Renaming Axiom for the inner scope. Choosing fresh name z, we get

$$=\ (\lambda y \cdot\ x\quad y\quad (\lambda z \cdot\ z\quad y\quad)\quad x\quad y\quad)\, x$$

by renaming, and then substitution gives

$$=\ (\quad x\quad x\quad (\lambda z \cdot\ z\quad x\quad)\quad x\quad x\quad)$$

——————————————————————————————End of Scope and Substitution

——————————————————————————————————End of Functions

Quantifiers

Now that we have functions, we can define a variety of <u>quantifiers</u>. Any binary symmetric associative operator can be used to define a quantifier. Here are four examples: the operators $\land\ \lor\ +\ \times$ are used to define, respectively, the quantifiers $\forall\ \exists\ \Sigma\ \Pi$. If p is a predicate, then $\forall p$ is the boolean result of applying p to all its domain elements and conjoining all the results. Similarly, $\exists p$ is the boolean result of applying p to all its domain elements and disjoining all the results. If f is a function with a numeric result, then Σf is the numeric result of applying f to all its domain elements and adding up all the results; and Πf is the numeric result of applying f to all its domain elements and multiplying together all the results. Here are four examples.

$\forall \lambda r : rat \cdot\ r{<}0 \lor r{=}0 \lor r{>}0$	"for all r in rat ..."
$\exists \lambda n : nat \cdot\ n{=}0$	"there exists n in nat such that ..."
$\Sigma \lambda n : nat{+}1 \cdot\ 1/2^n$	"the sum, for n in $nat{+}1$, of ..."
$\Pi \lambda n : nat{+}1 \cdot\ (4n^2)/(4n^2{-}1)$	"the product, for n in $nat{+}1$, of ..."

For the sake of convenience and tradition, we allow two abbreviated quantifier notations. First, we allow a λ following a quantifier to be omitted. For example we write

$$\forall r : rat \cdot\ r{<}0 \lor r{=}0 \lor r{>}0$$
$$\Sigma n : nat{+}1 \cdot\ 1/2^n$$

Second, we can group the variables in a repeated quantification. In place of

$$\forall x : rat \cdot\ \forall y : rat \cdot\ x = y{+}1\ \Rightarrow\ x > y$$

we can write

$$\forall x, y : rat \cdot\ x = y{+}1\ \Rightarrow\ x > y$$

and in place of

$$\Sigma n : 0,..10 \cdot\ \Sigma m : 0,..10 \cdot\ n{\times}m$$

we can write

$$\Sigma n, m : 0,..10 \cdot\ n{\times}m$$

The axioms for these quantifiers fall into two patterns, depending on whether the operator on which it is based is idempotent. The axioms are as follows (v is a name, A and B are bunches, b is a boolean expression, n is a number expression, and x is an element).

$$\forall v: null \cdot\ b$$
$$\forall v: x \cdot\ b\ =\ (\lambda v: x \cdot\ b)\, x$$
$$\forall v: A, B \cdot\ b\ =\ (\forall v: A \cdot\ b) \wedge (\forall v: B \cdot\ b)$$

$$\neg \exists v: null \cdot\ b$$
$$\exists v: x \cdot\ b\ =\ (\lambda v: x \cdot\ b)\, x$$
$$\exists v: A, B \cdot\ b\ =\ (\exists v: A \cdot\ b) \vee (\exists v: B \cdot\ b)$$

$$\Sigma v: null \cdot\ n\ =\ 0$$
$$\Sigma v: x \cdot\ n\ =\ (\lambda v: x \cdot\ n)\, x$$
$$(\Sigma v: A, B \cdot\ n) + (\Sigma v: A\text{‘}B \cdot\ n)\ =\ (\Sigma v: A \cdot\ n) + (\Sigma v: B \cdot\ n)$$

$$\Pi v: null \cdot\ n\ =\ 1$$
$$\Pi v: x \cdot\ n\ =\ (\lambda v: x \cdot\ n)\, x$$
$$(\Pi v: A, B \cdot\ n) \times (\Pi v: A\text{‘}B \cdot\ n)\ =\ (\Pi v: A \cdot\ n) \times (\Pi v: B \cdot\ n)$$

Care is required when translating from the English words "all" and "some" to the formal notations $\forall$ and $\exists$. For example, the statement "All is not lost." should not be translated as $\forall x \cdot \neg\ lost\ x$, but as $\exists x \cdot \neg\ lost\ x$ or as $\neg \forall x \cdot\ lost\ x$ or as $\neg \forall lost$. Notice that when a quantifier is applied to a function with an empty domain, it gives the identity element of the operator it is based on. It is probably not a surprise to find that the sum of no numbers is 0, but it may surprise you to learn that the product of no numbers is 1. You probably agree that there is not an element in the empty domain with property b (no matter what b is), and so existential quantification over an empty domain gives the result you expect. You may find it harder to accept that all elements in the empty domain have property b, but look at it this way: to deny it is to say that there is an element in the empty domain without property b. Since there isn't any element in the empty domain (with or) without property b, all (zero) elements have the property.

We can also form quantifiers from functions that we define ourselves. For example, functions *min* and *max* are binary symmetric associative idempotent functions, so we can define corresponding quantifiers *MIN* and *MAX* as follows.

$$MIN\ v: null \cdot\ n\ =\ \infty$$
$$MIN\ v: x \cdot\ n\ =\ (\lambda v: x \cdot\ n)\, x$$
$$MIN\ v: A, B \cdot\ n\ =\ min\,(MIN\ v: A \cdot\ n)\,(MIN\ v: B \cdot\ n)$$

$$MAX \; v: null \cdot n \; = \; -\infty$$
$$MAX \; v: x \cdot n \; = \; (\lambda v: x \cdot n) \, x$$
$$MAX \; v: A, B \cdot n \; = \; max \, (MAX \; v: A \cdot n) \, (MAX \; v: B \cdot n)$$

Our final quantifier applies to predicates. The solution quantifier § ("solutions of", "those") gives the bunch of solutions of a predicate. Here are the axioms.

$$\S v: null \cdot b \; = \; null$$
$$\S v: x \cdot b \; = \; \mathbf{if} \, (\lambda v: x \cdot b) \, x \; \mathbf{then} \; x \; \mathbf{else} \; null$$
$$\S v: A, B \cdot b \; = \; (\S v: A \cdot b), (\S v: B \cdot b)$$

We have all practiced solving equations, and we are comfortable with

$$\S i: int \cdot i^2 = 4 \; = \; -2, 2 \qquad\qquad \text{"those } i \text{ in } int \text{ such that ... "}$$

Equations are just a special case of boolean expression; we can just as well talk about the solutions of any predicate. For example,

$$\S n: nat \cdot n{<}3 \; = \; 0,..3$$

At the back of the book there are laws concerning quantification. (When domains are infinite, the proofs of some laws require induction, which we postpone to Chapter 6.) These laws are used again and again during programming; they must be studied until they are all familiar. Some of them can be written in a nicer, though less traditional, way. For example, the Specialization and Generalization laws at the back say that if $x: D$,

$$\forall v: D \cdot b \; \implies \; (\lambda v: D \cdot b) \, x$$
$$(\lambda v: D \cdot b) \, x \; \implies \; \exists v: D \cdot b$$

Together they can be written as follows: if $x: \Delta f$

$$\forall f \; \implies \; f x \; \implies \; \exists f$$

—End of Quantifiers

Function Fine Points

Substitution versus Distribution

Some operators, such as $+$ and $\times$, were invented to apply to elements; they are extended to non-elementary bunch operands by distribution. Some operators, such as $:$ and $\not\subset$, were invented to apply to bunches; in general they are not distributed over the elements of their operands.

$$(0, 1) + (1, 2) \; = \; 0{+}1, \, 0{+}2, \, 1{+}1, \, 1{+}2$$
$$(0,1: 1,2) \; \neq \; (0: 1), (0: 2), (1: 1), (1: 2)$$

The distributing operators are listed in the final paragraph of this book.

When we write a function, we create a new operator. It will apply to elements in its domain according to the Application Axiom: substitute the argument for the variable in the body. If we want to apply our function to non-elementary bunch arguments, we have a choice: either we distribute over the elements of the argument, or we extend the Application Axiom to allow substitution of bunch arguments.

Here are two examples. First,

$$double = \lambda n: nat \cdot n+n$$

Now $double\ 2 = 4$. What about $double\ (2, 3)$? We state our intention by saying $double$ distributes, which means we add the axioms

$$double\ null = null$$
$$double\ (A, B) = double\ A, double\ B$$

Now $double\ (2, 3) = 4, 6$. The Application Axiom allows us to substitute elementary arguments, but does not allow us to say

$$(\lambda n: nat \cdot n+n)\ (2, 3)$$
$$= \quad (2, 3) + (2, 3)$$
$$= \quad 4, 5, 6$$

The other example is

$$tiny = \lambda B: nat \cdot \not c B < 3$$

This time we choose to extend the Application Axiom by saying: if $A: nat$, then

$$(\lambda B: nat \cdot \not c B < 3)\ A = (\text{substitute } A \text{ for } B \text{ in } \not c B < 3)$$

Now $tiny\ (0, 1, 2, 3) = \not c(0, 1, 2, 3) < 3 = 4 < 3 = \perp$. We are not allowed to distribute $tiny$ over the elements of its arguments and say

$$tiny\ (0, 1, 2, 3)$$
$$= \quad tiny\ 0, tiny\ 1, tiny\ 2, tiny\ 3$$
$$= \quad \top, \top, \top, \top$$
$$= \quad \top$$

Each time we write a function we have to choose between substitution and distribution if we ever want to apply it to non-elementary bunch arguments.

Sometimes substitution and distribution give the same result. They are obviously the same when the argument is an elementary bunch. Less trivially, if the body of a function uses its variable exactly once, and uses only distributing operators (and functions), then again substitution and distribution are the same.

―――――――――――――――――――――――――――――――――――――End of Substitution versus Distribution

Function Inclusion and Equality

Consider a function in which the body is a bunch: each element of the domain is mapped to zero or more elements of the range. For example,

 λ*n*: *nat*· *n*, *n*+1

maps each natural number to two natural numbers.

Application works as usual:

 (λ*n*: *nat*· *n*, *n*+1) 3 = 3, 4

A function that sometimes produces no result is called "partial". A function that always produces at least one result is called "total". A function that always produces at most one result is called "deterministic". A function that sometimes produces more than one result is called "nondeterministic". Here is a function that is both partial and nondeterministic.

 λ*n*: *nat*· 0,..*n*

Like list formation, function formation distributes over bunch union, so that

 λ*v*: *D*· *A*, *B* = (λ*v*: *D*· *A*), (λ*v*: *D*· *B*)

A function whose body is a union is equal to a union of functions. A union of functions applied to an argument gives the union of the results:

 (*f*, *g*) *x* = *fx*, *gx*

A function *f* is included in a function *g* according to the <u>Function Inclusion Axiom</u>:

 f: *g* = Δ*g*: Δ*f* ∧ ∀*x*: Δ*g*· *fx*: *gx*

Using it both ways round, we find function equality is as follows:

 f = *g* = Δ*f* = Δ*g* ∧ ∀*x*: Δ*f*· *fx* = *gx*

We now prove *suc*: *nat*→*nat* . Function *suc* was defined earlier as

 suc = λ*n*: *nat*· *n*+1

Function *nat*→*nat* is an abbreviation of λ*n*: *nat*· *nat* , which has an unused variable. It is a nondeterministic function whose result, for each element of its domain *nat* , is the bunch *nat* .

  suc: *nat*→*nat*   use Function Inclusion Axiom
 = *nat*: *nat* ∧ ∀*n*: *nat*· *suc* *n*: *nat*
 = ∀*n*: *nat*· *n*+1: *nat*

We can prove similar inclusions about the other functions defined in the opening section of this chapter.

max: $rat{\rightarrow}rat{\rightarrow}rat$

min: $rat{\rightarrow}rat{\rightarrow}rat$

$even$: $int{\rightarrow}bool$

odd: $int{\rightarrow}bool$

$divides$: $(nat{+}1){\rightarrow}int{\rightarrow}bool$

And, more generally,

f: $A{\rightarrow}B$ $=$ A: $\Delta f \land \forall a$: $A \cdot fa$: B

Here is a predicate whose parameter is a function.

λf: $0,..10{\rightarrow}int \cdot \forall n$: $0,..10 \cdot even\ (f\ n)$

This predicate checks whether a function, when applied to the first 10 natural numbers, produces only even integers. Let us call this function *check* . An argument for *check* must be a function whose domain includes $0,..10$ because *check* will be applying its argument to all elements in $0,..10$. An argument for *check* must be a function whose results, when applied to the first 10 natural numbers, are included in *int* because they will be tested for evenness. An argument for *check* may have a larger domain (extra domain elements will be ignored), and it may have a smaller range. If A: B and f: $B{\rightarrow}C$ and C: D then f: $A{\rightarrow}D$. Therefore

suc: $0,..10{\rightarrow}int$

We can apply *check* to *suc* and the result will be $\bot$.

We earlier defined *suc* by the axiom

suc = λn: $nat \cdot n{+}1$

This equation can be written instead as

$\Delta suc = nat$ $\land$ $\forall n$: $nat \cdot suc\ n = n{+}1$

It would have been wiser to define *suc* by the weaker axiom

nat: Δsuc $\land$ $\forall n$: $nat \cdot suc\ n = n{+}1$

which is just as useful in practice, and allows *suc* to be extended to a larger domain later, if desired. A similar comment holds for *max* , *min* , *even* , *odd* , and *divides* .

—————————————————————————————————End of Function Inclusion and Equality

After this section, we do not use function composition in this book. Uninterested readers may skip the following subsection without harm. Interested readers will be surprised at the new treatment of this old topic.

Function Composition

As we said earlier, operators and functions are really the same. We defined the unary minus (–) operator to apply to a number and produce a number. We want to be able to compose it with any function f that produces a number to obtain a new function.

$$(-f)\,x \;=\; -(f\,x)$$

For example, we want

$$(-suc)\,3 \;=\; -(suc\,3) \;=\; -4$$

Similarly if p is a predicate, then we want

$$(\neg p)\,x \;=\; \neg(p\,x)$$

We want to compose $\neg$ with *even* to obtain *odd* again.

$$\neg even \;=\; odd$$

We want to write the Duality Laws this way:

$$\neg\forall f \;=\; \exists\neg f$$
$$\neg\exists f \;=\; \forall\neg f$$

or even this way:

$$\neg\forall \;=\; \exists\neg$$
$$\neg\exists \;=\; \forall\neg$$

We also want functions we define ourselves to be composable.

Let f and g be functions such that f is not in the domain of g ($\neg f{:}\,\Delta g$). Then $g\,f$ is the <u>composition</u> of g and f, defined by the <u>Function Composition Axioms</u>:

$$\Delta(g\,f) \;=\; \S x{:}\,\Delta f{\cdot}\ fx{:}\,\Delta g$$
$$(g\,f)\,x \;=\; g\,(f\,x)$$

For example, assuming that $\neg\ suc{:}\,\Delta even$,

$$\Delta(even\ suc) \;=\; \S x{:}\,\Delta suc{\cdot}\ suc\,x{:}\,\Delta even \;=\; \S x{:}\,nat{\cdot}\ x{+}1{:}\,int \;=\; nat$$
$$(even\ suc)\,3 \;=\; even\,(suc\,3) \;=\; even\,4 \;=\; \mathsf{T}$$

Suppose x and y are not functions, f and g are functions of 1 variable, and h is a function of 2 variables. Then

	$h\,f\,x\,g\,y$	juxtaposition is left-associative
$=$	$(((h\,f)\,x)\,g)\,y$	use function composition on $h\,f$ (assuming $\neg f{:}\,\Delta h$)
$=$	$((h\,(f\,x))\,g)\,y$	use function composition on $(h\,(f\,x))\,g$ (assuming $\neg\,g{:}\,\Delta\,h(fx)$)
$=$	$(h\,(f\,x))\,(g\,y)$	drop superfluous parentheses
$=$	$h\,(f\,x)\,(g\,y)$	

The Composition Axiom says that we can write complicated combinations of functions and arguments without parentheses. They sort themselves out properly according to their functionality. (This is called "Polish prefix" notation.)

Composition and application are closely related. Suppose $f{:}\,A{\to}B$ and $g{:}\,B{\to}C$ and $\neg f{:}\,\Delta g$ so that g can be composed with f. Although g cannot be applied to f, we can change g into a function $g'{:}\,(A{\to}B){\to}(A{\to}C)$ that can be applied to f to obtain the same result as composition: $g'\,f = g\,f$. Here is an example. Define

$$double \;=\; \lambda n{:}\,nat{\cdot}\ n{+}n$$

We can compose *double* with *suc* .

           (*double suc*) 3   use composition

=   *double* (*suc* 3)   apply *double* to *suc* 3

=   *suc* 3 + *suc* 3

From *double* we can form a new function

           double' = $\lambda f \cdot \lambda n \cdot f\, n + f\, n$

which can be applied to *suc*

           (*double' suc*) 3   =   ($\lambda n \cdot$ *suc* n + *suc* n) 3   =   *suc* 3 + *suc* 3

to obtain the same result as before. This close correspondence has led people to take a notational shortcut: they go ahead and apply *double* to *suc* even though it does not apply, then distribute the next argument to all occurrences of *suc* . Beginning with

           (*double suc*) 3   they "apply" *double* to *suc*

           (*suc* + *suc*) 3   then distribute 3 to all occurrences of *suc*

           suc 3 + *suc* 3   and get the right answer.

As in this example, the shortcut usually works, but beware: it can sometimes lead to inconsistencies. (The word "apposition" has been suggested as a contraction of "application" and "composition", and it perfectly describes the notation, too!)

———End of Function Composition

List as Function

A list is a kind of function. The domain of list L is $0,..\#L$. Indexing a list is the same as function application, and the same notation $L\, n$ is used. List composition is the same as function composition, and the same notation $L\, M$ is used. It is handy, and not harmful, to mix lists and other functions in a composition. For example,

           suc [3; 5; 2] = [4; 6; 3]

We can also mix lists and other functions in a selective union. With function $1{\rightarrow}21$ as left operand, and list [10; 11; 12] as right operand, we get

           $1{\rightarrow}21\,|\,[10; 11; 12]$ = [10; 21; 12]

just as we defined it for lists.

We can apply quantifiers to lists. Since list L is the function $\lambda n: 0,..\#L \cdot Ln$, then ΣL is the same as $\Sigma n: 0,..\#L \cdot Ln$, and conveniently expresses the sum of the items of the list.

Not all functions are lists. Catenation and length apply to lists, not to all functions. Order is defined for lists, not for all functions.

———End of List as Function

———End of Function Fine Points

———End of Function Theory

4 Program Theory

Our theory for the description of computation is divided into two parts: space and time. The space part is concerned with the question: what results do we get? The time part is concerned with the question: when do we get them? One possible answer to the latter question is: never, or as we may say, at time infinity. Thus we place termination within the time part of our theory. Nontermination is just the extreme case of taking a long time.

We begin with a very simple model of computation. A computer has a memory, and we can observe its contents, or state. Our input to a computation is to provide an initial state, or prestate. After a time, the output from the computation is the final state, or poststate. In a later chapter we will consider communication during the course of a computation, but in this chapter we consider only an initial input and a final output. Also, for exposition, we start by ignoring time, and therefore also ignoring termination.

Although the memory contents may physically be a sequence of bits, we can consider it to be a list of any items; we only need to group the bits and view them through a code. A state σ (sigma) may, for example, be given by

$$\sigma = [-2; \ 15; \ `A; \ 3.14]$$

The indexes of the items in a state are usually called "addresses". The bunch of possible states is called the state space. For example, the state space might be

$$[int; \ (0,..20); \ char; \ rat]$$

Our example state space is infinite, and this is unrealistic; any physical memory is finite. We allow this deviation from reality as a simplification; the theory of integers is simpler than the theory of integers modulo 2^{32}, and the theory of rational numbers is much simpler than the theory of 32-bit floating-point numbers. In the design of any theory we must decide which aspects of the world to consider and which to leave to other theories. We are free to develop and use more complicated theories when necessary, but we will have difficulties enough without considering the finite limitations of a physical memory.

If the memory is in state σ, then the items in memory are $\sigma 0$, $\sigma 1$, $\sigma 2$, and so on. Instead of using addresses, we find it much more convenient to refer to items in memory by distinct names such as i, n, c, and x. Names that are used to refer to components of the state are called state variables. We must always say what the state variables are and what their domains are, but we do not bother to say which address a state variable corresponds to. A state is then an assignment of values to state variables.

Specifications

A <u>specification</u> is a boolean expression whose variables represent quantities of interest. We are specifying computer behavior, and (for now) the quantities of interest are the prestate σ and the poststate σ'. We provide a prestate as input. A computation then delivers (computes) a poststate as output. To satisfy a specification, a computation must deliver a satisfactory poststate. In other words, the given prestate and the computed poststate must make the specification true. We have an implementation when the specification describes (is true of) every computation. For a specification to be implementable, there must be at least one satisfactory output state for each input state.

Here are three definitions based on the number of satisfactory outputs for each input.

    Specification S is <u>unsatisfiable</u> for prestate σ: $\cent(\S\sigma'\cdot S) = 0$

    Specification S is <u>deterministic</u> for prestate σ: $\cent(\S\sigma'\cdot S) = 1$

    Specification S is <u>nondeterministic</u> for prestate σ: $\cent(\S\sigma'\cdot S) \geq 2$

By negating the first of these definitions, we can define

    Specification S is <u>satisfiable</u> for prestate σ: $\exists\sigma'\cdot S$

And finally,

    Specification S is <u>implementable</u>: $\forall\sigma\cdot \exists\sigma'\cdot S$

For convenience, we prefer to write specifications in the initial values x, y, ... and final values x', y', ... of some state variables (we make no typographic distinction between a state variable and its initial value). Each state variable x becomes two ordinary variables x and x' in a specification. If that is clear, we can say "variable" for both "state variable" and "ordinary variable", and distinguish them by context.

Here is an example. Suppose there are two (state) variables x and y each with domain *int* . Then

    $x' = x+1 \ \wedge \ y' = y$

specifies the behavior of a computer that increases the value of x by 1 and leaves y unchanged. Let us check that it is implementable. We replace $\forall\sigma\cdot$ by either $\forall x, y\cdot$ or $\forall y, x\cdot$ and we replace $\exists\sigma'\cdot$ by either $\exists x', y'\cdot$ or $\exists y', x'\cdot$; according to the Commutative Laws, the order does not matter. We find

        $\forall x, y\cdot \exists x', y'\cdot x' = x+1 \ \wedge \ y' = y$ One-Point Law twice

$= \quad \forall x, y\cdot \ \mathsf{T}$ Identity Law twice

The specification is implementable. In fact, it is deterministic for each prestate.

In the same variables, here is a second specification.

    $x' > x$

This specification is satisfied by a computation that increases x by any amount; it may leave y

unchanged or may change it to any integer. This specification is nondeterministic for each initial state.

At one extreme, we have the specification $\top$; it is the easiest specification to implement because all computer behavior satisfies it. At the other extreme is the specification $\bot$, which is not satisfied by any computer behavior. But $\bot$ is not the only unimplementable specification. Here is another.

$$x{\geq}0 \ \wedge \ y'{=}0$$

If the initial value of x is nonnegative, the specification can be satisfied by setting variable y to 0 . But if the initial value of x is negative, there is no way to satisfy the specification. Perhaps the specifier has no intention of providing a negative input, but to the implementer, every input is a possibility. The specifier should have written

$$x{\geq}0 \ \Rightarrow \ y'{=}0$$

For nonnegative initial x , this specification still requires variable y to be assigned 0 . If we never provide a negative value for x then we don't care what would happen if we did. That's what this specification says: for negative x any result is satisfactory. It allows an implementer to provide some kind of error indication when x is initially negative. If we want a particular error indication, we must strengthen the specification to say so.

Specification Notations

For our specification language we will not be definitive or restrictive; we allow any well understood notations. Often this will include notations from the application area. When it helps to make a specification clearer and more understandable, a new notation may be invented (and defined) on the spot.

In addition to the notations already presented, we add two more.

$$
\begin{aligned}
ok \quad &= \quad \sigma'{=}\sigma \\
&= \quad x'{=}x \ \wedge \ y'{=}y \ \wedge \ldots
\end{aligned}
$$

$$
\begin{aligned}
x{:=}\,e \quad &= \quad (\text{substitute } e \text{ for } x \text{ in } ok) \\
&= \quad x'{=}e \ \wedge \ y'{=}y \ \wedge \ldots
\end{aligned}
$$

The notation ok specifies that the final values of all variables equal the corresponding initial values. A computer can satisfy this specification by doing nothing. In the assignment notation, x is any state variable and e is any expression in the domain of x . For example, in integer variables x and y ,

$$x{:=}\,x{+}y \quad = \quad x'{=}x{+}y \ \wedge \ y'{=}y$$

specifies that the final value of x should be the sum of the initial values of x and y , and the value of y should be unchanged. The assignment $x{:=}\,e$ is pronounced " x gets e " or " x becomes e ".

Specifications are boolean expressions, and they can be combined using any operators of Boolean Theory. If S and R are specifications, then $S \land R$ is a specification that is satisfied by any computation that satisfies both S and R. Similarly, $S \lor R$ is a specification that is satisfied by any computation that satisfies either S or R. Similarly, $\neg S$ is a specification that is satisfied by any computation that does not satisfy S. A particularly useful operator is **if** b **then** S **else** R where b is a boolean expression of the initial state; it can be implemented by a computer that evaluates b, and then, depending on the value of b, behaves according to either S or R. The $\lor$ and **if then else** operators have the nice property that if their operands are implementable, so is the result; the operators $\land$ and $\neg$ do not have that property.

Specifications can also be combined by <u>dependent composition</u>, which describes sequential execution. If S and R are specifications, then $S.R$ is a specification that can be implemented by a computer that first behaves according to S, then behaves according to R, with the final state from S serving as initial state for R. (The symbol for dependent composition is pronounced "dot". This is not the same as the raised dot used to introduce a variable formally in a function.) Dependent composition is defined as follows.

$$S.R \;=\; \exists x'', y'', \dots \cdot \quad (\text{substitute } x'', y'', \dots \text{ for } x', y', \dots \text{ in } S)$$
$$\land \;(\text{substitute } x'', y'', \dots \text{ for } x, y, \dots \text{ in } R)$$

Here's an example. In one integer variable x, the specification $x'=x \lor x'=x+1$ says that the final value of x is either the same as the initial value or one greater. Let's compose it with itself.

$$x'=x \lor x'=x+1 \;.\; x'=x \lor x'=x+1$$
$$= \quad \exists x'' \cdot \; (x''=x \lor x''=x+1) \land (x'=x'' \lor x'=x''+1) \qquad\qquad \text{distribute } \land \text{ over } \lor$$
$$= \quad \exists x'' \cdot \; x''=x \land x'=x'' \lor x''=x+1 \land x'=x'' \lor x''=x \land x'=x''+1 \lor x''=x+1 \land x'=x''+1$$

distribute $\exists$ over $\lor$

$$= \qquad (\exists x'' \cdot x''=x \land x'=x'') \lor (\exists x'' \cdot x''=x+1 \land x'=x'')$$
$$\lor \;(\exists x'' \cdot x''=x \land x'=x''+1) \lor (\exists x'' \cdot x''=x+1 \land x'=x''+1) \qquad \text{One-Point, 4 times}$$
$$= \quad x'=x \lor x'=x+1 \lor x'=x+2$$

If we either leave x alone or add 1 to it, and then again we either leave x alone or add 1 to it, the net result is that we either leave it alone, add 1 to it, or add 2 to it.

Here is a picture of the same example. In the picture, an arrow from a to b means that the specification allows variable x to change value from a to b. We see that if x can change from a to b in the left operand of a dependent composition, and from b to c in the right operand, then it can change from a to c in the result.

Our equation for $S.R$ was partly informal; we need to clarify what was meant by (substitute x'', y'', ... for x', y', ... in S) and (substitute x'', y'', ... for x, y, ... in R). To begin with, you should not conclude that substitution is impossible since the names S and R do not mention any state variables; presumably S and R stand for, or are equated to, expressions that do mention some state variables. And second, when S or R is an assignment, the assignment notation should be replaced by its equal using ordinary variables x, x', y, y', ... Finally, when S or R is a dependent composition, the inner substitutions must be made first. Here is an example, again in integer variables x and y.

$$x:= 3.\ \ y:=x+y \qquad\qquad\qquad\qquad \text{eliminate assignments}$$
$$=\quad x'=3 \wedge y'=y.\ \ x'=x \wedge y'=x+y \qquad \text{now eliminate dependent composition}$$
$$=\quad \exists x'', y'': int\cdot\ x''=3 \wedge y''=y \wedge x'=x'' \wedge y'=x''+y'' \quad \text{use One-Point Law twice}$$
$$=\quad x'=3 \wedge y' = 3+y$$

Specification Laws

We have seen some of the following laws before. For specifications P, Q, R, and S, and boolean b,

$ok.\,P\ =\ P.\,ok\ =\ P$	Identity Law
$P.\,(Q.\,R)\ =\ (P.\,Q).\,R$	Associative Law
if b **then** P **else** $P\ =\ P$	Idempotent Law
if b **then** P **else** $Q\ =\ $ **if** $\neg b$ **then** Q **else** P	Case Reversal Law
$P\ =\ $ **if** b **then** $b \Rightarrow P$ **else** $\neg b \Rightarrow P$	Case Creation Law
if b **then** S **else** $R\ =\ b \wedge S \vee \neg b \wedge R$	Case Analysis Law
if b **then** S **else** $R\ =\ (b \Rightarrow S) \wedge (\neg b \Rightarrow R)$	Case Analysis Law
$P \vee Q.\ R \vee S\ =\ (P.\ R) \vee (P.\ S) \vee (Q.\ R) \vee (Q.\ S)$	Distributive Law
(**if** b **then** P **else** $Q) \wedge R\ =\ $ **if** b **then** $P \wedge R$ **else** $Q \wedge R$	Distributive Law

and all other operators in place of $\wedge$ including dependent composition:

(**if** b **then** P **else** $Q).\ R\ =\ $ **if** b **then** $(P.\ R)$ **else** $(Q.\ R)$	Distributive Law
$x:=$ **if** b **then** e **else** $f\ =\ $ **if** b **then** $x:= e$ **else** $x:= f$	Functional-Imperative Law
$x:= e.\ P\ =\ $ (for x substitute e in P)	Substitution Law

The Substitution Law is stated partly informally, so we must explain exactly how the substitution is to be made. Exercise 81 illustrates all the difficult cases, so let us do the exercise. The state variables are x and y.

(a) $x := y+1. \ \ y'>x'$

Since x does not occur in $y'>x'$, replacing it is no change.

$\qquad = \quad y'>x'$

(b) $x := x+1. \ \ y'>x \wedge x'>x$

Both occurrences of x in $y'>x \wedge x'>x$ must be replaced by $x+1$.

$\qquad = \quad y' > x+1 \ \wedge \ x' > x+1$

(c) $x := y+1. \ \ y' = 2x$

Because multiplication has precedence over addition, we must put parentheses around $y+1$ when we substitute it for x in $y' = 2x$.

$\qquad = \quad y' = 2(y+1)$

(d) $x := 1. \ \ x{\geq}1 \ \Rightarrow \ \exists x \cdot y' = 2x$

In $x{\geq}1 \ \Rightarrow \ \exists x \cdot y' = 2x$, the first occurrence of x is global, and the last occurrence is local. It is the global x that is being replaced. The local x could have been almost any other name, and probably should have been to avoid any possible confusion.

$\qquad = \quad 1{\geq}1 \ \Rightarrow \ \exists x \cdot y' = 2x$

$\qquad = \quad even \ y'$

(e) $x := y. \ \ x{\geq}1 \ \Rightarrow \ \exists y \cdot y' = x{\times}y$

Now we are forced to rename the local y before making the substitution, otherwise we would be placing the global y in the scope of the local y.

$\qquad = \quad y{\geq}1 \ \Rightarrow \ \exists k \cdot y' = y{\times}k$

(f) $x := 1. \ \ ok$

The name ok is defined by the axiom $ok \ = \ x'{=}x \wedge y'{=}y$, so it depends on x.

$\qquad = \quad x'{=}1 \wedge y'{=}y$

(g) $x := 1. \ \ y := 2$

Although x does not appear in $y := 2$, the answer is not $y := 2$. We must remember that $y := 2$ is defined by an axiom, and it depends on x.

$\qquad = \quad x'{=}1 \wedge y'{=}2$

(It is questionable whether $x'{=}1 \wedge y'{=}2$ is a "simplification" of $x := 1. \ \ y := 2$.)

(h) $x:= 1.\ P$ where $P = y:= 2$

This one just combines the points of parts (f) and (g).

$\quad = \quad x'=1 \wedge y'=2$

(i) $x:= 1.\ y:= 2.\ x:= x+y$

In part (g) we saw that $x:= 1.\ y:= 2\ =\ x'=1 \wedge y'=2$. If we use that, we are then faced with a dependent composition $x'=1 \wedge y'=2.\ x:= x+y$ for which the Substitution Law does not apply. In a sequence of assignments, it is much better to use the Substitution Law from right to left.

$\quad = \quad x:= 1.\ x' = x+2 \wedge y'=2$
$\quad = \quad x'=3 \wedge y'=2$

(j) $x:= 1.\ \textbf{if } y>x \textbf{ then } x:= x+1 \textbf{ else } x:= y$

This part is unremarkable. It just shows that the Substitution Law applies to **if**s.

$\quad = \quad \textbf{if } y>1 \textbf{ then } x:= 2 \textbf{ else } x:=y$

(k) $x:= 1.\ x'>x.\ x' = x+1$

We can use the Substitution Law on the first two pieces of this dependent composition to obtain

$\quad = \quad x'>1.\ x' = x+1$

Now we have to use the axiom for dependent composition to get a further simplification.

$\quad = \quad \exists x'', y''\cdot x''>1 \wedge x' = x''+1$
$\quad = \quad x'>2$

The error we avoided in the first step is to replace x with 1 in the third part of the composition $x' = x+1$.

——End of Specification Laws

Refinement

Two specifications P and Q are equivalent if and only if each is satisfied whenever the other is. Formally,

$\quad \forall \sigma, \sigma'\cdot P=Q$

If a customer gives us a specification and asks us to implement it, we can instead implement an equivalent specification, and the customer will still be satisfied.

Suppose we are given specification P and we implement a stronger specification S . Since S implies P , all computer behavior satisfying S also satisfies P , so the customer will still be satisfied. We are allowed to change the specification, but only to an equivalent or stronger specification.

Specification P is <u>refined</u> by specification S if and only if P is satisfied whenever S is satisfied.

$$\forall \sigma, \sigma' \cdot P \Leftarrow S$$

Refinement of a specification P simply means finding another specification S that is everywhere equal or stronger. We call P "the refinement problem" and S "the refinement solution". When it is obvious that we are talking about refinement, we say just "the problem" and "the solution". In practice, to prove that P is refined by S, we work within the universal quantifications and prove $P \Leftarrow S$. In this context, we can pronounce $P \Leftarrow S$ as " P is refined by S ".

Here are some examples of refinement.

$$x'>x \ \Leftarrow \ x'=x+1 \wedge y'=y$$
$$x'=x+1 \wedge y'=y \ \Leftarrow \ x:= x+1$$
$$x' \le x \ \Leftarrow \ \textbf{if } x=0 \textbf{ then } x'=x \textbf{ else } x'<x$$
$$x'>y'>x \ \Leftarrow \ y:= x+1.\ \ x:= y+1$$

In each, the problem (left side) follows from the solution (right side) for all initial and final values of all variables.

———End of Refinement

Conditions

A <u>condition</u> is a specification that refers to at most one state. A condition that refers to (at most) the initial state (prestate) is called an <u>initial condition</u> or <u>precondition</u>, and a condition that refers to (at most) the final state (poststate) is called a <u>final condition</u> or <u>postcondition</u>. In the following two definitions let P and S be specifications.

The <u>exact precondition</u> for P to be refined by S is $\forall \sigma' \cdot P \Leftarrow S$.

The <u>exact postcondition</u> for P to be refined by S is $\forall \sigma \cdot P \Leftarrow S$.

For example, although $x'>5$ is not refined by $x:= x+1$, we can calculate (in one integer variable)

(the exact precondition for $x'>5$ to be refined by $x:= x+1$)

$= \quad \forall x' \cdot x'>5 \Leftarrow (x:= x+1)$

$= \quad \forall x' \cdot x'>5 \Leftarrow x'=x+1 \qquad\qquad\qquad$ One-Point Law

$= \quad x+1 > 5$

$= \quad x > 4$

This means that a computation satisfying $x:= x+1$ will also satisfy $x'>5$ if and only if it starts with $x>4$. If we are interested only in prestates such that $x>4$, then we should weaken our problem with that antecedent, obtaining the refinement

$$x>4 \Rightarrow x'>5 \ \Leftarrow \ x:= x+1$$

There is a similar story for postconditions. For example, although $x>4$ is unimplementable,

>   (the exact postcondition for $x>4$ to be refined by $x:=x+1$)

$=$ $\forall x \cdot\ x>4 \Leftarrow (x:=x+1)$

$=$ $\forall x \cdot\ x>4 \Leftarrow x'=x+1$ One-Point Law

$=$ $x'-1 > 4$

$=$ $x' > 5$

This means that a computation satisfying $x:=x+1$ will also satisfy $x>4$ if and only if it ends with $x'>5$. If we are interested only in poststates such that $x'>5$, then we should weaken our problem with that antecedent, obtaining the refinement

> $x'>5 \Rightarrow x>4 \Longleftarrow x:=x+1$

For easier understanding, it may help to use the Contrapositive Law to rewrite the specification $x'>5 \Rightarrow x>4$ as the equivalent specification $x\leq 4 \Rightarrow x'\leq 5$.

We can now find the exact pre- and postcondition for P to be refined by S. Any precondition that implies the exact precondition is called a <u>sufficient precondition</u>. Any precondition implied by the exact precondition is called a <u>necessary precondition</u>. Any postcondition that implies the exact postcondition is called a <u>sufficient postcondition</u>. Any postcondition implied by the exact postcondition is called a <u>necessary postcondition</u>. The exact precondition is therefore the necessary and sufficient precondition, and similarly for postconditions.

Exercise 96(c) asks for the exact precondition and postcondition for $x:= x^2$ to move integer variable x farther from zero. To answer, we must first state formally what it means to move x farther from zero: $abs\ x' > abs\ x$ (where abs is the absolute value function; its definition can be found in Chapter 11). We now calculate

>   (the exact precondition for $abs\ x' > abs\ x$ to be refined by $x:= x^2$)

$=$ $\forall x' \cdot\ abs\ x' > abs\ x \Leftarrow x' = x^2$ One-Point Law

$=$ $abs\ (x^2) > abs\ x$ by the arithmetic properties of $abs\ x$ and x^2

$=$ $x \neq -1 \wedge x \neq 0 \wedge x \neq 1$

>   (the exact postcondition for $abs\ x' > abs\ x$ to be refined by $x:= x^2$)

$=$ $\forall x \cdot\ abs\ x' > abs\ x \Leftarrow x' = x^2$ by case analysis and arithmetic

$=$ $x' \neq 0 \wedge x' \neq 1$

If x starts anywhere but -1, 0, or 1, we can be sure it will move farther from zero; if x ends anywhere but 0 or 1, we can be sure it did move farther from zero.

Let P and Q be any specifications, and let C be a precondition, and let C' be the corresponding postcondition (in other words, C' is the same as C but with primes on all the variables). Then the following are all laws.

$$C \wedge (P.\ Q) \quad \Longleftarrow \quad C \wedge P.\ Q$$
$$(P.Q) \wedge C' \quad \Longleftarrow \quad P.\ Q \wedge C'$$
$$C \Rightarrow (P.Q) \quad \Longleftarrow \quad C \Rightarrow P.\ Q$$
$$P.\ C \wedge Q \quad \Longleftarrow \quad P \wedge C'.\ Q$$
$$P.\ Q \quad \Longleftarrow \quad P \wedge C'.\ C \Rightarrow Q$$

Precondition Law:

C is a sufficient precondition for P to be refined by S if and only if $C \Rightarrow P \Longleftarrow S$.

Postcondition Law:

C' is a sufficient postcondition for P to be refined by S if and only if $C' \Rightarrow P \Longleftarrow S$.

——End of Conditions

Programs

A <u>program</u> is a description or specification of computer behavior. A computer executes a program by behaving according to the program, by satisfying the program. People often confuse programs with computer behavior. They talk about what a program "does"; of course it just sits there on the page or screen; it is the computer that "does" something. They ask whether a program "terminates"; of course it does; it is the execution that may not terminate. A program is not behavior, but a specification of behavior. Furthermore, a computer may not behave as specified by a program for a variety of reasons: a disk head may crash, a compiler may have a bug, or a resource may become exhausted (stack overflow, number overflow), to mention a few. Then the difference between a program and the computer behavior is obvious.

A program is a specification of computer behavior; it is therefore a boolean expression relating prestate and poststate. Not every specification is a program. A program is an <u>implemented</u> specification, that is, a specification for which an implementation has been provided, so that a computer can execute it. In this chapter we need only a very few programming notations that are similar to those found in many popular programming languages. We take the following:

(a) ok is a program.

(b)   If x is any state variable and e is an implemented expression of the initial values, then $x := e$ is a program.

(c)   If b is an implemented boolean expression of the initial values, and P and Q are programs, then **if** b **then** P **else** Q is a program.

(d)   If P and Q are programs then $P.Q$ is a program.

(e)   If P is an implementable specification and S is a program such that $P \Longleftarrow S$ is a theorem, then P is a program.

For the "implemented expressions" referred to in (b) and (c), we take booleans, numbers, characters, and lists, with all their operators. We omit bunches, sets, and strings because we have lists, and we omit functions and quantifiers because they are harder to implement. All these notations, and others, are still welcome in specifications.

Part (e) states that any implementable specification P is a program if a program S is provided such that $P \Leftarrow S$ is a theorem. To execute P, just execute S. The refinement acts as a procedure declaration; P acts as the procedure name, and S as the procedure body; use of the name P acts as a call. Recursion is allowed; in part (e) we may use P as a program in order to obtain program S.

Here is an example refinement.

$$x'=0 \quad \Leftarrow \quad \textbf{if } x=0 \textbf{ then } ok \textbf{ else } (x:= x-1. \; x'=0)$$

The problem is $x'=0$. The solution is **if** $x=0$ **then** ok **else** $(x:= x-1. \; x'=0)$. In the solution, the problem reappears. According to (e), the problem $x'=0$ is a program if its solution is a program. And the solution is a program if $x'=0$ is a program. By saying "recursion is allowed" we break the impasse and declare that $x'=0$ is a program. A computer executes it by behaving according to the solution, and whenever the problem is encountered again, the behavior is again according to the solution. When we consider execution time, we will see that a result is obtained in finite time only when initially $x \geq 0$; but for now, we continue to ignore time.

We must prove the refinement, of course, so we do that now.

	if $x=0$ **then** ok **else** $(x:= x-1. \; x'=0)$	Substitution Law
$=$	**if** $x=0$ **then** $x'=x$ **else** $x'=0$	Case Absorption
$=$	**if** $x=0$ **then** $x'=x=0$ **else** $x'=0$	Case Absorption (other way)
$=$	**if** $x=0$ **then** $x'=0$ **else** $x'=0$	Case Idempotence
$=$	$x' = 0$	

Since the problem and solution are equal, the refinement is proven.

---End of Programs

A specification serves as a contract between a client who wants a computer to behave a certain way and a programmer who will program a computer to behave as desired. For this purpose, a specification must be written as clearly, as understandably, as possible. The programmer then refines the specification to obtain a program, which a computer can execute. Sometimes the clearest, most understandable specification is already a program. When that is so, there is no need for any other specification, and no need for refinement. However, the programming notations are only part of the specification notations: those that happen to be implemented. Specifiers should use whatever notations help to make their specifications clear, including but not limited to programming notations.

---End of Specifications

Program Development

Refinement Laws

Once we have a specification, we refine it until we have a program. We have only five programming notations to choose from when we refine. Two of them, *ok* and assignment, are programs and require no further refinement. The other three solve the given refinement problem by raising new problems to be solved by further refinement. When these new problems are solved, their solutions will contribute to the solution of the original problem, according to the first of our refinement laws.

<u>Refinement by Steps</u> (Stepwise Refinement) (monotonicity, transitivity)

       If $A \Leftarrow$ **if** b **then** C **else** D and $C \Leftarrow E$ and $D \Leftarrow F$ are theorems,

          then $A \Leftarrow$ **if** b **then** E **else** F is a theorem.

       If $A \Leftarrow B.C$ and $B \Leftarrow D$ and $C \Leftarrow E$ are theorems, then $A \Leftarrow D.E$ is a theorem.

       If $A \Leftarrow B$ and $B \Leftarrow C$ are theorems, then $A \Leftarrow C$ is a theorem.

Refinement by Steps allows us to introduce one programming construct at a time into our ultimate solution. The next law allows us to break the problem into parts in a different way.

<u>Refinement by Parts</u> (monotonicity, confutation)

       If $A \Leftarrow$ **if** b **then** C **else** D and $E \Leftarrow$ **if** b **then** F **else** G are theorems,

          then $A{\wedge}E \Leftarrow$ **if** b **then** $C{\wedge}F$ **else** $D{\wedge}G$ is a theorem.

       If $A \Leftarrow B.C$ and $D \Leftarrow E.F$ are theorems, then $A{\wedge}D \Leftarrow B{\wedge}E. C{\wedge}F$ is a theorem.

       If $A \Leftarrow B$ and $C \Leftarrow D$ are theorems, then $A{\wedge}C \Leftarrow B{\wedge}D$ is a theorem.

When we add to our repertoire of programming operators in later chapters, the new operators must obey similar Refinement by Steps and Refinement by Parts laws. Our final refinement law is

<u>Refinement by Cases</u>

       $P \Leftarrow$ **if** b **then** Q **else** R is a theorem if and only if

       $P \Leftarrow b \wedge Q$ and $P \Leftarrow \neg b \wedge R$ are theorems.

As an example of Refinement by Cases, we can prove

       $x' {\le} x \Leftarrow$ **if** $x{=}0$ **then** $x'{=}x$ **else** $x'{<}x$

by proving both

       $x'{\le}x \Leftarrow x{=}0 \wedge x'{=}x$

and

       $x'{\le}x \Leftarrow x{\ne}0 \wedge x'{<}x$

                                                                   —End of Refinement Laws

List Summation

As an example of program development, let us do Exercise 123: write a program to find the sum of a list of numbers. Let L be the list of numbers, and let s be a number variable whose final value will be the sum of the items in L . Now s is a state variable, so it corresponds to two ordinary variables s and s' . Our solution does not change list L , so we do not consider L to be a state variable; we could say it is a state constant; we can call it a parameter of the problem; it is just an ordinary variable or constant.

The first step is to express the problem as clearly and as simply as possible. One possibility is

$s := \Sigma L$

We are assuming the expression to the right of the assignment symbol is not implemented, so this specification is not a program until we refine it. But first we should be sure it is the specification we want. It says not only that s has the right final value, but also that all other variables are unchanged. The problem did not say that, so we can weaken our specification and make it easier to refine.

$s' = \Sigma L$

The algorithmic idea is obvious: consider each item of the list in order, accumulating the sum. To do so we need an accumulator variable, and we may as well use s for that. We also need a variable to serve as index in the list, saying how many items have been considered; let us take natural variable n for that. We must begin by assigning 0 to both s and n to indicate that we have summed zero items so far. We complete the task by adding the remaining items (which means all of them) to the sum.

$s' = \Sigma L \quad \Longleftarrow \quad s := 0.\ n := 0.\ s' = s + \Sigma L\ [n;..\#L]$

(Remember: list indexes start at 0 , and the list $[n;..\#L]$ includes n and excludes $\#L$.) This theorem is easily proven by two applications of the Substitution Law. We consider that we have solved the original problem, but now we have a new problem to solve: $s' = s + \Sigma L\ [n;..\#L]$. When we refine this new problem, we must ignore the context in which it arose; in particular, we ignore that $s=0 \wedge n=0$. The new specification represents the problem when n items have been summed and the rest remain to be summed, for arbitrary n . One of the possible values for n is $\#L$, which means that all items have been summed. That suggests that we use Case Creation next.

$s' = s + \Sigma L\ [n;..\#L] \quad \Longleftarrow \quad$ **if** $n=\#L$ **then** $n=\#L \ \Rightarrow\ s' = s + \Sigma L\ [n;..\#L]$
$\qquad\qquad\qquad\qquad\qquad\qquad\qquad$ **else** $n \neq \#L \ \Rightarrow\ s' = s + \Sigma L\ [n;..\#L]$

Now we have two new problems, but one is trivial.

$n=\#L \ \Rightarrow\ s' = s + \Sigma L\ [n;..\#L] \quad \Longleftarrow \quad ok$

In the other problem, not all items have been summed $(n \neq \#L)$. That means there is at least one more item to be added to the sum, so let us add one more item to the sum. To complete the refinement, we must also add any remaining items.

$$n \ne \#L \implies s' = s + \Sigma L [n;..\#L] \quad \Longleftarrow \quad s:= s+Ln. \ n:= n+1. \ s' = s + \Sigma L [n;..\#L]$$

This refinement is proven by two applications of the Substitution Law. The final specification has already been refined, so we have finished programming.

One point that deserves further attention is our use of $n \ne \#L$ to mean that not all items have been summed. We really need $n < \#L$ to say that there is at least one more item. The specification in which this appears

$$n \ne \#L \implies s' = s + \Sigma L [n;..\#L]$$

also uses the notation $n;..\#L$, which is defined only for $n \le \#L$. We may therefore consider that $n \le \#L$ is implicit in our use of the notation; this, together with $n \ne \#L$, tells us $n < \#L$ as required.

In our first refinement, we could have used a weaker specification to say that n items have been summed and the rest remain to be added. We could have said

$$s' = \Sigma L \quad \Longleftarrow \quad s:= 0. \ n:= 0. \ 0 \le n \le \#L \wedge s = \Sigma L [0;..n] \implies s' = s + \Sigma L [n;..\#L]$$

For those who were uncomfortable about the use of implicit information in the preceding paragraph, the first part of the antecedent $(0 \le n \le \#L)$ makes the needed bound on n explicit. The second part of the antecedent $(s = \Sigma L [0;..n])$ is not used anywhere.

When a compiler translates a program into machine language, it treats each refined specification as just an identifier. For example, the summation program looks like

$A \quad \Longleftarrow \quad s:= 0. \ n:= 0. \ B$

$B \quad \Longleftarrow \quad$ **if** $n=\#L$ **then** C **else** D

$C \quad \Longleftarrow \quad ok$

$D \quad \Longleftarrow \quad s:= s+Ln. \ n:= n+1. \ B$

to a compiler. Using the Law of Refinement by Steps, a compiler can compile the calls to C and D in-line (macro-expansion) creating

$B \quad \Longleftarrow \quad$ **if** $n=\#L$ **then** ok **else** $(s:= s+Ln. \ n:= n+1. \ B)$

So, for the sake of efficient execution, there is no need for us to put the pieces together, and we needn't worry about the number of refinements we use. Also, the call to B can be translated as just a branch (jump, go to) as can most calls, so we needn't worry about calls, even recursive calls, being inefficient.

If you want to execute this program on a computer, you must translate it to a programming language that is implemented on that computer. For example, you can translate the summation program to Pascal as follows.

```
s:= 0;  n:= 0;
10: if n < > lengthL then
        begin s:= s + L[n];  n:= n+1;  goto 10 end
```

——End of List Summation

Binary Exponentiation

Now let's try Exercise 130: given natural variables x and y, write a program for $y' = 2^x$ without using exponentiation. Here is a solution that is neither the simplest nor the most efficient. It has been chosen to illustrate several points.

$y'=2^x \iff$ **if** $x=0$ **then** $x=0 \Rightarrow y'=2^x$ **else** $x>0 \Rightarrow y'=2^x$

$x=0 \Rightarrow y'=2^x \iff y:= 1. \; x:= 3$

$x>0 \Rightarrow y'=2^x \iff x>0 \Rightarrow y'=2^{x-1}. \; y'=2y$

$x>0 \Rightarrow y'=2^{x-1} \iff x'=x-1. \; y'=2^x$

$y'=2y \iff y:= 2y. \; x:= 5$

$x'=x-1 \iff x:= x-1. \; y:= 7$

The first refinement divides the problem into two cases; in the second case $x \neq 0$, and since x is natural, $x>0$. In the second refinement, since $x=0$, we want $y'=1$, which we get by the assignment $y:= 1$. The other assignment $x:= 3$ is superfluous, and our solution would be simpler without it; we have included it just to make the point that it is allowed by the specification. The third refinement makes $y'=2^x$ in two steps: first $y'=2^{x-1}$ and then double y. The antecedent $x>0$ is needed so that 2^{x-1} will be natural. The fifth and sixth refinements again contain superfluous assignments. Without the theory of programming, we would be very worried that these superfluous assignments might in some way make the result wrong. With the theory, we only need to prove these six refinements, and we are confident that execution will not give us a wrong answer.

This solution has been constructed to make it difficult to follow the execution. Here's some advice: don't try. You can make the program look more familiar by replacing the nonprogramming notations with single letters.

$A \iff$ **if** $x=0$ **then** B **else** C

$B \iff y:= 1. \; x:= 3$

$C \iff D. \; E$

$D \iff F. \; A$

$E \iff y:= 2y. \; x:= 5$

$F \iff x:= x-1. \; y:= 7$

You can reduce the number of refinements by applying the Stepwise Refinement Law.

$A \iff$ **if** $x=0$ **then** $(y:= 1. \; x:= 3)$ **else** $(x:= x-1. \; y:= 7. \; A. \; y:= 2y. \; x:= 5)$

You can probably translate this quite easily into a programming language that is available on a computer near you. For example, in Pascal it becomes

var x, y: *integer*;

procedure A;

begin if $x=0$ **then begin** $y:= 1$; $x:= 3$ **end**

    else begin $x:= x-1$; $y:= 7$; A; $y:= 2*y$; $x:= 5$ **end**

end;

You can then test it on a variety of x values. For example, execution of

   $x:= 5$; A; $write(y)$

will print 32 . But you will find it easier to prove the refinements than to try to understand all possible executions of this program without any theory.

——End of Binary Exponentiation

——End of Program Development

Time

So far, we have talked only about the result of a computation, not about how long it takes. To talk about time, we just add a <u>time variable</u>. We do not change the theory at all; the time variable is treated just like any other variable, as part of the state. The state $\sigma = [t; x; y; ...]$ now consists of a time variable t and some <u>space variables</u> x , y , ... The interpretation of t as time is justified by the way we use it. In an implementation, the space variables require space in the computer's memory, but the time variable does not; it simply represents the time at which execution occurs.

We use t for the initial time, the time at which execution starts, and t' for the final time, the time at which execution ends. To allow for nontermination we take the domain of time to be a number system extended with ∞ . The number system we extend can be the naturals, or the integers, or the rationals, or the reals, whichever we prefer.

Time cannot decrease, therefore a specification S with time is <u>implementable</u> if and only if

   $\forall \sigma \cdot \exists \sigma' \cdot S \land t' \geq t$

For each initial state, there must be at least one satisfactory final state in which time has not decreased.

There are many ways to measure time. We present just two: <u>real time</u> and <u>recursive time</u>.

Real Time

Real time has the advantage of measuring the real execution time; for some applications, such as the control of a chemical or nuclear reaction, this is essential. It has the disadvantage of requiring intimate knowledge of the implementation (hardware and software).

To obtain the real execution time of a program, modify the program as follows.
•   Replace each assignment $x:= e$ by

      $t:= t+u$. $x:= e$

   where u is the time required to evaluate and store e .

- Replace each conditional **if** b **then** P **else** Q by

    $t := t+v$. **if** b **then** P **else** Q

    where v is the time required to evaluate b and branch.

- Replace each call P by

    $t := t+w$. P

    where w is the time required for the call and return. For a call that is implemented "in-line", this time will be zero. For a call that is executed last in a refinement solution, it may be just the time for a branch. Sometimes it will be the time required to push a return address onto a stack and branch, plus the time to pop the return address and branch back.

- Each refined specification can include time. For example, let f be a function of the initial state σ. Then

    $t' = t + f\sigma$

    specifies that $f\sigma$ is the execution time,

    $t' \le t + f\sigma$

    specifies that $f\sigma$ is an upper bound on the execution time, and

    $t' \ge t + f\sigma$

    specifies that $f\sigma$ is a lower bound on the execution time.

We could place the time increase after each of the programming notations instead of before. By placing it before, we make it easier to use the Substitution Law.

In an earlier section, we considered the example

   $x'=0 \impliedby$ **if** $x=0$ **then** ok **else** $(x := x-1.\ x'=0)$

Suppose that the **if**, the assignment, and the call each take time 1. Using P for the specification, the refinement becomes

   $P \impliedby t := t+1$. **if** $x=0$ **then** ok **else** $(t := t+1.\ x := x-1.\ t := t+1.\ P)$

This is still a theorem when $P = x'=0$ as before, but we can now include time in the specification. The refinement with time is a theorem when

   $P = x'=0 \land$ **if** $x \ge 0$ **then** $t'=t+3x+1$ **else** $t'=\infty$

Execution of this program always sets x to 0; when x starts with a nonnegative value, it takes time $3x+1$ to do so; when x starts with a negative value, it takes infinite time. It is strange to say that a result such as $x'=0$ is obtained at time infinity. This is really just a way of saying that a result is never obtained.

Even stranger things can be said about the values of space variables at time infinity. Consider the refinement

   $Q \impliedby t := t+1$. Q

Two implementable specifications for which this is a theorem are $Q = x'=2 \wedge t'=\infty$ and $Q = x'=3 \wedge t'=\infty$. We can show that the "final" value of x is 2 , and also 3 . But since $t'=\infty$, we are really saying in both cases that we never obtain a result. We could limit ourselves to specifications that do not mention any results at time infinity. For example, the refinement of the previous paragraph is also a theorem when

$$P = \text{if } x{\ge}0 \text{ then } x'{=}0 \wedge t' = t{+}3x{+}1 \text{ else } t'{=}\infty$$

and in this paragraph

$$Q = t'{=}\infty$$

But proofs of refinement are often easier when we separate results and timing into different conjuncts and use Refinement by Parts. So we just ignore anything about the values of space variables at time infinity.

———End of Real Time

Recursive Time

To free ourselves from having to know implementation details, we allow any arbitrary scheme for inserting time increments $t:= t{+}u$ into programs. Each scheme defines a new measure of time. In the recursive time measure,

*   Each recursive call costs time 1 .
*   All else is free.

This measure neglects the time for "straight-line" and "branching" programs, charging only for loops.

In the recursive measure, our earlier example becomes

$$P \Leftarrow \text{if } x{=}0 \text{ then } ok \text{ else } (x:= x{-}1. \ t:= t{+}1. \ P)$$

which is a theorem when

$$P = x'{=}0 \wedge \text{if } x{\ge}0 \text{ then } t' = t{+}x \text{ else } t'{=}\infty$$

That example was a direct recursion, but recursions can also be indirect. For example, problem A may be refined by a solution containing a call to B , whose refinement solution contains a call to C , whose refinement solution contains a call to A . The general rule of recursive time is that in every loop of calls, at least one call must be charged at least one time unit.

———End of Recursive Time

Let us prove a refinement with time (Exercise 102(b)):

$$R \Leftarrow \text{if } x{=}1 \text{ then } ok \text{ else } (x:= div \ x \ 2. \ t:= t{+}1. \ R)$$

where x is an integer variable, and

$$R = x'{=}1 \wedge \text{if } x{\ge}1 \text{ then } t' \le t + log \ x \text{ else } t'{=}\infty$$
$$= x'{=}1 \wedge (x{\ge}1 \Rightarrow t' \le t + log \ x) \wedge (x{<}1 \Rightarrow t'{=}\infty)$$

This exercise uses the functions *div* (divide and round down) and *log* (binary logarithm). Execution of this program always sets x to 1 ; when x starts with a positive value, it takes logarithmic time; when x starts nonpositive, it takes infinite time. Thanks to Refinement by Parts, it is sufficient to verify the three conjuncts of R separately:

$x'=1 \ \Longleftarrow \ $ **if** $x=1$ **then** *ok* **else** $(x:= div\ x\ 2.\ \ t:= t+1.\ \ x'=1)$

$x \geq 1 \ \Rightarrow\ t' \leq t + log\ x \ \Longleftarrow\ $ **if** $x=1$ **then** *ok*

$\qquad\qquad\qquad\qquad$ **else** $(x:= div\ x\ 2.\ \ t:= t+1.\ \ x \geq 1 \Rightarrow t' \leq t + log\ x)$

$x<1 \ \Rightarrow\ t'=\infty \ \Longleftarrow\ $ **if** $x=1$ **then** *ok* **else** $(x:= div\ x\ 2.\ \ t:= t+1.\ \ x<1 \ \Rightarrow\ t'=\infty)$

We can apply the Substitution Law to rewrite these three parts as follows:

$x'=1 \ \Longleftarrow\ $ **if** $x=1$ **then** $x'=x \wedge t'=t$ **else** $x'=1$

$x \geq 1 \ \Rightarrow\ t' \leq t + log\ x \ \Longleftarrow\ $ **if** $x=1$ **then** $x'=x \wedge t'=t$

$\qquad\qquad\qquad\qquad$ **else** $div\ x\ 2 \geq 1 \ \Rightarrow\ t' \leq t+1 + log\ (div\ x\ 2)$

$x<1 \ \Rightarrow\ t'=\infty \ \Longleftarrow\ $ **if** $x=1$ **then** $x'=x \wedge t'=t$ **else** $div\ x\ 2 < 1 \ \Rightarrow\ t'=\infty$

Now we break each of these three parts in two using Refinement by Cases. We must prove

$x'=1 \ \Longleftarrow\ x=1 \wedge x'=x \wedge t'=t$

$x'=1 \ \Longleftarrow\ x \neq 1 \wedge x'=1$

$x \geq 1 \ \Rightarrow\ t' \leq t + log\ x \ \Longleftarrow\ x=1 \wedge x'=x \wedge t'=t$

$x \geq 1 \ \Rightarrow\ t' \leq t + log\ x \ \Longleftarrow\ x \neq 1 \wedge (div\ x\ 2 \geq 1 \ \Rightarrow\ t' \leq t+1 + log\ (div\ x\ 2))$

$x<1 \ \Rightarrow\ t'=\infty \ \Longleftarrow\ x=1 \wedge x'=x \wedge t'=t$

$x<1 \ \Rightarrow\ t'=\infty \ \Longleftarrow\ x \neq 1 \wedge (div\ x\ 2 < 1 \ \Rightarrow\ t'=\infty)$

We'll prove each of these in turn. First,

$\qquad x'=1 \ \Longleftarrow\ x=1 \wedge x'=x \wedge t'=t \qquad\qquad$ by transitivity and specialization

Next,

$\qquad x'=1 \ \Longleftarrow\ x \neq 1 \wedge x'=1 \qquad\qquad$ by specialization

Next,

$\qquad (x \geq 1 \ \Rightarrow\ t' \leq t + log\ x \ \Longleftarrow\ x=1 \wedge x'=x \wedge t'=t)$

Use the first Law of Portation to move the initial antecedent over to the solution side where it becomes a conjunct.

$\qquad =\quad t' \leq t + log\ x \ \Longleftarrow\ x=1 \wedge x'=x \wedge t'=t \qquad\qquad$ and note that $log\ 1 = 0$.

Next comes the hardest one of the six.

$\qquad (x \geq 1 \ \Rightarrow\ t' \leq t + log\ x \ \Longleftarrow\ x \neq 1 \wedge (div\ x\ 2 \geq 1 \ \Rightarrow\ t' \leq t+1 + log\ (div\ x\ 2)))$

Again use the first Law of Portation to move the initial antecedent over to the solution side where it becomes a conjunct.

$$= \quad t'\le t+ log\ x \ \Leftarrow\ x{>}1 \wedge (div\ x\ 2 \ge 1\ \Rightarrow\ t'\le t + 1 + log\ (div\ x\ 2))$$

Since x is integer, $x{>}1\ =\ div\ x\ 2 \ge 1$, so by the first Law of Discharge,

$$= \quad t'\le t+ log\ x \ \Leftarrow\ x{>}1\ \wedge\ t'\le t+1+ log\ (div\ x\ 2)$$

By the first Law of Portation, move $t'\le t+1+ log\ (div\ x\ 2)$ over to the left side.

$$= \quad (t'\le t+1+ log\ (div\ x\ 2)) \Rightarrow t'\le t+ log\ x)\ \Leftarrow\ x{>}1$$

Note that $(t'{\le}a \Rightarrow t'{\le}b)\ \Leftarrow\ a{\le}b$.

$$\Leftarrow \quad t+1+ log\ (div\ x\ 2)\le t+ log\ x\ \Leftarrow\ x{>}1 \qquad\qquad \text{subtract } t+1 \text{ from each side}$$

$$= \quad log\ (div\ x\ 2)\le log\ x-1\ \Leftarrow\ x{>}1$$

$$= \quad log\ (div\ x\ 2)\le log\ (x/2)\ \Leftarrow\ x{>}1 \qquad\qquad log \text{ is monotonic for } x{>}0$$

$$\Leftarrow \quad div\ x\ 2 \le x/2 \qquad\qquad\qquad\qquad\qquad\qquad div \text{ is / and then round down}$$

The next one is trivial.

$$\qquad (x{<}1\ \Rightarrow\ t'{=}\infty\ \Leftarrow\ x{=}1 \wedge x'{=}x \wedge t'{=}t) \qquad \text{Law of Portation}$$

$$= \quad t'{=}\infty\ \Leftarrow\ \perp \wedge x'{=}x \wedge t'{=}t \qquad\qquad\qquad \text{first Base Law}$$

$$= \quad t'{=}\infty\ \Leftarrow\ \perp \qquad\qquad\qquad\qquad\qquad\qquad \text{fourth Base Law}$$

And finally,

$$\qquad (x{<}1\ \Rightarrow\ t'{=}\infty\ \Leftarrow\ x{\ne}1 \wedge (div\ x\ 2 {<} 1\ \Rightarrow t'{=}\infty)) \ \text{Law of Portation}$$

$$= \quad t'{=}\infty\ \Leftarrow\ x{<}1 \wedge (div\ x\ 2 {<} 1\ \Rightarrow\ t'{=}\infty) \qquad \text{Discharge}$$

$$= \quad t'{=}\infty\ \Leftarrow\ x{<}1 \wedge t'{=}\infty \qquad\qquad\qquad\qquad \text{Specialization}$$

And that completes the proof.

Termination

A customer arrives with the specification

(a) $x'{=}2$

He evidently wants a computation in which variable x has final value 2 . A programmer provides it in the usual way: she refines his specification by a program and executes it. There are many ways to refine this specification. Perversely but legitimately, the refinement she chooses, including recursive time, is

$$\qquad x'{=}2\ \Leftarrow\ t{:=}t{+}1.\ \ x'{=}2$$

and execution begins. The customer waits for his result, and after a time becomes impatient. The programmer tells him to wait longer. After more time has passed, the customer sees the weakness in his specification and decides to strengthen it. He wants a computation that finishes at a finite time, and specifies it thus:

(b) $x'{=}2 \wedge t'{<}\infty$

The programmer rejects (b) because it is unimplementable: (b) $\wedge\ t' \ge t$ is unsatisfiable for $t{=}\infty$. It may seem strange to reject a specification just because it cannot be satisfied with nondecreasing time when started at time ∞ . After all, we never want to start at time ∞ . But consider the dependent composition $P.Q$ with P taking infinite time. Then Q starts at time ∞ (in other words, it never starts), and the theory must be good for this case too. An implementable specification must be satisfiable with nondecreasing time for all initial states, even for initial time ∞ . So the customer weakens his specification a little:

(c) $x'=2 \;\wedge\; (t<\infty \Rightarrow t'<\infty)$

He says he does not care how long it takes, except that it must not take forever. The programmer can refine (c) with exactly the same construction as (a)! Including recursive time, her refinement is

$\qquad x'=2 \wedge (t<\infty \Rightarrow t'<\infty) \;\; \Leftarrow \;\; t:= t+1. \;\; x'=2 \wedge (t<\infty \Rightarrow t'<\infty)$

Execution begins. When the customer becomes restless she again tells him to wait longer. After a while he decides to change his specification again:

(d) $x'=2 \wedge t'=t$

He not only wants his result in finite time, he wants it instantly. Now she must abandon her recursive construction, and she refines

$\qquad x'=2 \wedge t'=t \;\; \Leftarrow \;\; x:= 2$

Execution provides the customer with the desired result at the desired time.

Under specification (a) the customer is entitled to complain about a computation if and only if it terminates in a state in which $x'\neq 2$. Under specification (c) he can complain about a computation if it delivers a final state in which $x'\neq 2$ or it takes forever. But of course there is never a time when he can complain that a computation has taken forever, so the circumstances in which he can complain that specification (c) has not been met are exactly the same as for specification (a). This fact is accurately reflected in the theory, which allows the same refinement constructions for (c) as for (a). Specification (d) gives a time bound, therefore more circumstances in which to complain, therefore fewer refinements.

As this story shows, it is meaningless to request or to promise results in a "finite but unbounded" time. One might suggest that a time bound of a million years is also untestable in practice, but the distinction is one of principle, not practicality. A time bound is a line that divides shorter computations from longer ones. There is no line dividing finite computations from infinite ones.

Given a specification P and a prestate σ , we can say that termination is required within some time bound as follows:

$\qquad \exists n\colon nat\cdot\; \forall \sigma'\cdot\; t' \le t+n \;\Leftarrow\; P$

This may be called "the exact precondition for termination". And

$\qquad \forall \sigma\cdot\; \exists n\colon nat\cdot\; \forall \sigma'\cdot\; t' \le t+n \;\Leftarrow\; P$

says that P always requires termination within some time bound. This can be restated equivalently as

$\qquad \exists f\cdot\; \forall \sigma,\, \sigma'\cdot\; t' \le t+f\sigma \;\Leftarrow\; P$

where f is a nonnegative finite function of the state.

_____End of Termination

Linear Search

Exercise 134: Write a program to find the first occurrence of a given item in a given list. The execution time must be linear in the length of the list.

Let the list be L and the value we are looking for be x (these are not state variables). Our program will assign natural variable h (here it is) the index of the first occurrence of x in L if x is there. If x is not there, its "first occurrence" is not defined; it will be convenient to indicate that x is not in L by assigning h the length of L .

Let us call the part of the specification that refers to the result R , and formalize it as

$$R \;=\; \neg\, x\!: L\,(0,..h') \;\wedge\; (Lh'\!=\!x \,\vee\, h'\!=\!\#L)$$

The full specification is $R \wedge t' \le t+\#L$. But first, let us consider just R . The idea, of course, is to look at each item in the list, in order, starting at item 0 , until we either find x or run out of items. At each stage in the search, all previous items differ from x . We can represent this fact by condition A , defined as

$$A \;=\; \neg\, x\!: L\,(0,..h)$$

We are now ready to solve problem R as follows:

$$R \;\Longleftarrow\; h\!:=\!0.\;\; h\!\le\!\#L \wedge A \Rightarrow R$$

The new problem $h\!\le\!\#L \wedge A \Rightarrow R$ is weaker than the original problem R , so it is easier to solve. We have made progress. In the new problem, we have seen h items that differ from x . We can obtain the first conjunct of R by doing nothing, since it is A' (identical to A except that h' replaces h). To obtain the second conjunct, we need to test either $Lh\!=\!x$ or $h\!=\!\#L$. To test $Lh\!=\!x$ we need to know $h\!<\!\#L$, so we have to test $h\!=\!\#L$ first.

$$h\!\le\!\#L \wedge A \Rightarrow R \;\Longleftarrow\; \textbf{if } h\!=\!\#L \textbf{ then } ok \textbf{ else } h\!<\!\#L \wedge A \Rightarrow R$$

In the remaining problem we are able to test $Lh\!=\!x$.

$$h\!<\!\#L \wedge A \Rightarrow R \;\Longleftarrow\; \textbf{if } Lh\!=\!x \textbf{ then } ok \textbf{ else } (h\!:=\!h\!+\!1.\;\; h\!\le\!\#L \wedge A \Rightarrow R)$$

Now for the timing:

$$t' \le t+\#L \;\Longleftarrow\; h\!:=\!0.\;\; h\!\le\!\#L \Rightarrow t' \le t+\#L-h$$

$$h\!\le\!\#L \Rightarrow t' \le t+\#L-h \;\Longleftarrow\; \textbf{if } h\!=\!\#L \textbf{ then } ok \textbf{ else } h\!<\!\#L \Rightarrow t' \le t+\#L-h$$

$$h\!<\!\#L \Rightarrow t' \le t+\#L-h \;\Longleftarrow\; \textbf{if } Lh\!=\!x \textbf{ then } ok$$
$$\textbf{else } (h\!:=\!h\!+\!1.\;\; t\!:=\!t\!+\!1.\;\; h\!\le\!\#L \Rightarrow t' \le t+\#L-h)$$

Refinement by Parts says that if the same refinement structure can be used for two specifications, then it can be used for their conjunction. We have just used the same refinement structure for both R and $t' \le t+\#L$, so we know it works for their conjunction, and that solves the original problem.

Condition A talks about indexes $0,..h$. This makes sense only if $h\!\le\!\#L$. We might therefore consider that $h\!\le\!\#L$ is implicit in A and shorten $h\!\le\!\#L \wedge A$ to just A. For the timing we needed $h\!\le\!\#L$ but not A .

It is not really necessary to take such small steps in programming. We could have written

$R \wedge t' \le t+\#L \quad \Longleftarrow \quad h:= 0. \quad h{\le}\#L \wedge A \Rightarrow R \wedge t' \le t+\#L{-}h$

$h{\le}\#L \wedge A \Rightarrow R \wedge t' \le t+\#L{-}h \quad \Longleftarrow$

   if $h = \#L$ **then** *ok*

   else if $L\,h = x$ **then** *ok*

   else $(h:= h+1. \quad t:= t+1. \quad h{\le}\#L \wedge A \Rightarrow R \wedge t' \le t+\#L{-}h)$

But now, suppose we learn that the given list L is known to be nonempty. To take advantage of this new information, we rewrite the first refinement

$R \wedge t' \le t+\#L \quad \Longleftarrow \quad h:= 0. \quad h{<}\#L \wedge A \Rightarrow R \wedge t' \le t+\#L{-}h$

and that's all; the new problem is already solved if we haven't made our steps too large. (Note: Using the recursive time measure, there is no advantage to rewriting the first refinement this way. Using the real time measure, there is a small advantage.) As a habit, we write information about constants once, rather than in every specification. Here, for instance, we should say $\#L{>}0$ once so that we can use it when we prove our refinements, but we did not repeat it in each specification.

We can sometimes improve the execution time (real measure) by a technique called the <u>sentinel</u>. We need list L to be a variable so we can catenate one value to the end of it. If we can do so cheaply enough, we should begin by catenating x . Then the search is sure to find x , and we can skip the test $h = \#L$ each iteration. The program, ignoring time, becomes

$R \quad \Longleftarrow \quad L:= L^+[x]. \quad h:= 0. \quad Q$

$Q \quad \Longleftarrow \quad$ **if** $Lh{=}x$ **then** *ok* **else** $(h:= h+1. \quad Q)$

where

$Q \;=\; L\,(\#L{-}1) = x \wedge h{<}\#L \wedge A \;\Rightarrow\; A' \wedge Lh'{=}x$

End of Linear Search

Binary Search

Exercise 135: Write a program to find a given item in a given sorted list. The execution time must be logarithmic in the length of the list. The strategy is to identify which half of the list contains the item if it occurs at all, then which quarter, then which eighth, and so on.

As in the previous subsection, let the list be L and the value we are looking for be x (these are not state variables). Our program will again assign natural variable h the index of an occurrence of x in L if x is there. But this time, let's indicate whether x is present in L by assigning boolean variable p the value $\top$ if it is and $\bot$ if not. Ignoring time for the moment, the problem R is

$R \;=\; (x{:}\, L\,(0,..\#L) \;=\; p' \;\Longrightarrow\; Lh' = x)$

As the search progresses, we narrow the segment of the list that may contain x ; let us introduce variables i and j to keep track of this segment, and condition A to say that x does not occur outside the segment $i,..j$.

$$A \ = \ \neg \ x{:}\ L\ (0,..i\ ,\ \ j,..\#L)$$

According to A , if x occurs, it occurs within the segment $i,..j$.

We can now solve the problem.

$$R \ \Longleftarrow \ i{:=}\ 0.\ \ j{:=}\ \#L.\ \ i{\leq}j \wedge A \Rightarrow R$$

$$i{\leq}j \wedge A \Rightarrow R \ \Longleftarrow \ \mathbf{if}\ i{=}j\ \mathbf{then}\ p{:=}\ \perp\ \mathbf{else}\ i{<}j \wedge\ A \Rightarrow R$$

$$i{<}j \wedge\ A \Rightarrow R \ \Longleftarrow \ i{<}j \ \Rightarrow\ h'{:}\ i,..j \wedge i'{=}i \wedge j'{=}j.$$
$$\mathbf{if}\ Lh{=}x\ \mathbf{then}\ p{:=}\ \mathsf{T}$$
$$\mathbf{else}\ (\ \mathbf{if}\ Lh{<}x\ \mathbf{then}\ i{:=}\ h{+}1\ \mathbf{else}\ j{:=}\ h.$$
$$i{\leq}j \wedge A \Rightarrow R\ )$$

To get the correct result, it does not matter how we choose $h'{:}\ i,..j$. If we refine it as $h{:=}\ i$, we have a linear search. To obtain the best execution time on average, we should choose h so it splits the segment $i;..j$ into two segments in which there is an equal probability of finding x . In the absence of further information about probabilities, we should split $i;..j$ into two segments of equal size.

$$i{<}j \ \Rightarrow\ h'{:}\ i,..j \wedge i'{=}i \wedge j'{=}j \ \Longleftarrow \ h{:=}\ div\ (i{+}j)\ 2$$

This equal split also gives us the smallest maximum execution time.

The recursive execution time is found by putting $t{:=}\ t{+}1$ before the final, recursive call. We will have to prove

$$T \ \Longleftarrow \ i{:=}\ 0.\ \ j{:=}\ \#L.\ \ U$$

$$U \ \Longleftarrow \ \mathbf{if}\ i{=}j\ \mathbf{then}\ p{:=}\ \perp\ \mathbf{else}\ V$$

$$V \ \Longleftarrow \ h{:=}\ div\ (i{+}j)\ 2.$$
$$\mathbf{if}\ Lh{=}x\ \mathbf{then}\ p{:=}\ \mathsf{T}$$
$$\mathbf{else}\ (\ \mathbf{if}\ Lh{<}x\ \mathbf{then}\ i{:=}\ h{+}1\ \mathbf{else}\ j{:=}\ h.$$
$$t{:=}\ t{+}1.\ \ U\ )$$

for a suitable choice of timing expressions T , U , V . We might guess that T will be something like $t' \leq t + log\ (\#L)$, but it cannot be exactly that since the empty list does not take time $-\infty$ to search. If we do not see how to adjust this formula, we can always try executing the program a few times to see what we get. The worst case occurs when the item sought is smaller than all items in the list. For this case we get

$$\#L \quad = \qquad 0 \;\; 1 \;\; 2 \;\; 3 \;\; 4 \;\; 5 \;\; 6 \;\; 7 \;\; 8 \;\; 9 \;\; 10 \;\; 11 \;\; 12 \;\; 13 \;\; 14 \;\; 15 \;\; 16 \;\; 17 \;\; 18 \ldots$$
$$t'-t \quad = \qquad 0 \;\; 1 \;\; 2 \;\; 2 \;\; 3 \;\; 3 \;\; 3 \;\; 3 \;\; 4 \;\; 4 \;\; 4 \;\; 4 \;\; 4 \;\; 4 \;\; 4 \;\; 4 \;\; 5 \;\; 5 \;\; 5 \ldots$$

from which we define

$$T \;=\; \textbf{if } \#L{=}0 \textbf{ then } t'{=}t \textbf{ else } t' \le t + 1 + log\,(\#L)$$
$$U \;=\; (i{=}j \Rightarrow t'{=}t) \wedge (i{<}j \Rightarrow t' \le t + 1 + log\,(j{-}i))$$
$$V \;=\; i{<}j \Rightarrow t' \le t + 1 + log\,(j{-}i)$$

and prove the three refinements. The refinements for T and U are easy, and so is the first case $(Lh{=}x)$ of the refinement for V . The second and third cases require us to prove

$$V \;\Longleftarrow\; h{:=} \, div\,(i{+}j)\,2. \;\; i{:=}h{+}1. \;\; t{:=}t{+}1. \;\; U$$
$$V \;\Longleftarrow\; h{:=} \, div\,(i{+}j)\,2. \;\; j{:=}h. \;\; t{:=}t{+}1. \;\; U$$

We leave them to the industrious reader.

The program we have just developed, the standard binary search, is ugly in two places. First, it is ugly that i and j are changed asymmetrically: $i{:=}h{+}1$ and $j{:=}h$. That may seem to be a problem of using the asymmetric interval $i,..j$. Second, the time bound has a special case for the empty list. Perhaps the time bound can be excused because it is logarithmic; there is no zero on a logarithmic scale. But we might be able to do better if we treat the empty list separately, and we can certainly improve the way we divide the remaining interval.

$$R \;\Longleftarrow\; \textbf{if } \#L{=}0 \textbf{ then } p{:=}\perp \textbf{ else } (h{:=}0. \;\; j{:=}\#L. \;\; B \Rightarrow R)$$

where

$$B \;=\; h{<}j \wedge (x{:}\, L\,(0,..\#L) \;\Rightarrow\; x{:}\, L\,(h,..j))$$

B says that the interval $h,..j$ is nonempty, and if x is anywhere, it's in that interval. From now on, we will keep that interval nonempty. And one more trick: we won't test for the presence of x until the interval size is 1 .

$$B \Rightarrow R \;\Longleftarrow\; \textbf{if } j{-}h = 1 \textbf{ then } p{:=}Lh{=}x$$
$$\textbf{else } (\, m{:=} \, div\,(h{+}j)\,2.$$
$$\qquad \textbf{if } Lm{\le}x \textbf{ then } h{:=}m \textbf{ else } j{:=}m.$$
$$\qquad B \Rightarrow R \,)$$

It is prettier, but let's see what prettiness costs. For the main loop we prove

$$h{<}j \;\Rightarrow\; t' \le t + ceil\,(log\,(j{-}h)) \;\Longleftarrow$$
$$\qquad \textbf{if } j{-}h = 1 \textbf{ then } p{:=}Lh{=}x$$
$$\qquad \textbf{else } (\; m{:=} \, div\,(h{+}j)\,2.$$
$$\qquad\qquad \textbf{if } Lm{\le}x \textbf{ then } h{:=}m \textbf{ else } j{:=}m.$$
$$\qquad\qquad t{:=}t{+}1. \;\; h{<}j \;\Rightarrow\; t' \le t + ceil\,(log\,(j{-}h)) \,)$$

where $ceil$ is the function that rounds up. Using Refinement by Cases, we divide the proof into the following three cases.

$h<j \Rightarrow t' \le t + ceil\ (log\ (j-h)) \; \Longleftarrow \; j-h = 1 \; \wedge \; (p:= Lh=x)$

$h<j \Rightarrow t' \le t + ceil\ (log\ (j-h)) \; \Longleftarrow$
$\qquad j-h \neq 1 \; \wedge \; (\; m:= div\ (h+j)\ 2.$
$\qquad\qquad\qquad Lm{\le}x \; \wedge \; (h:= m.\ \ t:= t+1.\ \ h<j \Rightarrow t' \le t + ceil\ (log\ (j-h))))\ )$

$h<j \Rightarrow t' \le t + ceil\ (log\ (j-h)) \; \Longleftarrow$
$\qquad j-h \neq 1 \; \wedge \; (\; m:= div\ (h+j)\ 2.$
$\qquad\qquad\qquad Lm{>}x \; \wedge \; (j:= m.\ \ t:= t+1.\ \ h<j \Rightarrow t' \le t + ceil\ (log\ (j-h))))\ )$

In the first case, on the right side we have $j-h = 1$ and, from the assignment, $t'=t$. Together they imply the left side since $log\ 1 = 0$.

The second case to be proven was

$$(h<j \Rightarrow t' \le t + ceil\ (log\ (j-h)))$$
$$\Longleftarrow \qquad j-h \neq 1 \; \wedge \; (\; m:= div\ (h+j)\ 2.$$
$$\qquad\qquad\qquad\qquad Lm{\le}x \; \wedge \; (h:= m.\ \ t:= t+1.\ \ h<j \Rightarrow t' \le t + ceil\ (log\ (j-h))))\ )$$

Use Portation to move $h<j$ to the right side where it conjoins with $j-h \neq 1$ to give $j-h > 1$. Also, drop $Lm{\le}x$ because it won't help; this weakens an antecedent and so strengthens the implication. Also, use the Substitution Law for each assignment.

$$\Longleftarrow \qquad t' \le t + ceil\ (log\ (j-h))$$
$$\Longleftarrow j-h > 1 \wedge (div\ (h+j)\ 2 < j \Rightarrow t' \le t + 1 + ceil\ (log\ (j - div\ (h+j)\ 2)))$$

On the right side, we must use $j-h > 1$ to discharge the antecedent $div\ (h+j)\ 2 < j$. Here is a proof that it does.

    if $even\ (h+j)$
    then ($div\ (h+j)\ 2 < j$
         $=$ $(h+j)/2 < j$
         $=$ $j-h > 0$
         $\Longleftarrow$ $j-h > 1$)
    else ($div\ (h+j)\ 2 < j$
         $=$ $(h+j-1)/2 < j$
         $=$ $j-h > -1$
         $\Longleftarrow$ $j-h > 1$)

Resuming the main proof,

    $=$ $t' \le t + ceil\ (log\ (j-h)) \; \Longleftarrow \; j-h > 1 \; \wedge \; t' \le t + 1 + ceil\ (log\ (j - div\ (h+j)\ 2))$
    $=$ $j-h > 1 \Rightarrow 1 + ceil\ (log\ (j - div\ (h+j)\ 2)) \le ceil\ (log\ (j-h))$

To prove the inequality, it is again necessary to look at even and odd cases separately.

if *even* (*h*+*j*)

then   1 + *ceil* (*log* (*j* − *div* (*h*+*j*) 2))

=   *ceil* (1 + *log* (*j* − (*h*+*j*)/2))

=   *ceil* (*log* (*j*−*h*))

else   1 + *ceil* (*log* (*j* − *div* (*h*+*j*) 2))

=   *ceil* (1 + *log* (*j* − (*h*+*j*−1)/2))

=   *ceil* (*log* (*j*−*h*+1))   If *h*+*j* is odd then *j*−*h* is odd and can't be a power of 2

=   *ceil* (*log* (*j*−*h*))

and that completes the second our our three cases.

Finally we have to prove

$$(h<j \ \Rightarrow \ t' \leq t + ceil \ (log \ (j-h)))$$
$$\Leftarrow \quad j-h \neq 1 \ \wedge \ (\ m:= div \ (h+j) \ 2.$$
$$Lm>x \ \wedge \ (j:= m. \ t:= t+1. \ h<j \ \Rightarrow \ t' \leq t + ceil \ (log \ (j-h)))\ )$$

We use Portation exactly as before, we drop *Lm*>*x* , and we use the Substitution Law for each assignment.

$$\Leftarrow \qquad t' \leq t + ceil \ (log \ (j-h))$$
$$\Leftarrow j-h > 1 \wedge (h < div \ (h+j) \ 2 \ \Rightarrow \ t' \leq t + 1 + ceil \ (log \ (div \ (h+j) \ 2 - h)))$$

On the right side, we must use *j*−*h* > 1 to discharge the antecedent *h* < *div* (*h*+*j*) 2 . Here is a proof that it does.

$$h < div \ (h+j) \ 2$$
$$\Leftarrow \quad h < (h+j-1)/2$$
$$= \quad j-h > 1$$

Resuming the main proof,

$$= \qquad t' \leq t + ceil \ (log \ (j-h)) \ \Leftarrow \ j-h > 1 \ \wedge \ t' \leq t + 1 + ceil \ (log \ (div \ (h+j) \ 2 - h))$$
$$= \qquad j-h > 1 \ \Rightarrow \ 1 + ceil \ (log \ (div \ (h+j) \ 2 - h)) \leq ceil \ (log \ (j-h))$$

Now taking the consequent by itself,

$$1 + ceil \ (log \ (div \ (h+j) \ 2 - h))$$
$$= \quad ceil \ (1 + log \ (div \ (h+j) \ 2 - h))$$
$$\leq \quad ceil \ (1 + log \ ((h+j)/2 - h))$$
$$= \quad ceil \ (1 + log \ ((j-h)/2))$$
$$= \quad ceil \ (log \ (j-h))$$

We have proven that *ceil* (*log* (*j*−*h*)) is an upper bound on the execution time of the main loop, so it is a small step to show that **if** #*L*=0 **then** 0 **else** *ceil* (*log* (#*L*)) is an upper bound for the entire execution. The worst case execution time is actually a tiny bit less for the prettier program! Of course, the best case execution time is now greater. (More importantly, we state without proof that the average execution time is a tiny bit less. The real time measure is also less, since the loop now includes only two tests in place of the former three.)

_____End of Binary Search

Fast Exponentiation

Exercise 132: Given rational variables x and z and natural variable y, write a program for $z' = x^y$ that runs fast without using exponentiation.

This specification does not say how fast the execution should be; let's make it as fast as we can. The idea is to accumulate a product, using variable z as accumulator. Define

$$P \ = \ z' = z \times x^y$$

We can solve the problem as follows, though this solution does not give the fastest possible computation.

$z'=x^y \quad \Longleftarrow \quad z:= 1. \ P$

$P \quad \Longleftarrow \quad \textbf{if } y=0 \textbf{ then } ok \textbf{ else } y{>}0 \Rightarrow P$

$y{>}0 \Rightarrow P \quad \Longleftarrow \quad z:= z \times x. \ y:= y{-}1. \ P$

To speed up the computation, we change our refinement of $y{>}0 \Rightarrow P$ to test whether y is even or odd; in the odd case we make no improvement but in the even case we can cut y in half.

$y{>}0 \Rightarrow P \quad \Longleftarrow \quad \textbf{if } even \ y \textbf{ then } even \ y \wedge y{>}0 \Rightarrow P \textbf{ else } odd \ y \Rightarrow P$

$even \ y \wedge y{>}0 \Rightarrow P \quad \Longleftarrow \quad x:= x \times x. \ y:= y/2. \ P$

$odd \ y \Rightarrow P \quad \Longleftarrow \quad z:= z \times x. \ y:= y{-}1. \ P$

Each of these refinements is easily proven.

We have made the major improvement, but there are still several minor speedups. For most purposes, the minor speedups are not worth the effort. We make them partly as an exercise in squeezing out the last drop of speed possible, and mainly as an example of program modification. To begin, if y is even and greater than 0, it is at least 2; after cutting it in half, it is at least 1; let us not waste that information. We re-refine

$even \ y \wedge y{>}0 \Rightarrow P \quad \Longleftarrow \quad x:= x \times x. \ y:= y/2. \ y{>}0 \Rightarrow P$

If y is initially odd and 1 is subtracted, then it must become even; let us not waste that information. We re-refine

$odd \ y \Rightarrow P \quad \Longleftarrow \quad z:= z \times x. \ y:= y{-}1. \ even \ y \Rightarrow P$

$even \ y \Rightarrow P \quad \Longleftarrow \quad \textbf{if } y = 0 \textbf{ then } ok \textbf{ else } even \ y \wedge y{>}0 \Rightarrow P$

And one more very minor improvement: if the program is used to calculate x^0 less often than x to an odd power (a reasonable assumption), it would be better to start with the test for evenness rather than the test for zeroness. We re-refine

$P \quad \Longleftarrow \quad \textbf{if } even \ y \textbf{ then } even \ y \Rightarrow P \textbf{ else } odd \ y \Rightarrow P$

Program modification, whether to gain a tiny bit of speed or for any other purpose, can be dangerously error-prone when practiced without the proper theory. Try writing this program in your favorite standard programming language, starting with the first simple solution, and making the same modifications. The first modification introduces a new case within a loop; the second modification changes one of the cases into an inner loop; the third modification changes the outer loop into a case within the inner loop, with an intermediate exit; the final modification changes the loop entry-point to a choice of two other entry-points. The flow chart looks like this.

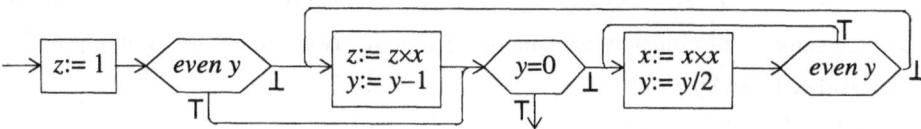

Without the theory, this sort of program surgery is bound to introduce a few bugs. With the theory we have a better chance of making the modifications correctly because each new refinement is an easy theorem.

Before we consider time, here is the fast exponentiation program again.

$z'=x^y \quad \Longleftarrow \quad z:= 1. \ P$

$P \quad \Longleftarrow \quad \textbf{if } even \ y \textbf{ then } even \ y \Rightarrow P \textbf{ else } odd \ y \Rightarrow P$

$even \ y \Rightarrow P \quad \Longleftarrow \quad \textbf{if } y=0 \textbf{ then } ok \textbf{ else } even \ y \wedge y>0 \Rightarrow P$

$odd \ y \Rightarrow P \quad \Longleftarrow \quad z:= z \times x. \ y:= y-1. \ even \ y \Rightarrow P$

$even \ y \wedge y>0 \Rightarrow P \quad \Longleftarrow \quad x:= x \times x. \ y:= y/2. \ y>0 \Rightarrow P$

$y>0 \Rightarrow P \quad \Longleftarrow \quad \textbf{if } even \ y \textbf{ then } even \ y \wedge y>0 \Rightarrow P \textbf{ else } odd \ y \Rightarrow P$

In the recursive time measure, every loop of calls must include a time increment. In this program, a single time increment charged to the call $y>0 \Rightarrow P$ does the trick.

$even \ y \wedge y>0 \Rightarrow P \quad \Longleftarrow \quad x:= x \times x. \ y:= y/2. \ t:= t+1. \ y>0 \Rightarrow P$

To help us decide what time bounds we might try to prove, we can execute the program on some test cases. We find, for each natural n ,

$y: 2^n,..2^{n+1} \Rightarrow t' = t+n$

plus the isolated case

$y=0 \Rightarrow t'=t$

We therefore define the timing specification

$T \quad = \quad \textbf{if } y=0 \textbf{ then } t'=t \textbf{ else } t' \leq t + log \ y$

Then we prove

$z'=x^y \wedge T \quad \Longleftarrow \quad z:= 1. \ P \wedge T$

$P \wedge T \quad \Longleftarrow \quad \textbf{if } even \ y \textbf{ then } even \ y \Rightarrow P \wedge T \textbf{ else } odd \ y \Rightarrow P \wedge T$

$even \ y \Rightarrow P \wedge T \quad \Longleftarrow \quad \textbf{if } y=0 \textbf{ then } ok \textbf{ else } even \ y \wedge y>0 \Rightarrow P \wedge T$

$odd \ y \Rightarrow P \wedge T \quad \Longleftarrow \quad z:= z \times x. \ y:= y-1. \ even \ y \Rightarrow P \wedge T$

$even \ y \wedge y>0 \Rightarrow P \wedge T \quad \Longleftarrow \quad x:= x \times x. \ y:= y/2. \ t:= t+1. \ y>0 \Rightarrow P \wedge T$

$y>0 \Rightarrow P \wedge T \quad \Longleftarrow \quad \textbf{if } even \ y \textbf{ then } even \ y \wedge y>0 \Rightarrow P \wedge T \textbf{ else } odd \ y \Rightarrow P \wedge T$

With only a little more effort, we can show the exact execution time by replacing T with

$$T \quad = \quad \textbf{if } y{=}0 \textbf{ then } t'{=}t \textbf{ else } t' = t + floor \ (log \ y)$$

where *floor* is the function that rounds down.

We could use Refinement by Parts to separate the results from the timing. In the above, just omit the initial "$z'{=}x^y \land$" and all occurrences of "$P \land$". It does not matter that two of the specifications are now the same. Unfortunately we cannot separate the two parts of the timing proof. We can prove the isolated case by itself:

$$y{=}0 \Rightarrow t'{=}t \quad \Longleftarrow \quad z{:=}1.\ y{=}0 \Rightarrow t'{=}t$$
$$y{=}0 \Rightarrow t'{=}t \quad \Longleftarrow \quad \textbf{if } even \ y \textbf{ then } y{=}0 \Rightarrow t'{=}t \textbf{ else } T$$
$$y{=}0 \Rightarrow t'{=}t \quad \Longleftarrow \quad \textbf{if } y{=}0 \textbf{ then } ok \textbf{ else } T$$
$$T \quad \Longleftarrow \quad z{:=} z{\times}x.\ y{:=} y{-}1.\ y{=}0 \Rightarrow t'{=}t$$
$$T \quad \Longleftarrow \quad x{:=} x{\times}x.\ y{:=} y/2.\ t{:=} t{+}1.\ T$$
$$T \quad \Longleftarrow \quad \textbf{if } even \ y \textbf{ then } T \textbf{ else } T$$

Again, it does not matter that some of the specifications are refined more than once; they will be distinguished when we conjoin specifications using Refinement by Parts. But the timing for $y{>}0$ cannot be separated because it depends on the timing for $y{=}0$ in the refinement containing $y{:=} y{-}1$.

———————————————————————————————————End of Fast Exponentiation

Fibonacci Numbers

In this subsection, we tackle Exercise 195. The definition of the Fibonacci numbers

$$f\ 0 \ = \ 0$$
$$f\ 1 \ = \ 1$$
$$f\ (n{+}2) \ = \ f\ n + f\ (n{+}1)$$

immediately suggests a recursive function definition

$$f \quad = \quad 0{\rightarrow}0\ |\ 1{\rightarrow}1\ |\ \lambda n{:}\ nat{+}2{\cdot}\ f\ (n{-}2) + f\ (n{-}1)$$
$$= \quad \lambda n{:}\ nat{\cdot}\ \textbf{if } n{<}2 \textbf{ then } n \textbf{ else } f\ (n{-}2) + f\ (n{-}1)$$

We did not include functions in our programming language, so we still have some work to do. Besides, the functional solution we have just given has exponential execution time, and we can do much better.

For $n \geq 2$, we can find a Fibonacci number if we know the previous pair of Fibonacci numbers. That suggests we keep track of a pair of numbers. Let x , y , and n be natural variables. We refine

$$x' = f\ n \quad \Longleftarrow \quad P$$

where P is the problem of finding a pair of Fibonacci numbers.

$$P \;=\; x' = f\,n \;\wedge\; y' = f\,(n+1)$$

When $n=0$, the solution is easy. When $n \geq 1$, we can decrease it by 1, find a pair of Fibonacci numbers at that previous argument, and then move x and y along one place.

$$P \;\Longleftarrow\; \textbf{if } n=0 \textbf{ then } (x:=0.\;\; y:=1) \textbf{ else } (n:=n-1.\;\; P.\;\; x'=y \;\wedge\; y' = x+y)$$

To move x and y along we need a third variable. We could use a new variable, but we already have n; is it safe to use n for this purpose? The specification $x'=y \;\wedge\; y' = x+y$ clearly allows n to change, so we can use it if we want.

$$x'=y \;\wedge\; y' = x+y \;\Longleftarrow\; n:=x.\;\; x:=y.\;\; y:=n+y$$

The time for this solution is linear. To prove it, we keep the same refinement structure, but we replace the specifications with new ones concerning time. We replace P by $t' = t+n$ and add $t:= t+1$ in front of its use; we also change $x'=y \;\wedge\; y = x+y$ into $t'=t$.

$$t' = t+n \;\Longleftarrow\; \textbf{if } n=0 \textbf{ then } (x:=0.\;\; y:=1) \textbf{ else } (n:=n-1.\;\; t:=t+1.\;\; t'=t+n.\;\; t'=t)$$

$$t'=t \;\Longleftarrow\; n:=x.\;\; x:=y.\;\; y:=n+y$$

Linear time is a lot better than exponential time, but we can do even better. Exercise 195 asks for a solution with logarithmic time. To get it, we need to take the hint offered in the exercise and use the equations

$$f(2k+1) \;=\; f\,k^2 + f(k+1)^2$$

$$f(2k+2) \;=\; 2\,f\!k\;f(k+1) + f(k+1)^2$$

These equations allow us to find a pair $f(2k+1),\, f(2k+2)$ in terms of a previous pair $f\!k,\, f(k+1)$ at half the argument. We refine

$$P \;\Longleftarrow\; \textbf{if } n=0 \textbf{ then } (x:=0.\;\; y:=1)$$
$$\qquad\qquad \textbf{else if } \textit{even } n \textbf{ then } \textit{even } n \wedge n > 0 \Rightarrow P$$
$$\qquad\qquad \textbf{else } \textit{odd } n \Rightarrow P$$

Let's take the last new problem first. If n is odd, we can cut it down from $2k+1$ to k by the assignment $n:= (n-1)/2$, then call P to obtain $f\!k$ and $f(k+1)$, then use the equations to obtain $f(2k+1)$ and $f(2k+2)$.

$$\textit{odd } n \Rightarrow P \;\Longleftarrow\; n:= (n-1)/2.\;\; P.\;\; x' = x^2 + y^2 \;\wedge\; y' = 2xy + y^2$$

The case $\textit{even } n \;\wedge\; n > 0$ is a little harder. We can decrease n from $2k+2$ to k by the assignment $n:= n/2 - 1$, then call P to obtain $f\!k$ and $f(k+1)$, then use the equations to obtain $f(2k+1)$ and $f(2k+2)$ as before, but this time we want $f(2k+2)$ and $f(2k+3)$. We can get $f(2k+3)$ as the sum of $f(2k+1)$ and $f(2k+2)$.

$$\textit{even } n \wedge n > 0 \Rightarrow P \;\Longleftarrow\; n:= n/2 - 1.\;\; P.\;\; x' = 2xy + y^2 \;\wedge\; y' = x^2 + y^2 + x'$$

The remaining two problems to find x' and y' in terms of x and y require a third variable as before, and as before, we can use n.

$$x' = x^2 + y^2 \;\wedge\; y' = 2xy + y^2 \;\; \Longleftarrow \;\; n := x. \;\; x := x^2 + y^2. \;\; y := 2ny + y^2$$
$$x' = 2xy + y^2 \;\wedge\; y' = x^2 + y^2 + x' \;\; \Longleftarrow \;\; n := x. \;\; x := 2xy + y^2. \;\; y := n^2 + y^2 + x$$

To prove that this program is now logarithmic time, we redefine

$$P \;=\; t' \leq t + log\,(n{+}1)$$

we replace the previous two problems with $t' = t$, and we put $t := t{+}1$ before calls to P. We must now prove

$$n{=}0 \Rightarrow P \;\; \Longleftarrow \;\; x := 0. \;\; y := 1$$
$$odd\ n \Rightarrow P \;\; \Longleftarrow \;\; n := (n{-}1)/2. \;\; t := t{+}1. \;\; P. \;\; t' = t$$
$$even\ n \wedge n{>}0 \Rightarrow P \;\; \Longleftarrow \;\; n := n/2 - 1. \;\; t := t{+}1. \;\; P. \;\; t' = t$$
$$t' = t \;\; \Longleftarrow \;\; n := x. \;\; x := x^2 + y^2. \;\; y := 2ny + y^2$$
$$t' = t \;\; \Longleftarrow \;\; n := x. \;\; x := 2xy + y^2. \;\; y := n^2 + y^2 + x$$

The first one and last two are easy. Here are the other two.

$$(odd\ n \Rightarrow t' \leq t + log\,(n{+}1)) \;\; \Longleftarrow \;\; (n := (n{-}1)/2. \;\; t := t{+}1. \;\; t' \leq t + log\,(n{+}1). \;\; t' = t)$$
$$= \quad (odd\ n \Rightarrow t' \leq t + log\,(n{+}1)) \;\; \Longleftarrow \;\; t' \leq t{+}1 + log\,((n{-}1)/2{+}1)$$

note that $(a \Rightarrow b) \Longleftarrow c \;=\; a \Rightarrow (b \Longleftarrow c)$

$$= \quad odd\ n \Rightarrow (t' \leq t + log\,(n{+}1) \;\Longleftarrow\; t' \leq t{+}1 + log\,((n{-}1)/2{+}1))$$
$$= \quad odd\ n \Rightarrow 1 + log\,((n{-}1)/2{+}1) \leq log\,(n{+}1)$$
$$= \quad odd\ n \Rightarrow log\,(n{-}1{+}2) \leq log\,(n{+}1)$$
$$= \quad odd\ n \Rightarrow log\,(n{+}1) \leq log\,(n{+}1)$$

$$(even\ n \wedge n{>}0 \Rightarrow t' \leq t + log\,(n{+}1)) \Longleftarrow (n := n/2 - 1. \;\; t := t{+}1. \;\; t' \leq t + log\,(n{+}1). \;\; t' = t)$$

by the same steps

$$= \quad even\ n \wedge n{>}0 \Rightarrow 1 + log\,(n/2 - 1{+}1) \leq log\,(n{+}1)$$
$$= \quad even\ n \wedge n{>}0 \Rightarrow log\ n \leq log\,(n{+}1)$$

——End of Fibonacci Numbers

——End of Time

Robustness

A program is robust if it describes reasonable behavior even when it is misused or used in error. What is "reasonable" is a matter of opinion, but we can illustrate some possibilities with a small example. Let i be an integer variable, and consider specification S defined by

$$S \;=\; i \geq 0 \;\Rightarrow\; i' = 0 \wedge t' \leq t{+}i$$

Clearly the specifier does not care what happens when initially $i < 0$; presumably S is intended to be used in a context where $i \geq 0$. But suppose someone makes a mistake and uses S in a context where $i < 0$. What will happen? That depends on how S is refined. Here are two possibilities.

(a) $S \Leftarrow i := 0$

(b) $S \Leftarrow$ **if** $i \geq 0$ **then** $i := 0$ **else** *print* "error: $i < 0$"

Both of these refinements are correct, so how do we choose between them? Clearly (a) is simplest, and fastest in execution. According to refinement (a), if by accident $i < 0$ initially, variable i will still be assigned 0 and execution will continue as though nothing were wrong. Perhaps later in the computation a disaster will occur; probably the bug will be hard to find. Refinement (b) provides an error message to pinpoint the problem, and so it is more robust. But robustness is not free; it costs a test even when all is well. In this simple example the test is small, but in a realistic example it may cost a considerable amount, even as much as the rest of the computation, to test whether the input satisfies the antecedent of a specification. There is a tradeoff between robustness and economy, and some judgment must be used.

A specifier who cares how the tradeoff is made can certainly strengthen the specification to say what result is wanted when $i < 0$, and say how much expense is acceptable more precisely using the real time measure. The purpose of this section is to consider the options when the specifier does not say.

To make a point about loops, here are two similar refinements.

(c) $S \Leftarrow$ **if** $i = 0$ **then** *ok* **else** $(i := i{-}1. \ S)$

(d) $S \Leftarrow$ **if** $i \leq 0$ **then** *ok* **else** $(i := i{-}1. \ S)$

Again, both are correct. When $i \geq 0$ they cost the same. With refinement (c), when $i < 0$ execution will take forever and will not progress to any further computation. An infinite loop is not as good as an error message, but after a while we will probably suspect that something is wrong. With refinement (d), when $i < 0$ execution will take zero time and will continue as though nothing were wrong. In that sense, (c) is more robust than (d).

———————————————————————————————————End of Robustness

Refinement in Place

It is sometimes convenient to refine a specification where it is used, rather than separately afterward. Instead of writing

$$x := 5. \ y' > x. \ z := y$$

and then separately

$$y' > x \Leftarrow y := x+1$$

we may write

$x:= 5$.

$y'{>}x \ :: \ y:= x{+}1$.

$z:= y$

The double colon signifies refinement in place. When we are considering the context in which a refinement in place appears, we ignore its solution (right side). In our example, we take the middle line to mean $y'{>}x$, hence the three lines together are equal to

$y' = z' > 5$

We are not allowed to use the way $y'{>}x$ is refined and conclude $x'{=}5 \wedge y'{=}z'{=}6$.

Refinement in place can be recursive, and thus serve as a loop. For example,

$x{\geq}0 \Rightarrow y'{=}\Pi[1;..x{+}1] \wedge t'{=}t{+}x \ ::$

$\quad (\ y:= 1$.

$\quad\quad x{\geq}0 \Rightarrow y'{=}y{\times}\Pi[1;..x{+}1] \wedge t'{=}t{+}x \ ::$

$\quad\quad\quad$ **if** $x{=}0$ **then** ok

$\quad\quad\quad$ **else** $(\ y:= y{\times}x. \ \ x:= x{-}1. \ \ t:= t{+}1$.

$\quad\quad\quad\quad\quad x{\geq}0 \Rightarrow y'{=}y{\times}\Pi[1;..x{+}1] \wedge t'{=}t{+}x \ ) \ )$

There are two theorems to be proven here. The first is

$x{\geq}0 \Rightarrow y'{=}\Pi[1;..x{+}1] \wedge t'{=}t{+}x \ \ \Longleftarrow \ \ y:= 1. \ \ x{\geq}0 \Rightarrow y'{=}y{\times}\Pi[1;..x{+}1] \wedge t'{=}t{+}x$

Note that the body of the loop is not used in this theorem. The other is

$x{\geq}0 \Rightarrow y'{=}y{\times}\Pi[1;..x{+}1] \wedge t'{=}t{+}x \ \ \Longleftarrow$

$\quad$ **if** $x{=}0$ **then** ok

$\quad$ **else** $(\ y:= y{\times}x. \ \ x:= x{-}1. \ \ t:= t{+}1$.

$\quad\quad\quad x{\geq}0 \Rightarrow y'{=}y{\times}\Pi[1;..x{+}1] \wedge t'{=}t{+}x \ )$

With refinement in place we indent the inner refinements; this makes our programs look more traditional. The preceding program looks structurally like its Pascal counterpart

$\quad$ 10: $y:= 1$;

$\quad\quad$ 20:   **if** $x{=}0$ **then** ok

$\quad\quad\quad$ **else   begin** $y:= y{*}x; \ \ x:= x{-}1$;

$\quad\quad\quad\quad\quad$ **goto** 20 **end**

Refinement in place has the advantage of saving us from writing a specification one extra time. With repeated use there is the disadvantage that parts of a program are crowded over on the right side of the page.

——————————————————————————————End of Refinement in Place

——————————————————————————————End of Program Theory

5   Programming Language

We have been using a very simple programming language consisting of only ok , assignment, **if then else** , dependent (sequential) composition, and refined specifications. In this chapter we enrich our repertoire by considering some of the notations found in some popular languages. We will not consider independent (parallel) composition and communication (input and output) just yet; they get their own chapters later.

Scope

Variable Declaration

The ability to declare a new state variable within a local scope is so useful that it is provided by every decent programming language. A declaration may look something like this:

var $x: T$

where x is the variable being declared, and T , called the type, indicates what values x can be assigned. There must be a rule to say what scope the declaration has; in other words, we must say what it applies to. We consider that a variable declaration applies to what follows it, with the same precedence as dependent composition. In program theory, it is essential that each of our notations apply to all specifications, not just to programs. That way we can introduce a local variable as part of the programming process, before its scope is refined.

We can express a variable declaration together with the specification to which it applies as a boolean expression in the initial and final state.

var $x: T \cdot P$ $=$ $\exists x, x': T \cdot P$

Specification P is an expression in the initial and final values of all global (already declared) variables plus the newly declared local variable. Specification **var** $x: T \cdot P$ is an expression in the global variables only. For a variable declaration to be implementable, its type must be nonempty. As a simple example, suppose the global variables are integer variables y and z . Then

$$\mathbf{var}\ x: int \cdot\ x:= 2.\ \ y:= x{+}z$$
$$=\quad \exists x, x': int \cdot\ x'{=}2\ \land\ y' = 2{+}z\ \land\ z'{=}z$$
$$=\quad y' = 2{+}z\ \land\ z'{=}z$$

According to our definition of variable declaration, the initial value of the local variable is an arbitrary value of its type.

$$\mathbf{var}\ x: int \cdot\ y:= x$$
$$=\quad \exists x, x': int \cdot\ x'{=}x \land y'{=}x \land z'{=}z$$
$$=\quad z'{=}z$$

which says that z is unchanged. Variable x is not mentioned because it is not one of the global variables, and variable y is not mentioned because its final value is unknown. However

$$\textbf{var } x \text{: } int \cdot \ \ y := x - x$$
$$= \quad y' = 0 \wedge z' = z$$

In some languages, a newly declared variable has a special value called "the undefined value" which cannot participate in any expressions. To write such declarations as boolean expressions, we introduce the expression *undefined* but we do not give any axioms about it, so nothing can be proven about it. Then

$$\textbf{var } x \text{: } T \cdot P \quad = \quad \exists x \text{: } undefined \cdot \exists x' \text{: } T, \ undefined \cdot P$$

For this kind of variable declaration, it is not necessary for the type to be nonempty.

An initializing assignment is easily defined in the same way.

$$\textbf{var } x \text{: } T := e \cdot \ P \quad = \quad \exists x \text{: } e \cdot \exists x' \text{: } T \cdot P$$

assuming e is of type T.

As in many programming languages, we can declare several variables in one declaration. For example,

$$\textbf{var } x, y, z \text{: } T \cdot P \quad = \quad \exists x, x', y, y', z, z' \text{: } T \cdot P$$

--End of Variable Declaration

It is a service to the world to make variable declarations as local as possible. That way, the state space outside the local scope is not polluted with unwanted variables. Inside the local scope, there are all the global variables plus the local ones; there are more variables to keep track of locally. Next, we consider a kind of local "undeclaration" so that we can narrow our focus temporarily.

Variable Suspension

Suppose the state consists of variables w, x, y, and z. We may wish, temporarily, to consider a subspace of the state space, consisting of only the variables w and x. We indicate this with the notation

$$\textbf{frame } w, x$$

It applies to what follows it, with the same precedence as dependent composition, just like **var**. Formally,

$$\textbf{frame } w, x \cdot P \ = \ P \wedge y' = y \wedge z' = z$$

Within P the state variables are w and x. This is similar to the "import" statement of some languages, though not identical. It allows P to refer to y and z, but only as local constants (ordinary variables, not state variables). The **frame** notation is the formal way of saying "and all other variables are unchanged".

Assignment and **frame** are related by the equation

$$x := e \ = \ \textbf{frame } x \cdot \ x' = e$$

--End of Variable Suspension

We specified the list summation problem in the previous chapter as $s' = \Sigma L$. We took s to be a state variable, and L to be a constant. We might have preferred the specification $s := \Sigma L$ saying that s has the right final value and that all other variables are unchanged, but our solution included a variable n which began at 0 and ended at $\#L$. We now have the formal notations needed.

$$s := \Sigma L \quad \Longleftarrow \quad \textbf{frame } s \cdot \textbf{ var } n : nat \cdot \ s' = \Sigma L$$

First we reduce the state space to s; if L was a state variable, it is now a constant. Next we introduce local variable n. Then we proceed as before.

───End of Scope

Data Structures

Arrays

In most popular programming languages there is the notion of subscripted variable, or indexed variable, usually called an array. Each element of an array is a variable. Element 2 of array A can be assigned the value 3 by a notation such as

$$A(2) := 3$$

Perhaps the brackets are square; let us dispense with the brackets. We can write an array element assignment as a boolean expression in the initial and final state as follows. Let A be an array name, let i be any expression of the index type, and let e be any expression of the element type. Then

$$Ai := e \quad = \quad A'i = e \ \wedge \ (\forall j \cdot j \neq i \Rightarrow A'j = Aj) \ \wedge \ x' = x \ \wedge \ y' = y \ \wedge \ldots$$

This says that after the assignment, element i of A equals e, all other elements of A are unchanged, and all other variables are unchanged. If you are unsure of the placement of the primes, consider the example

$$A(A2) := 3$$
$$= \quad A'(A2) = 3 \ \wedge \ (\forall j \cdot j \neq A2 \Rightarrow A'j = Aj) \ \wedge \ x' = x \ \wedge \ y' = y \ \wedge \ldots$$

The Substitution Law

$$x := e. \ P \quad = \quad (\text{for } x \text{ substitute } e \text{ in } P)$$

is very useful, but unfortunately it does not apply to array elements. For example,

$$A2 := 3. \ \ i := 2. \ \ Ai := 4. \ \ Ai = A2$$

should equal $\top$, because $i = 2$ just before the final boolean expression, and $A2 = A2$ certainly equals $\top$. If we try to apply the Substitution Law, we get

$$A2 := 3. \ \ i := 2. \ \ Ai := 4. \ \ Ai = A2$$
$$= \quad A2 := 3. \ \ i := 2. \ \ 4 = A2$$
$$= \quad A2 := 3. \ \ 4 = A2$$
$$= \quad 4 = 3$$
$$= \quad \bot$$

Here is a second example of the failure of the Substitution Law for array elements.

      $A2:=2.\ \ A(A2):=3.\ \ A2=2$

This should equal $\perp$ because $A2=3$ just before the final boolean expression. But the Substitution Law says

      $A2:=2.\ \ A(A2):=3.\ \ A2=2$

$=$ $A2:=2.\ \ A2=2$

$=$ $2=2$

$=$ $\top$

The Substitution Law works only when the assignment has a simple name to the left of $:=$. Fortunately we can always rewrite an array element assignment in that form.

      $Ai:=e$

$=$ $A'i{=}e \ \wedge\ (\forall j\cdot\ j{\neq}i \Rightarrow A'j{=}Aj)\ \wedge\ x'{=}x\ \wedge\ y'{=}y\ \wedge\ldots$

$=$ $A'=i{\rightarrow}e\,|\,A\ \wedge\ x'{=}x\ \wedge\ y'{=}y\ \wedge\ldots$

$=$ $A:=i{\rightarrow}e\,|\,A$

Let us look again at the examples for which the Substitution Law did not work, this time using the notation $A:=i{\rightarrow}e\,|\,A$.

      $A:=2{\rightarrow}3\,|\,A.\ \ i:=2.\ \ A:=i{\rightarrow}4\,|\,A.\ \ Ai=A2$

$=$ $A:=2{\rightarrow}3\,|\,A.\ \ i:=2.\ \ (i{\rightarrow}4\,|\,A)i=(i{\rightarrow}4\,|\,A)2$

$=$ $A:=2{\rightarrow}3\,|\,A.\ \ (2{\rightarrow}4\,|\,A)2=(2{\rightarrow}4\,|\,A)2$

$=$ $A:=2{\rightarrow}3\,|\,A.\ \ \top$

$=$ $\top$

      $A:=2{\rightarrow}2\,|\,A.\ \ A:=A2{\rightarrow}3\,|\,A.\ \ A2=2$

$=$ $A:=2{\rightarrow}2\,|\,A.\ \ (A2{\rightarrow}3\,|\,A)2=2$

$=$ $((2{\rightarrow}2\,|\,A)2{\rightarrow}3\,|\,2{\rightarrow}2\,|\,A)\,2=2$

$=$ $(2{\rightarrow}3\,|\,2{\rightarrow}2\,|\,A)\,2=2$

$=$ $3=2$

$=$ $\perp$

The only thing to remember about array element assignment is this: change $Ai:=e$ to $A:=i{\rightarrow}e\ |\ A$ before applying any programming theory. A two-dimensional array element assignment $Aij:=e$ must be changed to $A:=(i;j){\rightarrow}e\,|\,A$, and similarly for more dimensions.

——End of Arrays

Records

Without inventing anything new, we can already build a record structure similar to that found in several languages. Let us define *person* as follows.

$$person = \quad \text{"name"} \rightarrow text$$
$$| \text{ "age"} \rightarrow nat$$

We declare

var p: *person*

and assign p as follows.

p:= "name" $\rightarrow$ "Josh" | "age" $\rightarrow$ 17

We can reassign p the same way we make an array element assignment, either as

p "age":= 18

or preferably

p:= "age" $\rightarrow$ 18 | p

No new theory is needed for records.

―――End of Records
―――――――――――――――――――――――――――――――――――――――End of Data Structures

Control Structures

While Loop

The **while**-loop of several languages has the syntax

while b **do** P

where b is boolean and P is a program. To execute it, evaluate b, and if its value is $\bot$ then you're done, but if its value is $\top$ then execute P and start over. We do not equate the **while**-loop to a boolean expression the way we have defined previous programming notations. Instead, we consider

$W \quad \Longleftarrow \quad$ **while** b **do** P

to be an abbreviation of

$W \quad \Longleftarrow \quad$ **if** b **then** $(P. \ W)$ **else** ok

For example, to prove

$s' = s + \Sigma L \ [n;..\#L] \ \wedge \ t' = t + \#L - n \ \Longleftarrow$
$\quad$ **while** $n \neq \#L$ **do** $(s:= s + Ln. \ n:= n+1. \ t:= t+1)$

prove instead

$s' = s + \Sigma L \ [n;..\#L] \ \wedge \ t' = t + \#L - n \ \Longleftarrow$
$\quad$ **if** $n \neq \#L$ **then** $(s:= s + Ln. \ n:= n+1. \ t:= t+1. \ s' = s + \Sigma L \ [n;..\#L] \ \wedge \ t' = t+\#L-n)$
$\quad$ **else** ok

During programming, we may happen to refine a specification W by **if** b **then** $(P. \quad W)$ **else** ok . If so, we may abbreviate it as a while-loop. This is particularly valuable when the implementation of call is poor, and does not use a branch instruction in this situation.

This account of **while**-loops is adequate for practical purposes: it tells us where we can use them in programming. But it does not allow us to prove as much as we might like; for example, we cannot prove

$$\textbf{while } b \textbf{ do } P \;\; = \;\; \textbf{if } b \textbf{ then } (P. \;\; \textbf{while } b \textbf{ do } P) \textbf{ else } ok$$

A different account of **while**-loops is given in Chapter 6.

——End of While Loop

Repeat Loop

The **repeat**-loop of Pascal has the syntax

repeat P **until** b

where b is boolean and P is a program. To execute it, execute P and then evaluate b and if its value is $\top$ you're done, and if its value is $\bot$ start over. Our treatment of **repeat**-loops is similar to our treatment of **while**-loops. Specifically, we consider

$$R \;\; \Longleftarrow \;\; \textbf{repeat } P \textbf{ until } b$$

to be an abbreviation of

$$R \;\; \Longleftarrow \;\; P. \;\; \textbf{if } b \textbf{ then } ok \textbf{ else } R$$

The comments of the previous subsection about implementation and adequacy apply here too.

——End of Repeat Loop

Exit Loop

Some languages provide a command to jump out of the middle of a loop. The syntax for a loop in such a language might be

loop P **end**

with the additional syntax

exit when b

allowed within P , where b is boolean. As in the previous two subsections, we consider refinement by a loop with exits to be an alternative notation. For example,

$$L \;\; \Longleftarrow \;\; \textbf{loop}$$
$$\qquad\qquad A.$$
$$\qquad\qquad \textbf{exit when } b.$$
$$\qquad\qquad C$$
$$\qquad\quad \textbf{end}$$

means

$$L \;\; \Longleftarrow \;\; A. \;\; \textbf{if } b \textbf{ then } ok \textbf{ else } (C. \;\; L)$$

Programmers who use loop constructs sometimes find that they reach their goal deep within several nested loops. The problem is how to get out. A boolean variable can be introduced for the purpose of recording whether the goal has been reached, and tested at each iteration of each level of loop to decide whether to continue or exit. Or a **go to** can be used to jump directly out of all the loops, saving all tests. Or perhaps the programming language provides a specialized **go to** for this purpose: a "deep exit". For example, we may have something like this:

> P:: **loop**
> A.
> Q:: **loop**
> C.
>   **exit from** P **when** b.
> D
>   **end** Q.
> E
>   **end** P

In general, loops with exits take a backward approach: when there is more to be done (another iteration), one says **end** , and when there is no more to be done, one says **exit** . Refinement is more straightforward: when there is no more to be done, one says ok , and when there is more to be done, one says exactly what is to be done. The refinement structure corresponding to the above loop is

> P:: (A.
> Q:: (C.
>   **if** b **then** ok
>   **else** (D.
> Q)))

using refinement in place.

The preceding example had a deep exit but no shallow exit, leaving E stranded in a dead area, with no counterpart in the refinements. Here is an example with both deep and shallow exits.

> P:: **loop**
> A.
> Q:: **loop**
> D.
>   **exit from** P **when** b.
> E.
>   **exit from** Q **when** c.
> F
>   **end** Q.
> G
>   **end** P

The refinement structure corresponding to the above loop is

P:: (A.
 $\quad$ Q:: (D.
 $\qquad$ **if** b **then** ok
 $\qquad$ **else** (E.
 $\qquad\quad$ **if** c **then** (G.
 $\qquad\qquad\qquad$ P)
 $\qquad\quad$ **else** (F.
 $\qquad\qquad\qquad$ Q))))

Loops with exits can always be translated easily to a refinement structure. But the reverse is not true; some refinement structures require the introduction of new variables and even whole data structures to encode them as loops with exits.

——End of Exit Loop

Two-Dimensional Search

To illustrate the preceding subsection, we can do Exercise 138: Write a program to find a given item in a given 2-dimensional array. The execution time must be linear in the product of the dimensions.

Let the array be A , let its dimensions be n by m , and let the item we seek be x . We will indicate the position of x in A by the final values of natural variables i and j . If x occurs more than once, any of its positions will do. If it does not occur, we will indicate that by assigning i and j the values n and m respectively. The problem, except for time, is then P where
$$P \;=\; \textbf{if}\, x: A\, (0,..n)\, (0,..m)\; \textbf{then}\; x = A\, i'\, j'\; \textbf{else}\; i'{=}n \wedge j'{=}m$$
We may as well search row 0 first, then row 1 , and so on. Accordingly, we define R to mean " x does not occur before row i ":
$$R \;=\; \neg\, x: A\, (0,..i)\, (0,..m)$$
Within each row, we search the columns in order, and so we define C to mean " x does not occur in row i before column j ":
$$C \;=\; \neg\, x: A\, i\, (0,..j)$$
With these definitions, we now solve the problem in five easy pieces.

$$P \;\Longleftarrow\; i{:=}\,0.\;\; i{\le}n \wedge R \Rightarrow P$$

$$i{\le}n \wedge R \Rightarrow P \;\Longleftarrow\; \textbf{if}\; i{=}n\; \textbf{then}\; j{:=}\,m\; \textbf{else}\; i{<}n \wedge R \Rightarrow P$$

$$i{<}n \wedge R \Rightarrow P \;\Longleftarrow\; j{:=}\,0.\;\; i{<}n \wedge R \wedge j{\le}m \wedge C \Rightarrow P$$

$i<n \wedge R \wedge j{\leq}m \wedge C \Rightarrow P \quad \Longleftarrow$
$\qquad$ **if** $j{=}m$ **then** $(i{:=} i{+}1. \quad i{\leq}n \wedge R \Rightarrow P)$
$\qquad$ **else** $i<n \wedge R \wedge j<m \wedge C \Rightarrow P$

$i<n \wedge R \wedge j<m \wedge C \Rightarrow P \quad \Longleftarrow \quad$ **if** $A\,i\,j = x$ **then** ok **else** $(j{:=} j{+}1. \quad i<n \wedge R \wedge j{\leq}m \wedge C \Rightarrow P)$

It is easier to see the execution pattern when we retain only enough information for execution. The non-program specifications are needed for understanding the purpose, and for proof, but not for execution. To a compiler, the program appears as follows:

$\quad i{:=} 0.$
$\quad Q{::} \ $ **if** $i{=}n$ **then** $j{:=} m$
$\qquad$ **else** $(\,j{:=} 0.$
$\qquad\qquad S{::} \ $ **if** $j{=}m$ **then** $(i{:=} i{+}1. \ \ Q)$
$\qquad\qquad\qquad$ **else** **if** $A\,i\,j = x$ **then** ok
$\qquad\qquad\qquad$ **else** $(j{:=} j{+}1. \ \ S)\,)$

In Pascal, this is

$\quad i{:=} 0;$
$\quad 10{:} \ $ **if** $i{=}n$ **then** $j{:=} m$
$\qquad$ **else** **begin** $j{:=} 0;$
$\qquad\qquad\qquad 20{:} \ $ **if** $j{=}m$ **then** **begin** $i{:=} i{+}1;$ **goto** 10 **end**
$\qquad\qquad\qquad$ **else** **if** $A[i, j] = x$ **then**
$\qquad\qquad\qquad$ **else** **begin** $j{:=} j{+}1;$ **goto** 20 **end** **end**

To add time, we put $t{:=} t{+}1$ just after $i{:=} i{+}1$ and after $j{:=} j{+}1$. We also change the five specifications we are refining to refer to time.

$t' \leq t + n(m{+}1) \quad \Longleftarrow \quad i{:=} 0. \ \ i{\leq}n \Rightarrow t' \leq t + (n{-}i)(m{+}1)$

$i{\leq}n \Rightarrow t' \leq t + (n{-}i)(m{+}1) \quad \Longleftarrow \quad$ **if** $i{=}n$ **then** $j{:=} m$ **else** $i<n \Rightarrow t' \leq t + (n{-}i)(m{+}1)$

$i<n \Rightarrow t' \leq t + (n{-}i)(m{+}1) \quad \Longleftarrow \quad j{:=} 0. \ \ i<n \wedge j{\leq}m \Rightarrow t' \leq t + (n{-}i)(m{+}1) - j$

$i<n \wedge j{\leq}m \Rightarrow t' \leq t + (n{-}i)(m{+}1) - j \quad \Longleftarrow$
$\qquad$ **if** $j{=}m$ **then** $(i{:=} i{+}1. \ \ t{:=} t{+}1. \ \ i{\leq}n \Rightarrow t' \leq t + (n{-}i)(m{+}1))$
$\qquad$ **else** $i<n \wedge j<m \Rightarrow t' \leq t + (n{-}i)(m{+}1) - j$

$i<n \wedge j<m \Rightarrow t' \leq t + (n{-}i)(m{+}1) - j \quad \Longleftarrow$
$\qquad$ **if** $A\,i\,j = x$ **then** ok
$\qquad$ **else** $(j{:=} j{+}1. \ \ t{:=} t{+}1. \ \ i<n \wedge j{\leq}m \Rightarrow t' \leq t + (n{-}i)(m{+}1) - j)$

———End of Two-Dimensional Search

For Loop

Let us use the syntax

  for $i:= m;..n$ **do** P

where i is a fresh name, m and n are integer expressions such that $m{\le}n$, and P is a specification, as an almost-typical notation for controlled iteration. The difference from popular languages is just that iteration continues up to but excluding $i=n$. To avoid some thorns, let us say also that i is not a state variable (so it cannot be assigned within P), and that the initial values of m and n control the iteration.

As with the previous loop constructs, we will not equate the **for**-loop to a boolean expression, but instead show how it is used in refinement. Let $A: int{\rightarrow}bool$, so that Ai is a condition. Then

  $Am{\Rightarrow}A'n \ \Longleftarrow \ $ **for** $i:= m;..n$ **do** $i: m,..n \wedge Ai \Rightarrow A'(i{+}1)$

For example, let the state consist of integer variable x , and let A be defined as

  $A \ = \ \lambda i: nat \cdot\ x{=}2^i$

Then we can solve the exponentiation problem $x'{=}2^n$ in three refinements:

  $x'{=}2^n \ \Longleftarrow \ x:= 1.\ A0{\Rightarrow}A'n$

  $A0{\Rightarrow}A'n \ \Longleftarrow \ $ **for** $i:= 0;..n$ **do** $i:\ 0,..n \wedge Ai \Rightarrow A'(i{+}1)$

  $i:\ 0,..n \wedge Ai \Rightarrow A'(i{+}1) \ \Longleftarrow \ x:= 2{\times}x$

The recursive time measure requires each loop to contain a time increment of at least one time unit. In general, the time taken by the body of a **for** loop may be a function f of the iteration i . Then

  $t' = t + \Sigma i{:}\ m,..n \cdot\ fi \ \Longleftarrow \ $ **for** $i:= m;..n$ **do** $t' = t{+}fi$

When the body takes constant time c , this simplifies to

  $t' = t + (n{-}m){\times}c \ \Longleftarrow \ $ **for** $i:= m;..n$ **do** $t' = t{+}c$

───End of For Loop

Minimum Sum Segment

Exercise 168: Given a list of integers, possibly including negatives, write a program to find the minimum sum of any segment (sublist of consecutive items).

Let L be the list. Formally, the problem is P where

  $P \ = \ s' = MIN\ i, j \cdot\ \Sigma\ L\ [i;..j]$

where $0 \le i \le j \le \#L$. We will solve the problem using a **for**-loop. The condition $A\ k$ will say that s is the minimum sum of any segment up to index k . For $k{=}0$ there is only one segment, the empty segment, and its sum is 0 . When $k{=}\#L$ all segments are included and we have the desired result. To go from $A\ k$ to $A\ (k{+}1)$ we have to consider those segments that end at index $k{+}1$. We could find the sum of each new segment, then take the minimum of those sums and of *s* to be the new value of *s* . But we can do better. Each segment ending at index *k*+1 is a one-item extension of a segment ending at index *k* with one exception: the empty segment ending at *k*+1 .

$$\begin{matrix} k & k+1 \\ \downarrow & \downarrow \end{matrix}$$
$$[\ 4 \ ; \ -2 \ ; \ -8 \ ; \ 7 \ ; \ 3 \ ; \ 0 \ ; \ -1 \ ]$$

If we know the minimum sum *c* of any segment ending at *k* , then *min* $(c + L\ k)\ 0$ is the minimum sum of any segment ending at *k*+1 . So we define, for $0 \le k \le \#L$,

$$A\ k \ = \quad s = (MIN\ i\colon 0,..k+1\cdot MIN\ j\colon i,..k+1\cdot \Sigma\ L\ [i;..j])$$
$$\wedge\ c = (MIN\ i\colon 0,..k+1\cdot \Sigma\ L\ [i;..k])$$

Now the program is easy.

$$P \ \Longleftarrow \ s:= 0.\ \ c:= 0.\ \ A\ 0 \Rightarrow A'(\#L)$$
$$A\ 0 \Rightarrow A'(\#L) \ \Longleftarrow \ \textbf{for}\ k:= 0;..\#L\ \textbf{do}\ k\colon 0,..\#L \wedge A\ k \Rightarrow A'(k+1)$$
$$k\colon 0,..\#L \wedge A\ k \Rightarrow A'(k+1) \ \Longleftarrow \ c:= min\ (c + L\ k)\ 0.\ \ s:= min\ c\ s$$

──End of Minimum Sum Segment

Go To

For every set of loop constructs that might be included in a programming language, there is some pattern of execution that cannot be conveniently expressed using those loop constructs. For that reason, many languages include a loop-building primitive: the **go to**. Programming texts often warn that the **go to** is harmful, and should be avoided, without saying why. The trouble with **go to** is that it cannot be considered a specification, and it does not refine any specification. It does not fit in any usable theory of programming. If you are not using any theory of programming, and your only understanding of programs is the ability to execute them, there is no further harm in using **go to**. Textbooks that do not present any theory of programming have no reason to avoid **go to**.

Refinement is more than any set of loop constructs; it provides not only tail recursions (branching) but also general recursions (stacking). It provides all possible patterns of execution. Its closest relative in many popular programming languages is the procedure declaration and call, but unfortunately the refinement aspect is usually coupled with parameterization and local scope aspects, and the implementation is often poor. For efficient execution, it may be necessary to code the refinements using the execution-control primitives, such as **go to**, that are provided in an available programming language.

──End of Go To

──End of Control Structures

Time Dependence

Some programming languages provide a clock, or a delay, or other time-dependent features. Our examples have used the time variable as a ghost, or auxiliary variable, never affecting the course of a computation. It was used as part of the theory, to prove something about the execution time. Used for that purpose only, it did not need representation in a computer. But if there is a readable clock available as a time source during a computation, it can be used to affect the computation. Both $x := t$ and

> $\textbf{if } t < [1994; 04; 09; 01; 30; 00.000] \textbf{ then } \dots \textbf{ else } \dots$

are allowed, but not

> $t := [1974; 06; 13; 05; 30; 00.000]$

We can look at the clock, but not reset it arbitrarily; all clock changes must correspond to the passage of time (according to some measure). (A computer operator may need to set the clock sometimes, but that is not part of the theory of programming.)

In programs that depend upon time, we should use the real time measure, rather than the recursive time measure. We also need to be more careful where we place our time increments. But we do not pursue the subject further in this book.

We may occasionally want to specify the passage of time. For example, we may want the computation to "wait until time w". Let us invent a notation for it, and define it formally as

> $\textbf{wait until } w \quad = \quad t := max\ t\ w$

(For simplicity we are considering time to be integer-valued, and using the recursive time measure. For real-valued time and the real time measure we need a slightly different definition of **wait until** w .) Because we are not allowed to reset the clock, $t := max\ t\ w$ is not acceptable as a program until we refine it. Including recursive time,

> $\textbf{wait until } w \quad \Longleftarrow \quad \textbf{if } t{\geq}w \textbf{ then } ok \textbf{ else } (t := t{+}1.\ \textbf{wait until } w)$

and we obtain a busy-wait loop. We can prove this refinement by cases. First,

> $\quad\quad t{\geq}w \wedge ok$
> $= \quad t{\geq}w \wedge (t := t)$
> $\Longrightarrow \quad t := max\ t\ w$

And second,

> $\quad\quad t{<}w \wedge (t := t{+}1.\ t := max\ t\ w)$

In the left conjunct, use $t: int$. In the right conjunct, use the Substitution Law.

> $= \quad t{+}1 \leq w \wedge (t := max\ (t{+}1)\ w)$
> $= \quad t{+}1 \leq w \wedge (t := w)$
> $= \quad t{<}w \wedge (t := max\ t\ w)$
> $\Longrightarrow \quad t := max\ t\ w$

End of Time Dependence

Assertions

Checking

As a safety check, some programming languages include the notation

    assert b

where b is boolean. It is executed by checking that b is true; if it is, execution continues normally, but if not, an error message is printed and execution is suspended. The intention is that in a correct program, the asserted expressions will always be true, and so all assertions are redundant. All error checking requires redundancy, and assertions help us to find errors and prevent subsequent damage to the state variables.

Assertions are defined as follows.

    assert b =   **if** b **then** ok **else** (*print* "error". $t:= \infty$)

If b is true, **assert** b is the same as ok. If b is false, execution cannot proceed in finite time to any following actions. Assertions are an easy way to make programs more robust.

———End of Checking

Backtracking

If P and Q are implementable specifications, so is $P \lor Q$. It can be implemented by choosing one of P or Q and satisfying it. We could make disjunction a programming connective, perhaps by using the notation **or** . This would sometimes save a programming step by making the implementation choose a disjunct. For example,

    $x:= 0$ **or** $x:= 1$

would be a program whose execution assigns either 0 or 1 to x.

The next construct radically changes the way we program. We introduce the notation

    ensure b

where b is boolean, and define it as follows.

    ensure b =   **if** b **then** ok **else** $\bot$

              = $b \land ok$

Like **assert** b, **ensure** b is equal to ok if b is true. But when b is false, there is a problem: it is unsatisfiable. By itself, this construct is unimplementable (unless b is identically true). However, in combination with other constructs, the whole may be implementable. Consider the following example in variables x and y.

        $x:= 0$ **or** $x:= 1$.   **ensure** $x=1$

= $\exists x'', y''\cdot (x''=0 \land y''=y \ \lor \ x''=1 \land y''=y) \ \land \ x''=1 \land x'=x'' \land y'=y''$

= $x'=1 \land y'=y$

= $x:= 1$

Although an implementation is given a choice between $x:=0$ and $x:=1$, it must choose the right one to satisfy a later condition. It can do so by making either choice (as usual), and when faced with a later **ensure** whose condition is false, it must backtrack and make another choice. Since choices can be nested within choices, a lot of bookkeeping is necessary.

Several popular programming languages, such as Prolog, feature backtracking. They may state that choices are made in a particular order (we have omitted that complication). Two warnings should accompany such languages. First, it is the programmer's responsibility to show that a program is implementable; the language does not guarantee it. Alternatively, the implementation does not guarantee that computations will satisfy the program, since it is sometimes impossible to satisfy it. The second warning is that the timing calculus does not work.

———End of Backtracking

———End of Assertions

Subprogram

Result Expression

Let P be a specification and e be an expression in unprimed variables. Then

> P **result** e

is an expression of the initial state. It expresses the result of executing P and then evaluating e . For example, the following expresses an approximation to the base of the natural logarithms.

> **var** *term, sum*: *rat* := $1 \cdot$
>
> **for** $i:= 1;..15$ **do** (*term*:= *term*/*i*. *sum*:= *sum*+*term*)
>
> **result** *sum*

The axiom for the **result** expression is

> $x' = (P \text{ result } e) \;=\; P. \; x'{=}e$

where x is any state variable of the right type.

The example introduces local variables *term* and *sum* , and no other variables are reassigned. So clearly the global state is unchanged. But consider

> $y:= y+1$ **result** y

The result is as if the assignment $y:= y+1$ were executed, then y is the result, except that the value of variable y is unchanged.

$$
\begin{aligned}
& x:= (y:= y+1 \text{ result } y) \\
=\;& x' = (y:= y+1 \text{ result } y) \;\land\; y'{=}y \\
=\;& (y:= y+1. \; x'{=}y) \;\land\; y'{=}y \\
=\;& x' = y+1 \;\land\; y'{=}y \\
=\;& x:= y+1
\end{aligned}
$$

When global variables seem to be changed (but they really aren't), implementation of **result** expressions presents a difficulty, although not an impossibility. To avoid the difficulty, we have a choice: we can forbid assignments to global variables within **result** expressions, or we can allow global variables to change with a warning that mathematical reasoning is no longer possible. For example, we cannot say $x+x = 2\times x$, nor even $x=x$, since x might be defined as

$x = (y:= y+1 \textbf{ result } y)$.

State changes resulting from the evaluation of an expression are called "side-effects". If side-effects are allowed, we have to get rid of **result** expressions before using any theory. For example,

$x:= (P \textbf{ result } e)$ becomes $(P. \ x:= e)$

after renaming local variables within P as necessary to avoid clashes with global variables, and allowing the scope of variables declared in P to extend through $x:= e$. For another example,

$x:= y + (P \textbf{ result } e)$ becomes $(\textbf{var } z:= y \cdot \ P. \ x:= z+e)$

with similar provisos.

The recursive time measure that we have been using neglects the time for expression evaluation. This is reasonable, in some applications, for expressions consisting of a few operations implemented in computer hardware. For expressions using operations not implemented in hardware (perhaps list catenation) it is questionable. For **result** expressions containing loops, it is unreasonable. We must find a time bound for the program part, and charge that much time. If the **result** expression does not contain any assignments to global space variables, we can use the translation of the previous paragraph to account for its time. The passage of time is a side-effect: it is an assignment to a global time variable.

——End of Result Expression

Function

In many popular programming languages, a function is a combination of name declaration, possibly parameterization, local scope, **result** expression, and assertion about the result. It's a "package deal". To write the successor function on integers in Pascal, you must write

       function $suc(n: integer)$: $integer$;

       begin $suc:= n+1$ **end**

instead of

       $\lambda n: int \cdot n+1$

Though you may not want to, you must name it, assert the result type, and write a program for the body. We have presented these programming features separately so that they can be understood separately. They can be combined in any way desired; for example, using the notations we have already introduced, we can write a binary exponential function as

$$bexp \;=\; \lambda n\text{: } nat\cdot$$
$$(\;\; \mathbf{var}\ r\text{: } nat := 1\cdot$$
$$\mathbf{for}\ i := 0;..n\ \mathbf{do}\ r := r\times 2$$
$$\mathbf{result}\ r\;\;)$$

The harm in providing one construct for the combination is its complexity. Programmers trained with these languages may be unable to separate the issues and realize that naming, parameterization, assertions, local scope, and **result** expressions are independently useful.

Even the form of function we are using in this book could be both simplified and generalized. Stating the domain of a parameter is a special case of axiom introduction, which can be separated from name introduction (see Exercise 77).

——End of Function

Procedure

The procedure, as it is found in many languages, is a "package deal" like the function. It combines name declaration, parameterization, and local scope. The comments of the previous subsection apply here too. There are also some new issues.

To use our theory for program development, not just verification, we must be able to talk about a procedure whose body is an unrefined specification, not yet a program. For example, we may want a procedure P with parameter x defined as

$$P \;=\; \lambda x\text{: } int\cdot\ a' < x < b'$$

that assigns variables a and b values that lie on opposite sides of a value to be supplied as argument. We can use procedure P before we refine its body. For example,

$$P\,3 \;=\; a' < 3 < b'$$
$$P\,(a{+}1) \;=\; a' < a{+}1 < b'$$

The body is easily refined as

$$a' < x < b' \;\;\Leftarrow\;\; a := x{-}1.\ \ b := x{+}1$$

Our choice of refinement does not alter our definition of P ; it is of no use when we are using P .

A procedure and argument can be translated to a local variable and initial value.

$$(\lambda p\text{: } D\cdot\ B)\ a \;=\; (\mathbf{var}\ p\text{: } D := a\cdot\ B)$$

This translation suggests that a parameter is really just a local variable whose initial value will be supplied as an argument. In many popular programming languages, that is exactly the case. This is an unfortunate confusion of specification and implementation. The decision to create a parameter, and the choice of its domain, are part of a procedural specification, and are of interest to a user of the procedure. The decision to create a local variable, and the choice of its domain, are normally part of refinement, part of the process of implementation, and should not be of concern to a user of the procedure. When a parameter is assigned a value within a procedure body, it is acting as a local variable and no longer has any connection to its former role as parameter.

Another kind of parameter, usually called a **var** parameter, does not act as a local variable, but stands for an unknown global variable to be supplied as argument. Here is an example.

$$(\lambda \textbf{var } x: int \cdot x:= 3. \ b:= a) \, a \ = \ a:= 3. \ b:= a \ = \ d = b' = 3$$

Formally, a **var** parameter is two parameters, one for the initial value and one for the final value, and the argument is correspondingly two arguments.

$$(\lambda \textbf{var } p: D \cdot B) \, a \ = \ (\lambda p, p': D \cdot B) \, a \, a'$$

Unfortunately, the arguments must be substituted for the parameters before any other manipulations are performed. We are prevented from manipulating the procedure body by itself, and must apply our programming theory separately for each call. In our example, we cannot say whether

$$x:= 3. \ b:= a \ = \ b:= a. \ x:= 3$$

without seeing the argument for parameter x . To a large degree, this contradicts the purpose of a procedure.

———————————————————————————————————End of Procedure
———————————————————————————————————End of Subprogram

Alias

Many popular programming languages present us with a model of computation in which there is a memory consisting of a large number of individual storage cells. Each cell contains a value. Via the programming language, cells have names. Here is a standard sort of picture.

v, i	2
p	25A7F1
	4
$A[0]$	1
$p\uparrow, A[1]$	3
$A[i], A[2]$	2
$A[3]$	3

In the picture, p is a pointer variable that currently points to $A[1]$, so $p\uparrow$ and $A[1]$ refer to the same memory cell. Since variable i currently has value 2 , $A[i]$ and $A[2]$ refer to the same cell. And v is a **var** parameter for which variable i has been supplied as argument, so v and i refer to the same cell. We see that a cell may have zero, one, two, or more names. When a cell has two or more names that are visible at the same time, the names are said to be "aliases".

As we have seen with arrays and with **var** parameters, aliasing prevents us from applying our theory of programming. Some programming languages prohibit aliasing. Unfortunately, aliasing is difficult to detect, especially during program construction before a specification has been fully refined as a program. To most people, prohibitions and restrictions are distasteful. To avoid the prohibition, we have a choice: we can complicate our theory of programming to handle aliasing, or we can simplify our model of computation to eliminate the possibility. If we redraw our picture slightly, we see that there are two mappings: one from names to cells, and one from cells to values.

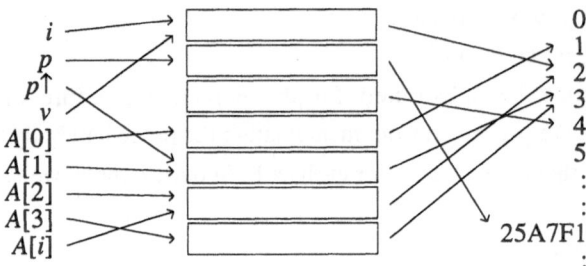

An assignment such as $p := \uparrow A[3]$ or $i := 4$ can change both mappings at once. An assignment to one name can change the value indirectly referred to by another name. To simplify the picture and eliminate the possibility of aliasing, we eliminate the cells and allow a richer space of values. Here is the new picture.

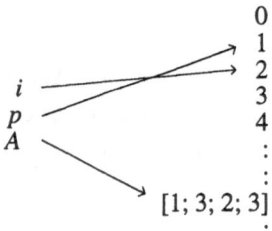

Pointer variables can be replaced by index variables dedicated to one structure so that they can be implemented as addresses. A procedure with **var** parameters can be replaced by a function that returns a structured value (not shown). The simpler picture is perfectly adequate, and the problem of aliasing disappears.

——End of Alias

Functional Programming

Most of this book is about a kind of programming that is sometimes called "imperative", which means that a program describes a change of state. This section presents an alternative: a program is a function from its input to its output. More generally, a specification is a function from possible inputs to desired outputs, and programs (as always) are implemented specifications. We take away assignment and dependent composition from our programming notations, and we add functions.

To illustrate, we look once again at the list summation problem (Exercise 123). This time, the specification is $\lambda L: [*rat]\cdot \Sigma L$. Assuming Σ is not an implemented operator, we still have some programming to do. We introduce variable n to indicate how much of the list has been summed; initially n is 0.

$$\Sigma L = (\lambda n: 0,..\#L+1\cdot \Sigma L [n;..\#L])\, 0$$

It saves some copying to write " $\Sigma L = ...$ " rather than " $\lambda L: [*rat]\cdot \Sigma L = ...$ ", but we must remember the domain of L. At first sight, the domain of n is annoying; it seems to be one occasion when an interval notation that includes both endpoints would be preferable. On second look, it's trying to tell us something useful: the domain is really composed of two parts that must be treated differently.

$$0,..\#L+1 \quad = \quad 0,..\#L \;,\; \#L$$

We divide the function into a selective union

$$\lambda n: 0,..\#L+1\cdot \Sigma L [n;..\#L] \quad = \quad (\lambda n: 0,..\#L\cdot \Sigma L [n;..\#L])\,|\,(\lambda n: \#L\cdot \Sigma L [n;..\#L])$$

and continue with each part separately. In the left part, we have $n < \#L$, and in the right part $n = \#L$.

$$\lambda n: 0,..\#L\cdot \Sigma L [n;..\#L] \quad = \quad \lambda n: 0,..\#L\cdot Ln + \Sigma L [n+1;..\#L]$$
$$\lambda n: \#L\cdot \Sigma L [n;..\#L] \quad = \quad \lambda n: \#L\cdot 0$$

This time we copied the domain of n to indicate which part of the selective union is being considered. The one remaining problem is solved by recursion.

$$\Sigma L [n+1;..\#L] \quad = \quad (\lambda n: 0,..\#L+1\cdot \Sigma L [n;..\#L])\,(n+1)$$

In place of the selective union we could have used **if then else** ; they are related by the law

$$(\lambda v: A\cdot x)\,|\,(\lambda v: B\cdot y) \quad = \quad \lambda v: A, B\cdot \textbf{if}\; v: A \;\textbf{then}\; x \;\textbf{else}\; y$$

When we are interested in the execution time rather than the result, we replace the body of each function with its time according to some measure. For example, in the list summation problem, we might decide to charge time 1 for each addition and 0 for everything else. The specification becomes $\lambda L: [*rat]\cdot \#L$, meaning for any list, the execution time is its length. We now must make exactly the same programming steps as before. The first step was to introduce variable n ; we do the same now, but we choose a new body for the new function to indicate its execution time.

$$\#L = (\lambda n: 0,..\#L+1\cdot \#L-n)\, 0$$

The second step was to decompose the function into a selective union; we do so again.

$$\lambda n: 0,..\#L+1\cdot \#L-n \quad = \quad (\lambda n: 0,..\#L\cdot \#L-n)\,|\,(\lambda n: \#L\cdot \#L-n)$$

The left side of the selective union became a function with one addition in it, so our timing function must become a function with a charge of 1 in it. To make the equation correct, the time for the remaining summation must be adjusted.

$$\lambda n: 0,..\#L\cdot \#L-n \quad = \quad \lambda n: 0,..\#L\cdot 1 + \#L-n-1$$

The right side of the selective union became a function with a constant body; according to our measure, its time must be 0.

$$\lambda n: \#L\cdot \#L-n \quad = \quad \lambda n: \#L\cdot 0$$

The remaining problem was solved by a recursive call; the corresponding call solves the remaining time problem.

$$\#L{-}n{-}1 \quad = \quad (\lambda n{:}\ 0,..\#L{+}1 \cdot\ \#L{-}n)\ (n{+}1)$$

And that completes the proof that execution time (according to this measure) is the length of the list.

In the recursive time measure, we charge nothing for any operation except recursive call, and we charge 1 for that. Let's redo the timing proof with this measure. Again, the time specification is $\lambda L{:}\ [*rat] \cdot\ \#L$.

$$\#L \ =\ (\lambda n{:}\ 0,..\#L{+}1 \cdot\ \#L{-}n)\ 0$$
$$\lambda n{:}\ 0,..\#L{+}1 \cdot\ \#L{-}n \ =\ (\lambda n{:}\ 0,..\#L \cdot\ \#L{-}n)\ |\ (\lambda n{:}\ \#L \cdot\ \#L{-}n)$$
$$\lambda n{:}\ 0,..\#L \cdot\ \#L{-}n \ =\ \lambda n{:}\ 0,..\#L \cdot\ \#L{-}n$$
$$\lambda n{:}\ \#L \cdot\ \#L{-}n \ =\ \lambda n{:}\ \#L \cdot\ 0$$
$$\#L{-}n \ =\ 1 + (\lambda n{:}\ 0,..\#L{+}1 \cdot\ \#L{-}n)\ (n{+}1)$$

Function Refinement

In imperative programming, we can write a nondeterministic specification such as $x'{:}\ 2, 3, 4$ that allows the result to be any one of several possibilities. In functional programming, a nondeterministic specification is a bunch consisting of more than one element. The specification $2, 3, 4$ allows the result to be any one of those three numbers.

Functional specifications can be classified the same way as imperative specifications, based on the number of satisfactory outputs for each input.

Functional specification S is unsatisfiable for domain element x : $¢\,Sx = 0$

Functional specification S is deterministic for domain element x : $¢\,Sx = 1$

Functional specification S is nondeterministic for domain element x : $¢\,Sx \geq 2$

Functional specification S is satisfiable for domain element x : $\exists y \cdot\ y{:}\ Sx$

Functional specification S is implementable: $\forall x \cdot\ \exists y \cdot\ y{:}\ Sx$

(x is quantified over the domain of S , and y is quantified over the range of S .) Implementability can be restated as $\forall x \cdot\ Sx \neq null$.

Consider the problem of searching for an item in a list of integers. Our first attempt at specification might be

$$\lambda L{:}\ [*int] \cdot\ \lambda x{:}\ int \cdot\ \S n{:}\ 0,..\#L \cdot\ Ln = x$$

which says that for any list L and item x , we want an index of L where x occurs. If x occurs several times in L , any of its indexes will do. Unfortunately, if x does not occur in L , we are left without any possible result, so this specification is unimplementable. We must decide what we want when x does not occur in L ; let's say any natural that is not an index of L will do.

$$\lambda L{:}\ [*int] \cdot\ \lambda x{:}\ int \cdot\ \textbf{if}\ x{:}\ L\ (0,..\#L)\ \textbf{then}\ \S n{:}\ 0,..\#L \cdot\ Ln = x\ \textbf{else}\ \#L,..\infty$$

This specification is implementable, and often nondeterministic.

Functional refinement is similar to imperative refinement. Functional specification P (the problem) is refined by functional specification S (the solution) if and only if all results that are satisfactory according to S are also satisfactory according to P. Formally, this is just inclusion $S: P$. Now we have a most annoying notational problem. Typically, we like to write the problem on the left, then the refinement symbol, then the solution on the right; we want to write $S: P$ the other way round. Inclusion is antisymmetric, so its symbol should not be symmetric, but unfortunately it is. Let us write $:\cdot$ for "backwards colon", so that " P is refined by S " is written $P :\cdot S$.

To refine our search specification, we create a linear search program, starting the search with index 0 and increasing the index until either x is found or L is exhausted. First we introduce the index.

> $(\textbf{if}\ x: L\ (0,..\#L)\ \textbf{then}\ \S n:\ 0,..\#L\cdot\ Ln = x\ \textbf{else}\ \#L,..\infty)\ :\cdot$
>
> $\quad(\lambda i:\ nat\cdot\ \textbf{if}\ x: L\ (i,..\#L)\ \textbf{then}\ \S n:\ i,..\#L\cdot\ Ln = x\ \textbf{else}\ \#L,..\infty)\ 0$

The two sides of this refinement are equal, so we could have written $=$ instead of $:\cdot$. We could have been more precise about the domain of i, and then we probably would decompose the function into a selective union, as we did in the previous problem. But this time let's use an **if then else**.

> $(\textbf{if}\ x: L\ (i,..\#L)\ \textbf{then}\ \S n:\ i,..\#L\cdot\ Ln = x\ \textbf{else}\ \#L,..\infty)\ :\cdot$
>
> $\quad\textbf{if}\ i = \#L\ \textbf{then}\ \#L$
>
> $\quad\textbf{else}\ \ \textbf{if}\ x = Li\ \textbf{then}\ i$
>
> $\quad\textbf{else}\ (\lambda i\cdot\ \textbf{if}\ x: L\ (i,..\#L)\ \textbf{then}\ \S n:\ i,..\#L\cdot\ Ln = x\ \textbf{else}\ \#L,..\infty)\ (i+1)$

The timing specification, recursive measure, is $\lambda L\cdot\ \lambda x\cdot\ 0,..\#L+1$, which means that the time is less than $\#L+1$. Here's the proof.

> $0,..\#L+1\ \ :\cdot\ \ (\lambda i\cdot\ 0,..\#L-i+1)\ 0$

> $0,..\#L-i+1\ :\cdot\ \ \textbf{if}\ i = \#L\ \textbf{then}\ 0$
>
> $\qquad\qquad\qquad\ \textbf{else}\ \ \textbf{if}\ x = Li\ \textbf{then}\ 0$
>
> $\qquad\qquad\qquad\ \textbf{else}\ 1 + (\lambda i\cdot\ 0,..\#L-i+1)\ (i+1)$

———End of Function Refinement

Functional and imperative programming are not really competitors; they can be used together. We cannot ignore imperative programming if ever we want to pause, to stop computing for a while, and resume later from the same state. Imperative programming languages all include a functional (expression) sublanguage, so we cannot ignore functional programming either.

———End of Functional Programming
———End of Programming Language

6   Recursive Definition

Recursive Data Definition

We are free to invent new syntax and rules for its use, as long as the new syntax and rules do not conflict with those already in use. In this section we are concerned with the definition of infinite bunches. Our first example is *nat* , the natural numbers. We have been using this syntax, but we have not yet defined it formally. Let us pretend we have not seen it before, and define it now. To do so requires axioms called <u>construction</u> and <u>induction</u>.

Construction and Induction

To define *nat* , we need to say what its elements are. We can start by saying that 0 is an element

$\quad$ 0: *nat*

and then say that for every element of *nat* , adding 1 gives another element

$\quad$ *nat*+1: *nat*

These axioms are called the *nat* construction axioms, and 0 and *nat*+1 are called the *nat* <u>constructors</u>. Using these axioms, we can "construct" the elements of *nat* as follows.

	0: *nat*	add 1 to each side
$\Rightarrow$	0+1: *nat*+1	by arithmetic, 0+1 = 1 . By the axiom *nat*+1: *nat* .
$\Rightarrow$	1: *nat*	add 1 to each side
$\Rightarrow$	1+1: *nat*+1	by arithmetic, 1+1 = 2 . By the axiom *nat*+1: *nat* .
$\Rightarrow$	2: *nat*	

and so on.

From the construction axioms we can prove 2: *nat* but we cannot prove $\neg$ –2: *nat* . That is why we need the induction axiom. The construction axioms tell us that the natural numbers are in *nat* , and the induction axiom tells us that nothing else is. Here is the *nat* induction axiom.

$\quad$ 0: B $\wedge$ B+1: B $\Rightarrow$ *nat*: B

(Note: we have introduced *nat* as new syntax, like *null* and 0 and + . It is not a variable, and cannot be instantiated. But B is a variable, to be instantiated at will.)

The two construction axioms can be combined into one, and induction can be restated, as follows:

$\quad$ 0, *nat*+1: *nat* $\qquad\qquad$ *nat* construction

$\quad$ 0, B+1: B $\Rightarrow$ *nat*: B $\qquad$ *nat* induction

There are many bunches satisfying the inclusion 0, B+1: B , such as: the naturals, the integers, the integers and half-integers, the rationals. Induction says that of all these bunches, *nat* is the smallest.

We have presented *nat* construction and *nat* induction using bunch notation. We now present equivalent axioms using predicate notation. We begin with induction.

In predicate notation, the *nat* induction axiom can be stated as follows: If $P: nat \rightarrow bool$,

$$P0 \land \forall n: nat \cdot Pn \Rightarrow P(n+1) \quad \Longrightarrow \quad \forall n: nat \cdot Pn$$

We prove first that the bunch form implies the predicate form.

$$0: B \ \land \ B+1: B \ \Rightarrow \ nat: B$$

Let $P: nat \rightarrow bool$ and let $B = \S n: nat \cdot Pn$. Then $B: nat$,

$$\Longrightarrow \quad 0: B \ \land (\forall n: nat \cdot n: B \ \Rightarrow \ n+1: B) \ \Rightarrow \ \forall n: nat \cdot n: B$$

and $\forall n: nat \cdot (n: B) = Pn$.

$$= \quad P0 \land (\forall n: nat \cdot Pn \Rightarrow P(n+1)) \ \Rightarrow \ \forall n: nat \cdot Pn$$

The reverse is proven similarly.

$$P0 \land (\forall n: nat \cdot Pn \Rightarrow P(n+1)) \ \Rightarrow \ \forall n: nat \cdot Pn$$

For arbitrary bunch B , let $P = \lambda n: nat \cdot n: B$. Then again $\forall n: nat \cdot Pn = (n: B)$.

$$\Longrightarrow \quad 0: B \ \land \ (\forall n: nat \cdot n: B \ \Rightarrow \ n+1: B) \ \Rightarrow \ \forall n: nat \cdot n: B$$

$$= \quad 0: B \ \land \ (\forall n: nat\text{'}B \cdot n+1: B) \ \Rightarrow \ \forall n: nat \cdot n: B$$

$$= \quad 0: B \ \land \ (nat\text{'}B)+1: B \ \Rightarrow \ nat: B$$

$$\Longrightarrow \quad 0: B \ \land \ B+1: B \ \Rightarrow \ nat: B$$

Therefore the bunch and predicate forms of *nat* induction are equivalent.

The predicate form of *nat* construction can be stated as follows: If $P: nat \rightarrow bool$,

$$P0 \land \forall n: nat \cdot Pn \Rightarrow P(n+1) \quad \Longleftarrow \quad \forall n: nat \cdot Pn$$

This is the same as induction but with the main implication reversed. We prove first that the bunch form implies the predicate form.

	$\forall n: nat \cdot Pn$	domain change using *nat* construction, bunch version
$\Longrightarrow$	$\forall n: 0, nat+1 \cdot Pn$	axiom about $\forall$
$=$	$(\forall n: 0 \cdot Pn) \land (\forall n: nat+1 \cdot Pn)$	One-Point Law and variable change
$=$	$P0 \land \forall n: nat \cdot P(n+1)$	
$\Longrightarrow$	$P0 \land \forall n: nat \cdot Pn \Rightarrow P(n+1)$	

And now we prove that the predicate form implies the bunch form .

	$P0 \land (\forall n: nat \cdot Pn \Rightarrow P(n+1)) \ \Leftarrow \ \forall n: nat \cdot Pn$	Let $P = \lambda n: nat \cdot n: nat$
$\Longrightarrow$	$0: nat \land (\forall n: nat \cdot n: nat \ \Rightarrow \ n+1: nat) \ \Leftarrow \ \forall n: nat \cdot n: nat$	
$=$	$0: nat \land (\forall n: nat \cdot n+1: nat) \ \Leftarrow \ \top$	
$=$	$0: nat \ \land \ nat+1: nat$	

A corollary is that *nat* can be defined by the single axiom

$$P0 \land \forall n: nat \cdot Pn \Rightarrow P(n+1) \ = \ \forall n: nat \cdot Pn$$

There are other predicate versions of induction; here is the usual one again plus three more.

$$P0 \land \forall n\text{: } nat\cdot\ Pn \Rightarrow P(n+1) \;\Longrightarrow\; \forall n\text{: } nat\cdot\ Pn$$
$$P0 \lor \exists n\text{: } nat\cdot\ \neg Pn \land P(n+1) \;\Longleftarrow\; \exists n\text{: } nat\cdot\ Pn$$
$$\forall n\text{: } nat\cdot\ Pn \Rightarrow P(n+1) \;\Longrightarrow\; \forall n\text{: } nat\cdot\ P0 \Rightarrow Pn$$
$$\exists n\text{: } nat\cdot\ \neg Pn \land P(n+1) \;\Longleftarrow\; \exists n\text{: } nat\cdot\ \neg P0 \land Pn$$

The first version says that to prove P of all naturals, prove it of 0, and assuming it of natural n, prove it of $n+1$. In other words, you get to all naturals by starting at 0 and repeatedly adding 1. The second version is obtained from the first by the duality laws and a renaming. The third is the prettiest; it says that if you can "go" from any natural to the next, then you can "go" from 0 to any natural. (It is very much like the **for**-loop rule.)

Here are two laws that are consequences of induction.

$$\forall n\text{: } nat\cdot\ (\forall m\text{: } nat\cdot\ m<n \Rightarrow Pm) \Rightarrow Pn \;\Longrightarrow\; \forall n\text{: } nat\cdot\ Pn$$
$$\exists n\text{: } nat\cdot\ (\forall m\text{: } nat\cdot\ m<n \Rightarrow \neg Pm) \land Pn \;\Longleftarrow\; \exists n\text{: } nat\cdot\ Pn$$

The first is like the first version of induction, except that the base case $P0$ is not explicitly stated, and the step uses the assumption that all previous naturals satisfy P, rather than just the one previous natural. The last one says that if there is a natural with property P then there is a first natural with property P (all previous naturals don't have it).

Now that we have an infinite bunch, it is easy to define others. For example, we can define pow to be the powers of 2 either by the equation

$$pow \;=\; 2^{nat}$$

or by using the solution quantifier

$$pow \;=\; \S p\text{: } nat\cdot\ \exists m\text{: } nat\cdot\ p = 2^m$$

But let us do it the same way we defined nat. The pow construction axiom is

$$1,\ 2{\times}pow\text{: } pow$$

and the pow induction axiom is

$$1,\ 2{\times}B\text{: } B \;\Rightarrow\; pow\text{: } B$$

Induction is not just for nat. In predicate form, we can define pow with the axiom

$$P1 \;\land\; \forall p\text{: } pow\cdot\ Pp \Rightarrow P(2{\times}p) \;=\; \forall p\text{: } pow\cdot\ Pp$$

We can define the bunch of integers as

$$int \;=\; nat,\ -nat$$

or equivalently we can use the construction and induction axioms

$$0,\ int+1,\ int-1\text{: } int$$
$$0,\ B+1,\ B-1\text{: } B \;\Rightarrow\; int\text{: } B$$

or we can use the axiom

$$P0 \land (\forall i\text{: } int\cdot\ Pi \Rightarrow P(i+1)) \land (\forall i\text{: } int\cdot\ Pi \Rightarrow P(i-1)) \;=\; \forall i\text{: } int\cdot\ Pi$$

Whichever we choose as axiom(s), the others are theorems.

Similarly we can define the bunch of rationals as

$$rat = int/(nat+1)$$

or equivalently by the construction and induction axioms

$$1, rat+rat, rat-rat, rat\times rat, rat/(\S r\cdot rat\cdot r\neq 0): rat$$
$$1, B+B, B-B, B\times B, B/(\S b: B\cdot b\neq 0): B \;\Rightarrow\; rat: B$$

or with the axiom (quantifying over rat , of course)

$$P1$$
$$\wedge\,(\forall r, s\cdot Pr \wedge Ps \Rightarrow P(r+s))$$
$$\wedge\,(\forall r, s\cdot Pr \wedge Ps \Rightarrow P(r-s))$$
$$\wedge\,(\forall r, s\cdot Pr \wedge Ps \Rightarrow P(r\times s))$$
$$\wedge\,(\forall r, s\cdot Pr \wedge Ps \wedge s\neq 0 \Rightarrow P(r/s))$$
$$= \quad \forall r\cdot Pr$$

As the examples suggest, we can define a bunch by construction and induction axioms using any number of constructors. To end this section, we define a bunch using zero constructors. In general, we have one construction axiom per constructor, so there aren't any construction axioms. But there is still an induction axiom. With no constructors, the antecedent becomes trivial and disappears, and we are left with the induction axiom

$$null: B$$

where $null$ is the bunch being defined. As always, induction says that, apart from elements due to construction axioms, nothing else is in the bunch being defined. This is exactly how we defined $null$ in Chapter 2.

———————————————————————————————————————End of Construction and Induction

Least Fixed-Points

We have defined nat by a construction axiom and an induction axiom

$$0, nat+1: nat \qquad\qquad\qquad nat \text{ construction}$$
$$0, B+1: B \;\Rightarrow\; nat: B \qquad\qquad nat \text{ induction}$$

We now prove two similar-looking theorems:

$$nat = 0, nat+1 \qquad\qquad\qquad nat \text{ fixed-point construction}$$
$$B = 0, B+1 \;\Rightarrow\; nat: B \qquad\qquad nat \text{ fixed-point induction}$$

A <u>fixed-point</u> of a function f is an element x of its domain such that f maps x to itself: $x = fx$. A <u>least fixed-point</u> of f is a smallest such x . Fixed-point construction has the form

$$name = (\text{expression involving } name)$$

and so it says that $name$ is a fixed-point of the expression on the right. Fixed-point induction tells us that $name$ is the smallest bunch satisfying fixed-point construction, and in that sense it is the least fixed-point of the constructor.

We first prove *nat* fixed-point construction. It is stronger than *nat* construction, so the proof will also have to use *nat* induction. Let us start there.

$$0, B+1: B \implies nat: B \qquad \text{replace } B \text{ with } 0, nat+1$$
$$\implies \quad 0, (0, nat+1)+1: 0, nat+1 \implies nat: 0, nat+1$$

strengthen the antecedent by cancelling the "0"s and "+1"s from the two sides of the first ":"

$$\implies \quad 0, nat+1: nat \implies nat: 0, nat+1$$

the antecedent is the *nat* construction axiom, so we can delete it, and use it again to strengthen the consequent

$$= \quad nat = 0, nat+1$$

We prove *nat* fixed-point induction just by strengthening the antecedent of *nat* induction.

In similar fashion we can prove that *pow*, *int*, and *rat* are all least fixed-points of their constructors. In fact, we could have defined *nat* and each of these bunches as least fixed-points of their constructors. It is quite common to define a bunch of strings by a fixed-point construction axiom called a grammar. For example,

$$exp = \text{"x"}, \; exp; \text{"+"}; exp$$

In this context, union is usually denoted by | and catenation is usually denoted by nothing. The other axiom, to say that *exp* is the least of the fixed-points, is usually stated informally by saying that only constructed elements are included.

——End of Least Fixed-Points

Recursive Data Construction

Recursive construction is a procedure for constructing least fixed-points from constructors. It usually works, but not always. We seek the smallest solution of

$$name = (\text{expression involving } name)$$

Here are the steps of the procedure.

0. Construct a sequence of bunches $name_0 \; name_1 \; name_2 \; ...$ beginning with

$$name_0 = null$$

and continuing with

$$name_{n+1} = (\text{expression involving } name_n)$$

We can thus construct a bunch $name_n$ for any natural number n.

1. Next, try to find an expression for $name_n$ that may involve n but does not involve *name*.

$$name_n = (\text{expression involving } n \text{ but not } name)$$

2. Now form a bunch $name_\infty$ by replacing n with ∞.

$name_\infty$ = (expression involving neither n nor $name$)

3. The bunch $name_\infty$ is usually the least fixed-point of the constructor, but not always, so we must test it. First we test to see if it is a fixed-point.

$name_\infty$ = (expression involving $name_\infty$)

4. Then we test $name_\infty$ to see if it is the least fixed-point.

B = (expression involving B) $\implies$ $name_\infty$: B

We illustrate recursive construction on the constructor for pow , which is $1, 2{\times}pow$.

0. Construct the sequence

pow_0 = $null$

pow_1 = $1, 2{\times}pow_0$

= $1, 2{\times}null$

= $1, null$

= 1

pow_2 = $1, 2{\times}pow_1$

= $1, 2{\times}1$

= $1, 2$

pow_3 = $1, 2{\times}pow_2$

= $1, 2{\times}(1, 2)$

= $1, 2, 4$

The first bunch pow_0 tells us all the elements of the bunch pow that we know without looking at its constructor. In general, pow_n represents our knowledge of pow after n uses of its constructor.

1. Perhaps now we can guess the general member of this sequence

pow_n = $2^{0,..n}$

We could prove this by nat induction, but it is not really necessary. The proof would only tell us about pow_n for n: nat and we want pow_∞. Besides, we will test our final result.

2. Now that we can express pow_n , we can define pow_∞ as

pow_∞ = $2^{0,..\infty}$

= 2^{nat}

and we have found a likely candidate for the least fixed-point of the pow constructor.

3. We must test pow_∞ to see if it is a fixed-point.

$$2^{nat} = 1, 2{\times}2^{nat}$$
$$= \quad 2^{nat} = 2^0, 2^1{\times}2^{nat}$$
$$= \quad 2^{nat} = 2^0, 2^{1+nat}$$
$$= \quad 2^{nat} = 2^{0,\ 1+nat}$$
$$\Leftarrow \quad nat = 0, nat+1$$

The last line is a theorem, so the first line is a theorem too.

4. We must test pow_∞ to see if it is the least fixed-point.

$$2^{nat}\colon B$$

$=$	$\forall n\colon nat{\cdot}\ 2^n\colon B$	use the predicate form of nat induction
$\Leftarrow$	$2^0\colon B \ \wedge\ \forall n\colon nat{\cdot}\ 2^n\colon B \ \Rightarrow\ 2^{n+1}\colon B$	change variable
$=$	$1\colon B \ \wedge\ \forall m\colon 2^{nat}{\cdot}\ m\colon B \ \Rightarrow\ 2m\colon B$	increase domain
$\Leftarrow$	$1\colon B \ \wedge\ \forall m\colon nat{\cdot}\ m\colon B \ \Rightarrow\ 2m\colon B$	
$=$	$1\colon B \ \wedge\ \forall m\colon nat`B{\cdot}\ 2m\colon B$	increase domain
$\Leftarrow$	$1\colon B \ \wedge\ \forall m\colon B{\cdot}\ 2m\colon B$	
$=$	$1\colon B \ \wedge\ 2{\times}B\colon B$	
$\Leftarrow$	$B = 1, 2{\times}B$	

Since 2^{nat} is the least fixed-point of the pow constructor, we conclude $pow = 2^{nat}$.

───End of Recursive Data Construction

Whenever we add axioms, we must be careful to remain consistent with the theory we already have. A badly chosen axiom can cause inconsistency. Here is an example. Suppose we make

$$bad = \S n\colon nat{\cdot}\ \neg\ n\colon bad$$

an axiom. Thus bad is defined as the bunch of all naturals that are not in bad. From this axiom we find

$$0\colon bad \quad = \quad 0\colon \S n\colon nat{\cdot}\ \neg\ n\colon bad$$
$$= \quad \neg\ 0\colon bad$$

is a theorem. From the Completion Rule we find that $0\colon bad = \neg\ 0\colon bad$ is also an antitheorem. To avoid the inconsistency, we must withdraw this axiom.

Sometimes recursive construction does not produce any answer. For example, the fixed-point equation of the previous paragraph results in the sequence of bunches

$$bad_0 = null$$
$$bad_1 = nat$$
$$bad_2 = null$$

and so on, alternating between $null$ and nat. We cannot say what bad_∞ is because we cannot say whether ∞ is even or odd. We should not blame recursive construction for failing to find a fixed-point when there is none. However, it sometimes fails to find a fixed-point when there is one (see Exercise 275(a)).

───End of Recursive Data Definition

Recursive Program Definition

Programs, and more generally, specifications, can be defined by axioms just as data can. For our first example, let x and y be integer variables. The name zap is introduced, and the fixed-point equation

$$zap \;\; = \;\; \textbf{if } x{=}0 \textbf{ then } y{:=} 0 \textbf{ else } (x{:=} x{-}1.\;\; t{:=} t{+}1.\;\; zap)$$

is given as an axiom. The right side of the equation is the constructor. Here are six solutions to this equation.

(a) $x{\geq}0 \;\Rightarrow\; x'{=}y'{=}0 \wedge t' = t{+}x$

(b) $\textbf{if } x{\geq}0 \textbf{ then } x'{=}y'{=}0 \wedge t' = t{+}x \textbf{ else } t'{=}\infty$

(c) $x'{=}y'{=}0 \wedge (x{\geq}0 \Rightarrow t' = t{+}x)$

(d) $x'{=}y'{=}0 \wedge \textbf{if } x{\geq}0 \textbf{ then } t' = t{+}x \textbf{ else } t'{=}\infty$

(e) $x'{=}y'{=}0 \wedge t' = t{+}x$

(f) $x{\geq}0 \wedge x'{=}y'{=}0 \wedge t' = t{+}x$

Solution (a) is the weakest and solution (f) is the strongest, although the solutions are not totally ordered. We can express their order by the following picture.

Solutions (e) and (f) are so strong that they are unimplementable. Solution (d) is deterministic, so it is a strongest implementable solution.

We could now give a second axiom to define zap as the weakest (least strong) fixed-point of the constructor, but there is no need to do so. If the fixed-point equation is all we know about zap, then we cannot say that it is equal to a particular one of the solutions. But we can say this: it refines the weakest solution

$$x{\geq}0 \Rightarrow x'{=}y'{=}0 \wedge t' = t{+}x \;\; \Longleftarrow \;\; zap$$

so we can use it to solve problems. And it is refined by its constructor

$$zap \;\; \Longleftarrow \;\; \textbf{if } x{=}0 \textbf{ then } y{:=} 0 \textbf{ else } (x{:=} x{-}1.\;\; t{:=} t{+}1.\;\; zap)$$

so we can execute it. For all practical purposes, that is all we need.

Recursive Program Construction

Recursive program construction is similar to recursive data construction, and serves a similar purpose. We illustrate the procedure using the example zap . We start with zap_0 describing the computation as well as we can without looking at the definition of zap . Of course, if we don't look at the definition, we have no idea what computation zap is describing, so our description must be one that is satisfied by every computation. Let us start with

$$zap_0 \;=\; \top$$

We obtain the next description of zap by substituting zap_0 for zap in the constructor, and so on.

$$
\begin{aligned}
zap_1 \;&=\; \textbf{if } x{=}0 \textbf{ then } y{:=}0 \textbf{ else } (x{:=}x{-}1. \;\; t{:=}t{+}1. \;\; zap_0)\\
\;&=\; x{=}0 \;\Rightarrow\; x'{=}y'{=}0 \wedge t'{=}t\\
zap_2 \;&=\; \textbf{if } x{=}0 \textbf{ then } y{:=}0 \textbf{ else } (x{:=}x{-}1. \;\; t{:=}t{+}1. \;\; zap_1)\\
\;&=\; 0{\leq}x{<}2 \;\Rightarrow\; x'{=}y'{=}0 \wedge t' = t{+}x
\end{aligned}
$$

In general, zap_n describes the computation as well as possible after n uses of the constructor. We can now guess (and prove using nat induction if we want)

$$zap_n \;=\; 0{\leq}x{<}n \;\Rightarrow\; x'{=}y'{=}0 \wedge t' = t{+}x$$

The next step is to replace n with ∞ .

$$zap_\infty \;=\; 0{\leq}x{<}\infty \;\Rightarrow\; x'{=}y'{=}0 \wedge t' = t{+}x$$

Finally, we must test the result to see if it satisfies the axiom.

$$
\begin{aligned}
&\quad\; \text{(right side of equation with } zap_\infty \text{ for } zap)\\
=\;& \textbf{if } x{=}0 \textbf{ then } y{:=}0 \textbf{ else } (x{:=}x{-}1. \;\; t{:=}t{+}1. \;\; 0{\leq}x \;\Rightarrow\; x'{=}y'{=}0 \wedge t' = t{+}x)\\
=\;& \textbf{if } x{=}0 \textbf{ then } x'{=}y'{=}0 \wedge t'{=}t \textbf{ else } 0{\leq}x{-}1 \;\Rightarrow\; x'{=}y'{=}0 \wedge t' = t{+}x\\
=\;& 0{\leq}x \;\Rightarrow\; x'{=}y'{=}0 \wedge t' = t{+}x\\
=\;& \text{(left side of equation with } zap_\infty \text{ for } zap)
\end{aligned}
$$

It satisfies the fixed-point equation, and in fact it is the weakest fixed-point.

If we are not considering time, then $\top$ is all we can say about an unknown computation, and we must start our recursive construction there. With time, we can say more than just $\top$; we can say that time does not decrease. Starting with $t' \geq t$ we can construct a stronger fixed-point.

$$
\begin{aligned}
zap_0 \;&=\; t' \geq t\\
zap_1 \;&=\; \textbf{if } x{=}0 \textbf{ then } y{:=}0 \textbf{ else } (x{:=}x{-}1. \;\; t{:=}t{+}1. \;\; zap_0)\\
\;&=\; \textbf{if } x{=}0 \textbf{ then } x'{=}y'{=}0 \wedge t'{=}t \textbf{ else } t' \geq t{+}1\\
zap_2 \;&=\; \textbf{if } x{=}0 \textbf{ then } y{:=}0 \textbf{ else } (x{:=}x{-}1. \;\; t{:=}t{+}1. \;\; zap_1)\\
\;&=\; \textbf{if } x{=}0 \textbf{ then } x'{=}y'{=}0 \wedge t'{=}t \textbf{ else } \textbf{if } x{=}1 \textbf{ then } x'{=}y'{=}0 \wedge t'{=}t{+}1 \textbf{ else } t' \geq t{+}2\\
\;&=\; \textbf{if } 0{\leq}x{<}2 \textbf{ then } x'{=}y'{=}0 \wedge t' = t{+}x \textbf{ else } t' \geq t{+}2
\end{aligned}
$$

In general, zap_n describes what we know up to time n . We can now guess (and prove using nat induction if we want)

zap_n $=$ **if** $0\leq x<n$ **then** $x'=y'=0 \wedge t'=t+x$ **else** $t' \geq t+n$

We replace n with ∞

zap_∞ $=$ **if** $0\leq x$ **then** $x'=y'=0 \wedge t'=t+x$ **else** $t'=\infty$

and test the result

(right side of equation with zap_∞ for zap)

$=$ **if** $x=0$ **then** $y:= 0$ **else** $(x:= x-1.$ $t:= t+1.$ **if** $0\leq x$ **then** $x'=y'=0 \wedge t'=t+x$ **else** $t'=\infty)$

$=$ **if** $x=0$ **then** $x'=y'=0 \wedge t'=t$ **else**   **if** $0\leq x-1$ **then** $x'=y'=0 \wedge t'=t+x$ **else** $t'=\infty$

$=$ **if** $0\leq x$ **then** $x'=y'=0 \wedge t' = t+x$ **else** $t'=\infty$

$=$ (left side of equation with zap_∞ for zap)

Beginning our recursive construction with $t' \geq t$, we have constructed a stronger but still implementable fixed-point. If we begin our recursive construction with $\perp$ we obtain the strongest fixed-point, which is unimplementable.

——————————————————————————————————End of Recursive Program Construction

Loop Definition

Loops can be defined by construction and induction. The axioms for the **while**-loop are

if b **then** $(P.$ **while** b **do** $P)$ **else** ok $\Longleftarrow$ **while** b **do** P

$\forall\sigma, \sigma'\cdot$ (**if** b **then** $(P.$ $W)$ **else** $ok \Longleftarrow W)$ $\Longrightarrow$ $\forall\sigma, \sigma'\cdot$ (**while** b **do** $P \Longleftarrow W)$

and the axioms for the **repeat**-loop are

$P.$ **if** b **then** ok **else** **repeat** P **until** b $\Longleftarrow$ **repeat** P **until** b

$\forall\sigma, \sigma'\cdot$ $(P.$ **if** b **then** ok **else** $R \Longleftarrow R)$ $\Longrightarrow$ $\forall\sigma, \sigma'\cdot$ (**repeat** P **until** $b \Longleftarrow R)$ ˙

The **while**-loop construction axiom says that **while** b **do** P refines (implements) its first unrolling, and by Stepwise Refinement, it refines any of its unrollings. The induction axiom says that it is the weakest specification that does so. Similarly for **repeat**.

From these axioms we can prove theorems called fixed-point construction and fixed-point induction. For the **while**-loop they are

while b **do** P $=$ **if** b **then** $(P.$ **while** b **do** $P)$ **else** ok

$\forall\sigma, \sigma'\cdot$ $(W$ $=$ **if** b **then** $(P.$ $W)$ **else** $ok)$ $\Longrightarrow$ $\forall\sigma, \sigma'\cdot$ (**while** b **do** $P \Longleftarrow W)$

and for the **repeat**-loop they are

repeat P **until** b $=$ $P.$ **if** b **then** ok **else** **repeat** P **until** b

$\forall\sigma, \sigma'\cdot$ $(R$ $=$ $P.$ **if** b **then** ok **else** $R)$ $\Longrightarrow$ $\forall\sigma, \sigma'\cdot$ (**repeat** P **until** $b \Longleftarrow R)$

This account differs from that presented in Chapter 5; we have gained some theorems, and also lost some theorems. For example, we can no longer prove

$t' \geq t$ $\Longleftarrow$ **while** b **do** $t' \geq t$

——————————————————————————————————End of Loop Definition

——————————————————————————————————End of Recursive Program Definition

The following section is optional.

Limits

Recursive construction, as it was presented, contains a step in which n is replaced with ∞ . From $name_n$ we obtain a candidate $name_\infty$ for a fixed-point of a constructor. This substitution is simple to perform, and the resulting candidate is usually satisfactory. But the result is sensitive to the way $name_n$ is expressed. From two expressions for $name_n$ that are equal for all finite n , we may obtain expressions for $name_\infty$ that are unequal. This section presents another way to obtain a candidate so that the result is not sensitive to the way $name_n$ is expressed.

The <u>limit</u> of a sequence of bunches $B_0\ B_1\ B_2\ ...$ is written $lim\ n \cdot\ B_n$ and defined by the two axioms

$$\exists p \cdot\ \forall n \cdot\ n{\geq}p \Rightarrow x{:}B_n \implies x{:}lim\ n \cdot\ B_n$$
$$\exists p \cdot\ \forall n \cdot\ n{\geq}p \Rightarrow \neg\, x{:}B_n \implies \neg\, x{:}lim\ n \cdot\ B_n$$

The first axiom says that x is in the limit bunch if there is a point in the sequence after which x is in all succeeding bunches. The second axiom says that x is not in the limit bunch if there is a point in the sequence after which x is not in all succeeding bunches. The two axioms can be written as one, giving a lower bound and an upper bound for limits, as follows:

$$\exists p \cdot\ \forall n \cdot\ n{\geq}p \Rightarrow x{:}B_n \implies x{:}lim\ n \cdot\ B_n \implies \forall p \cdot\ \exists n \cdot\ n{\geq}p \land x{:}B_n$$

For recursive data construction, in place of $name_\infty$, we can use $lim\ n \cdot\ name_n$ as our candidate.

The limit of a sequence of boolean expressions $b_0\ b_1\ b_2\ ...$ is written $lim\ n \cdot\ b_n$ and defined by the two axioms

$$\exists p \cdot\ \forall n \cdot\ n{\geq}p \Rightarrow b_n \implies lim\ n \cdot\ b_n$$
$$\exists p \cdot\ \forall n \cdot\ n{\geq}p \Rightarrow \neg b_n \implies \neg\ lim\ n \cdot\ b_n$$

The two axioms can be written as one, giving a strong bound and a weak bound, as follows:

$$\exists p \cdot\ \forall n \cdot\ n{\geq}p \Rightarrow b_n \implies lim\ n \cdot\ b_n \implies \forall p \cdot\ \exists n \cdot\ n{\geq}p \land b_n$$

For recursive program construction, in place of $name_\infty$, we can use $lim\ n \cdot\ name_n$ as our candidate.

Finding a limit is much harder than substituting ∞ for n , and it is still not guaranteed to produce a fixed-point. We can identify a special case that is sufficient to guarantee that the limit is the least fixed-point (the constructor is monotonic and continuous). But we leave the subject to other books.

———————————————————————————————————————End of Limits

———————————————————————————————————————End of Recursive Definition

7 Theory Design and Implementation

Programmers use the formalisms, abstractions, theories, structures that have been created for them by the designers and implementers of their programming languages. And with every program they write, with every name they introduce, programmers create new formalisms, abstractions, theories, structures. To make their creations as elegant and useful as possible, programmers should be aware of their role as theory designers and implementers, as well as theory users.

The stack, the queue, and the tree are standard data structures used frequently in programming. It is not the purpose of the present chapter to show their usefulness in applications; we leave that to books devoted to data structures. They are presented here as case studies in theory design and implementation. Each of these data structures contains items of some sort. For example, we can have stacks of integers, stacks of lists of booleans, even stacks of stacks. In this chapter, X is the bunch (or type) of items in a data structure.

Data Theories

Data-Stack Theory

The stack is a useful data structure for the implemention of programming languages. Its distinguishing feature is that, at any time, the item to be inspected or deleted next is always the newest remaining item. It is the structure with the motto: the last one in is the first one out.

We introduce the syntax *stack* , *empty* , *push* , *pop* , and *top* . Informally, they mean the following.

stack	a bunch consisting of all stacks of items of type X
empty	a stack containing no items
push	a function that, given a stack and an item, gives back the stack containing the same items plus the one new item
pop	a function that, given a stack, gives back the stack minus the newest remaining item
top	a function that, given a stack, gives back the newest remaining item

Here are the first four axioms.

> *empty*: *stack*
>
> *push*: *stack*→X→*stack*
>
> *pop*: *stack*→*stack*
>
> *top*: *stack*→X

We want *empty* and *push* to be *stack* constructors. We want a stack obtained by *pop* to be one that was constructed from *empty* and *push* , so we do not need *pop* to be a constructor. A construction axiom can be written in either of the following ways:

> *empty, push stack X: stack*
>
> $P\ empty \land \forall s: stack \cdot \forall x: X \cdot Ps \Rightarrow P(push\ s\ x)\ \Longleftarrow\ \forall s: stack \cdot Ps$

where *P: stack→bool* , but it is already implied by our first two axioms. To exclude anything else from being a stack requires an induction axiom, which can be written in many ways; here are two:

> *empty, push B X: B* $\Rightarrow$ *stack: B*
>
> $P\ empty \land \forall s: stack \cdot \forall x: X \cdot Ps \Rightarrow P(push\ s\ x)\ \Longrightarrow\ \forall s: stack \cdot Ps$

According to the axioms we have so far, it is possible that all stacks are equal. To say that the constructors always construct different stacks requires two more axioms. Let *s, t: stack* and *x, y: X* ; then

> *push s x* ≠ *empty*
>
> *push s x = push t y* = *s=t* ∧ *x=y*

And finally, two axioms are needed to say that stacks behave in "last in, first out" fashion.

> *pop (push s x) = s*
>
> *top (push s x) = x*

And that completes the data-stack axioms.

———————————————————————————————————End of Data-Stack Theory

Data-stack theory allows us to declare as many stack variables as we want and to use them in expressions according to the axioms. We can declare variables *a* and *b* of type *stack* , and then write the assignments *a:= empty* and *b:= push a* 2 .

Data-Stack Implementation

If you need a stack and stacks are not provided in your programming language, you will have to build your stack using the implemented data structures. Suppose the list structure is implemented. Then we can define a stack of integers as follows.

> *stack* = [**int*]
>
> *empty* = [*nil*]
>
> *push* = $\lambda s: stack \cdot \lambda x: int \cdot s^+[x]$
>
> *pop* = $\lambda s: stack \cdot$ **if** *s=empty* **then** *empty* **else** *s* [0;..#*s*−1]
>
> *top* = $\lambda s: stack \cdot$ **if** *s=empty* **then** 0 **else** *s* (#*s*−1)

To prove that these definitions implement stacks, we must prove that the stack axioms are satisfied. For example, the last axiom becomes

$$top \ (push \ s \ x) = x \qquad\qquad\qquad \text{replace } push$$

$$= \quad top \ ((\lambda s: stack \cdot \lambda x: int \cdot s^+[x]) \ s \ x) = x \qquad \text{apply function}$$

$$= \quad top \ (s^+[x]) = x \qquad\qquad\qquad \text{replace } top$$

$$= \quad (\lambda s: stack \cdot \textbf{if } s{=}empty \textbf{ then } 0 \textbf{ else } s \ (\#s{-}1)) \ (s^+[x]) = x$$

apply function and replace *empty*

$$= \quad (\textbf{if } s^+[x]{=}[nil] \textbf{ then } 0 \textbf{ else } (s^+[x]) \ (\#(s^+[x]){-}1)) = x \qquad \text{simplify the } \textbf{if} \text{ and the index}$$

$$= \quad (s^+[x]) \ (\#s) = x \qquad\qquad\qquad \text{index the list}$$

$$= \quad x = x \qquad\qquad\qquad\qquad \text{reflexive law}$$

——End of Data-Stack Implementation

Is stack theory consistent? Since we implemented it using list theory, we know that if list theory is consistent, so is stack theory. Is stack theory complete? To show that a boolean expression is unclassified, we must implement stacks twice, making the expression a theorem in one implementation, and an antitheorem in the other. The expressions

$$pop \ empty = empty$$

$$top \ empty = 0$$

are theorems in our implementation, but we can alter the implementation as follows

$$pop \ = \ \lambda s: stack \cdot \textbf{if } s{=}empty \textbf{ then } push \ empty \ 0 \textbf{ else } s \ [0;..\#s{-}1]$$

$$top \ = \ \lambda s: stack \cdot \textbf{if } s{=}empty \textbf{ then } 1 \textbf{ else } s \ (\#s{-}1)$$

to make them antitheorems. So stack theory is incomplete.

Stack theory specifies the properties of stacks. A person who implements stacks must ensure that *all* these properties are provided. A person who uses stacks must ensure that *only* these properties are relied upon. This point deserves emphasis: a theory is a contract between two parties, an implementer and a user (they may be one person with two hats, or two corporations). It makes clear what each party's obligations are to the other, and what each can expect from the other. If something goes wrong, it makes clear who is at fault. A theory makes it possible for each side to modify their part of a program without knowing how the other part is written. This is an essential principle in the construction of large-scale software. In our small example, the stack user must not use *pop empty = empty* even though the stack implementer has provided it; if the user wants it, it should be added to the theory.

Simple Data-Stack Theory

In the data-stack theory just presented, we have the axioms *empty*: *stack* and *pop*: *stack→stack* ; from them we can prove *pop empty*: *stack* . In other words, popping the empty stack gives a stack, though we do not know which one. An implementer is obliged to give a stack for *pop empty* , though it does not matter which one. If we never want to pop an empty stack, then the theory is too strong. We should weaken the axiom *pop*: *stack→stack* and remove the implementer's obligation to provide something that is not wanted. The weaker axiom

$s \neq empty \implies pop\ s: stack$

says that popping a nonempty stack yields a stack, but it is implied by the remaining axioms and so is unnecessary. Similarly from *empty*: *stack* and *top*: *stack*$\rightarrow X$ we can prove *top empty*: X ; deleting the axiom *top*: *stack*$\rightarrow X$ removes an implementer's obligation to provide an unwanted result for *top empty* .

We may decide that we have no need to prove anything about all stacks, and can do without *stack* induction. After a little thought, we may realize that we never need an empty stack, nor to test if a stack is empty. We can always work on top of a given (possibly non-empty) stack, and in most uses we are required to do so, leaving the stack as we found it. If we want to test whether a stack is empty, we should begin by pushing some special value, one that will not be pushed again, onto the stack; the empty test is then a test whether the top is the special value. We can delete the axiom *empty*: *stack* and all mention of *empty* . We must replace this axiom with the weaker axiom *stack* $\neq$ *null* so that we can still declare variables of type *stack* .

For most purposes, it is sufficient to be able to push items onto a stack, pop items off, and look at the top item. The theory we need is considerably simpler than the one presented previously. Our simpler data-stack theory introduces the names *stack* , *push* , *pop* , and *top* with the following four axioms: Let s: *stack* and x: X ; then

$stack \neq null$

$push\ s\ x: stack$

$pop\ (push\ s\ x) = s$

$top\ (push\ s\ x) = x$

──End of Simple Data-Stack Theory

For the purpose of studying stacks, as a mathematical activity, we want the strongest axioms possible so that we can prove as much as possible. As an engineering activity, theory design is the art of excluding all unwanted implementations while allowing all the others. It is counter-productive to design a stronger theory than necessary; it makes implementation harder, and it makes theory extension harder.

Data-Queue Theory

The queue data structure, also known as a buffer, is useful in simulations and scheduling. Its distinguishing feature is that, at any time, the item to be inspected or deleted next is always the oldest remaining item. It is the structure with the motto: the first one in is the first one out.

We introduce the syntax *queue* , *emptyq* , *join* , *leave* , and *front* with the following informal meaning:

queue	a bunch consisting of all queues of items of type X
emptyq	a queue containing no items
join	a function that, given a queue and an item, gives back the queue containing the same items plus the one new item
leave	a function that, given a queue, gives back the queue minus the oldest remaining item
front	a function that, given a queue, gives back the oldest remaining item

The same kinds of considerations that went into the design of stack theory also guide the design of queue theory. Let $q, r: queue$ and $x, y: X$. We certainly want the construction axioms

emptyq: *queue*

join q x: *queue*

If we want to prove things about the domain of *join* , then we must replace the second construction axiom by the stronger axiom

join: *queue*$\rightarrow$*X* $\rightarrow$*queue*

To say that the constructors construct distinct queues, with no repetitions, we need

join q x $\ne$ *emptyq*

join q x = join r y $=$ $q=r \wedge x=y$

We want a queue obtained by *leave* to be one that was constructed from *emptyq* and *join* , so we do not need

leave q: *queue*

for construction, and we don't want to oblige an implementer to provide a representation for *leave emptyq* , so perhaps we will omit that one. We do want to say

$q \ne emptyq$ $\Rightarrow$ *leave q*: *queue*

And similarly, we want

$q \ne emptyq$ $\Rightarrow$ *front q*: X

We may or may not want to prove something about all queues. If so we need *queue* induction:

emptyq, *join B X*: *B* $\Rightarrow$ *queue*: *B*

And finally, we need to give queues their "first in, first out" character:

leave (*join emptyq x*) $=$ *emptyq*

$q \ne emptyq$ $\Rightarrow$ *leave* (*join q x*) = *join* (*leave q*) *x*

front (*join emptyq x*) $=$ *x*

$q \ne emptyq$ $\Rightarrow$ *front* (*join q x*) = *front q*

If we have decided to keep the *queue* induction axiom, we can throw away the two earlier axioms

$q \ne emptyq$ $\Rightarrow$ *leave q*: *queue*

$q \ne emptyq$ $\Rightarrow$ *front q*: X

since they can now be proven.

——End of Data-Queue Theory

After data-stack implementation, data-queue implementation raises no new issues, so we leave it as Exercise 303.

Data-Tree Theory

We introduce the syntax

tree	a bunch consisting of all finite binary trees of items of type X
emptree	a tree containing no items
graft	a function that, given two trees and an item, gives back the tree with the item at the root and the two given trees as left and right subtree
left	a function that, given a tree, gives back its left subtree
right	a function that, given a tree, gives back its right subtree
root	a function that, given a tree, gives back its root item

For the purpose of studying trees, we want a strong theory. Let t, u, v, w: *tree* and x, y: X .

> *emptree*: *tree*
>
> *graft*: *tree*$\rightarrow$$X$$\rightarrow$*tree*$\rightarrow$*tree*
>
> *emptree*, *graft B X B*: B $\Rightarrow$ *tree*: B
>
> *graft t x u* $\neq$ *emptree*
>
> *graft t x u = graft v y w* $\ \equiv\ $ t=v $\wedge$ x=y $\wedge$ u=w
>
> *left* (*graft t x u*) = t
>
> *root* (*graft t x u*) = x
>
> *right* (*graft t x u*) = u

For most programming purposes, the following simpler, weaker theory is sufficient.

> *tree* $\neq$ *null*
>
> *graft t x u*: *tree*
>
> *left* (*graft t x u*) = t
>
> *root* (*graft t x u*) = x
>
> *right* (*graft t x u*) = u

As with stacks, we don't really need to be given an empty tree. As long as we are given some tree, we can build a tree with a distinguished root that serves the same purpose. And we probably don't need *tree* induction.

———End of Data-Tree Theory

Data-Tree Implementation

Suppose lists and recursive data definition are implemented. Then we can define a tree of integers as follows.

tree = *emptree, graft tree int tree*

emptree = [*nil*]

graft = λ*t*: *tree*· λ*x*: *int*· λ*u*: *tree*· [*t*; *x*; *u*]

left = λ*t*: *tree*· *t* 0

right = λ*t*: *tree*· *t* 2

root = λ*t*: *tree*· *t* 1

The procedure *graft* makes a list (or function) of three items; two of those items may be lists themselves. A reasonable implementation strategy for lists is to allocate a small space, one capable of holding an integer or data address, for each item. If an item is an integer, it is put in its place; if an item is a list, it is put somewhere else and a pointer to it (data address) is put in its place. In this implementation of lists, pointers are provided automatically when needed. For example, the tree

[[[*nil*]; 2; [[*nil*]; 5; [*nil*]]]; 3; [[*nil*]; 7; [*nil*]]]

looks like

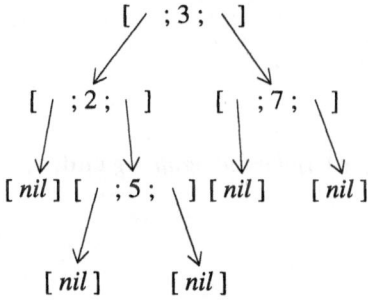

Here is another implementation of data-trees.

tree = *emptree, graft tree int tree*

emptree = 0

graft = λ*t*: *tree*· λ*x*: *int*· λ*u*: *tree*· "left"→*t* | "root"→*x* | "right"→*u*

left = λ*t*: *tree*· *t* "left"

right = λ*t*: *tree*· *t* "right"

root = λ*t*: *tree*· *t* "root"

With this implementation, a tree value looks like this.

        "left" →   ("left" → 0
                    | "root" → 2
                    | "right" → ("left" → 0
                                | "root" → 5
                                | "right" → 0))
    | "root" → 3
    | "right" → ("left" → 0
                | "root" → 7
                | "right" → 0)

If the implementation you have available does not include recursive data definition, you will have to build the pointer structure yourself. For example, in Pascal you can code the implementation of binary trees as follows.

```
type   tree = ↑somewhere;
       somewhere = record  left: tree;
                           root: integer;
                           right: tree
                   end;


var  a, b, c: tree;


function emptree: tree;
     begin emptree:= nil end;


function graft (t: tree; x: integer; u: tree): tree;
     var g: tree;
     begin new (g);  g↑.left:= t;  g↑.root:= x;  g↑.right:= u;  graft:= g end;


function left (t: tree): tree;
     begin left:= t↑.left end;


function root (t: tree): integer;
     begin root:= t↑.root end;


function right (t: tree): tree;
     begin right:= t↑.right end;
```

As you can see, the Pascal code is clumsy. It is not a good idea to apply Program Theory directly to the Pascal code. The use of pointers (data addresses) when recursive data definition is unimplemented is just like the use of **go to** (program addresses) when recursive program definition is unimplemented or implemented badly.

──End of Data-Tree Implementation

──End of Data Theories

A data theory creates a new type, or value space, or perhaps an extension of an old type. A program theory creates new programs, or rather, new specifications that become programs when the theory is implemented. These two styles of theory correspond to two styles of programming: functional and imperative.

Program Theories

In program theories, the state is divided into two kinds of variables: the <u>user's variables</u> and the <u>implementer's variables</u>. A user of the theory enjoys full access to the user's variables, but cannot directly access (see or change) the implementer's variables. A user gets access to the implementer's variables only through the theory. On the other side, an implementer of the theory enjoys full access to the implementer's variables, but cannot directly access (see or change) the user's variables. An implementer gets access to the user's variables only through the theory. Some programming languages have a "module" or "object" construct exactly for this purpose. In other languages we simply forbid the unauthorized use of variables on the wrong side of the boundary.

If we need only one stack or one queue or one tree, we can obtain an economy of expression and of execution by leaving it implicit. There is no need to say which stack to push onto if there is only one, and similarly for the other operations and data structures. Each of the program theories we present will provide only one of its data structure to the user, but it could be generalized by adding an extra parameter to each operation.

Program-Stack Theory

The simplest version of program-stack theory introduces three names: *push* (a procedure with parameter of type X), *pop* (a program), and *top* (of type X). In this theory, *push* 3 is a program (assuming $3: X$); it changes the state. Following this program, before any other pushes and pops, *print top* will print 3 . The following two axioms are sufficient.

$$top' = x \quad \Longleftarrow \quad push\ x$$
$$ok \quad \Longleftarrow \quad push\ x.\ pop$$

where $x: X$.

The second axiom says that a pop undoes a push. In fact, it says that any natural number of pushes are undone by the same number of pops.

ok	use second axiom
$\Longleftarrow$ *push x. pop*	*ok* is identity for dependent composition
$=$ *push x. ok. pop*	Refinement by Steps reusing the axiom
$\Longleftarrow$ *push x. push y. pop. pop*	

We can prove things like

$$top' = x \quad \Longleftarrow \quad push\ x.\ push\ y.\ push\ z.\ pop.\ pop$$

which say that when we push something onto the stack, we find it there later at the appropriate time. That is all we really want.

Program-Stack Implementation

To implement program-stack theory, we introduce an implementer's variable $s: [*X]$ and now we define

$push = \lambda x: X \cdot s := s^+[x]$

$pop = s := s\ [0;..\#s-1]$

$top = s\ (\#s-1)$

And, of course, we must show that these definitions satisfy the axioms. We'll do the first axiom, and leave the others as Exercise 305.

$\quad\quad\quad (top'=x \ \Leftarrow\ push\ x)$ \hfill use definition of $push$ and top

$=\quad (s'(\#s'-1)=x \ \Leftarrow\ s := s^+[x])$ \hfill List Theory

--End of Program-Stack Implementation

Fancy Program-Stack Theory

The program-stack theory just presented corresponds to the simpler data-stack theory presented earlier. A slightly fancier program-stack theory introduces two more names: *mkempty* (a program to make the stack empty) and *isempty* (a condition to say whether the stack is empty). Letting $x: X$, the axioms are

$top'=x \ \land\ \neg isempty' \ \Leftarrow\ push\ x$

$ok \ \Leftarrow\ push\ x.\ pop$

$isempty' \ \Leftarrow\ mkempty$

--End of Fancy Program-Stack Theory

Once we implement program-stack theory using lists, we know that program-stack theory is consistent if list theory is consistent. Program-stack theory, like data-stack theory, is incomplete. Incompleteness is a freedom for the implementer, who can trade economy against robustness. If we care how this trade will be made, we should strengthen the theory. For example, we could add the axiom

$print$ "error" $\ \Leftarrow\ mkempty.\ pop$

Weak Program-Stack Theory

The program-stack theory we presented first can be weakened and still retain its stack character. We must keep the axiom

$top'=x \ \Leftarrow\ push\ x$

but we do not need the composition $push\ x.\ pop$ to leave all variables unchanged. We do require that any natural number of pushes followed by the same number of pops gives back the original top. The axiom is

$$top' = top \impliedby balance$$

where *balance* is defined by the fixed-point construction

$$balance = ok \vee \exists x \cdot (push\ x.\ balance.\ pop)$$

This weaker theory allows an implementation in which popping does not restore the implementer's variable s to its pre-pushed value, but instead marks the last item as "garbage".

A weak theory can be extended in ways that are excluded by a strong theory. For example, we can add the names *count* (of type *nat*) and *start* (a program), with the axioms

$$count' = 0 \impliedby start$$
$$count' = count+1 \impliedby push\ x$$
$$count' = count+1 \impliedby pop$$

so that *count* counts the number of pushes and pops.

———End of Weak Program-Stack Theory

Program-Queue Theory

Program-queue theory introduces five names: *mkemptyq* (a program to make the queue empty), *isemptyq* (a condition to say whether the queue is empty), *join* (a procedure with parameter of type X), *leave* (a program), and *front* (of type X). The axioms are

$$isemptyq' \impliedby mkemptyq$$
$$isemptyq \Rightarrow front'=x \wedge \neg isemptyq' \impliedby join\ x$$
$$\neg isemptyq \Rightarrow front'=front \wedge \neg isemptyq' \impliedby join\ x$$
$$isemptyq \Rightarrow (join\ x.\ leave = mkemptyq)$$
$$\neg isemptyq \Rightarrow (join\ x.\ leave = leave.\ join\ x)$$

———End of Program-Queue Theory

Program-Tree Theory

As usual, there is more than one way to do it. Imagine a tree that is infinite in all directions; there are no leaves and no root. You are looking at one particular item in the tree. The name *node* (of type X) tells the value of that item; *change* (a procedure with parameter of type X) causes the value of that item to change; *goUp* (a program) changes your view to the parent of that item; *goLeft* changes your view to the left child of that item; *goRight* changes your view to the right child of that item. In the axioms, we use six auxiliary definitions: L means "go down left, then do anything except go back up (ending in the same place), then go back up"; R means "go down right, then do anything except go back up (ending in the same place), then go back up"; U means "go up, then do anything except go back down the way you came (ending in the same place), then go back down the way you came"; $\underline{L}$ means "do anything except for going down left (ending where you start)"; $\underline{R}$ means "do anything except for going down right (ending where you start)"; $\underline{U}$ means "do anything except for going up (ending where you start)". Here are the axioms.

$$node'=x \quad \Longleftarrow \quad change\ x$$
$$node'=node \quad \Longleftarrow \quad L \vee R \vee U$$
$$goLeft.\ goUp \quad = \quad goRight.\ goUp \quad = \quad ok$$

where

$$L \quad = \quad goLeft.\ \underline{U}.\ goUp$$
$$R \quad = \quad goRight.\ \underline{U}.\ goUp$$
$$goLeft.\ U \quad = \quad \underline{L}.\ goLeft$$
$$goRight.\ U \quad = \quad \underline{R}.\ goRight$$
$$\underline{L} \quad = \quad ok \vee (\exists x \cdot change\ x) \vee R \vee U \vee (\underline{L}.\ \underline{L})$$
$$\underline{R} \quad = \quad ok \vee (\exists x \cdot change\ x) \vee U \vee L \vee (\underline{R}.\ \underline{R})$$
$$\underline{U} \quad = \quad ok \vee (\exists x \cdot change\ x) \vee L \vee R \vee (\underline{U}.\ \underline{U})$$

———————————————————————————————————End of Program-Tree Theory

———————————————————————————————————End of Program Theories

To implement a data type, you must provide a representation for all values of the type, and implement all the operators. Someone who uses the type may need only some of its values, and some of its operators, and only in some special circumstances. If you are implementing the type only for that someone (who may even be yourself), you should wait to see its use before you provide the implementation.

Let's do Exercise 328 (parsing) to illustrate the principle. Define E as a bunch of strings of texts satisfying the fixed-point equation

$$E \quad = \quad \text{"x"}, \quad \text{"if"};\ E;\ \text{"then"};\ E;\ \text{"else"};\ E$$

Given a string s of texts, write a program to determine if $s: E$.

We can express the result as the final value of boolean variable q ; the problem is then $q' = (s:E)$. For the problem to be nontrivial, we assume that recursive data definition and bunch inclusion are not implemented operations. Although there are no bunch-valued variables, let us begin as though there were; we will eliminate them later. Let A be a variable whose values are bunches of strings of texts. Bunch A will consist of all strings in E that might possibly be s according to what we have seen of s . Initially, $A = E$, meaning that s might be any string in E . As we see more and more of s , we can eliminate some strings from A in the hope that this will make the inclusion question easier.

Our first decision is to parse from left to right, so we introduce natural variable n , increasing from 0 to at most $\#s$, indicating the current item s_n of the string we are parsing. (Reminder: $\#$ is string length.)

$$q' = (s: E) \quad \Longleftarrow \quad A := E. \quad n := 0. \quad P$$

where

$$P \;=\; 0 \le n \le \#s \;\wedge\; A = (\S e: E \cdot \#e \ge n \;\wedge\; e_{0;..n} = s_{0;..n}) \;\Rightarrow\; q' = (s: A)$$

In words, the new problem P says that if n indicates some point in s, and A consists of all strings of E that agree with s up to index n, then the question is whether s is in A. Here is its solution.

$$P \quad \Longleftarrow \quad \textbf{if } n = \#s \textbf{ then } n = \#s \Rightarrow P$$
$$\textbf{else } (A := (\S a \cdot A \cdot a_n = s_n). \quad n := n+1. \quad P)$$

Now we should begin to consider how to represent A. Notice that all strings in A are identical to s up to index n; this initial portion of each string does not need representation. We can replace A by B which consists of all possibilities for the remainder of s, the part not yet seen, rather than all of s. (This decision is called "top-down" parsing.) A and B are related by

$$A = s_{0;..n}; B$$

With this equation, we now replace A by B.

$A := E. \quad n := 0$ becomes $B := E. \quad n := 0$

P becomes $0 \le n \le \#s \wedge B = (\S b \cdot s_{0;..n}; b: E) \Rightarrow q' = (s_{n;..\#s}: B)$

$A := (\S a \cdot A \cdot a_n = s_n). \quad n := n+1$ becomes $B := (\S b \cdot s_n; b: B). \quad n := n+1$

We can refine

$$n = \#s \Rightarrow P \quad \Longleftarrow \quad q := nil: B$$

Now we must consider how to represent B. Let us replace it with variable r whose value is a string of texts. We represent bunch E with the text "$\langle E \rangle$", which we assume cannot be in the given string s. (In parsing theory "$\langle E \rangle$" is called a "nonterminal".) For example, the string of texts

"if"; "x"; "then"; "$\langle E \rangle$"; "else"; "$\langle E \rangle$"

represents the bunch of strings of texts

"if"; "x"; "then"; E; "else"; E

Now we replace all uses of B. First,

$B := E$ becomes $r := "\langle E \rangle"$

From the definition of E we see $\neg\, nil: E$. So if r consists of any items at all, whether "x", "if", "then", "else", or "$\langle E \rangle$", then nil is not in the bunch it represents. Thus

$nil: B$ becomes $r = nil$

For the assignment $B := (\S b \cdot s_n; b: B)$, we have four cases.

$\textbf{if } s_n = r_0 \textbf{ then } r := r_{1;..\#r}$

$\textbf{else if } s_n = "x" \wedge r_0 = "\langle E \rangle" \textbf{ then } r := r_{1;..\#r}$

$\textbf{else if } s_n = "if" \wedge r_0 = "\langle E \rangle" \textbf{ then } r := "\langle E \rangle"; "then"; "\langle E \rangle"; "else"; r$

$\textbf{else } B := null$

If $s_n = r_0$, then $r_{1;..\#r}$ represents all possibilities for the remainder of s . If r begins with "$\langle E\rangle$" , then all strings in the bunch represented by r begin with either "x" or "if" . To select just those that begin with "x" , we replace "$\langle E\rangle$" with "x" ; but we want just the remainders of these strings after the "x" , so again $r_{1;..\#r}$ represents all possibilities. When $s_n =$ "if" $\wedge$ $r_0 =$ "$\langle E\rangle$" we want to replace the "$\langle E\rangle$" with "if"; "$\langle E\rangle$"; "then"; "$\langle E\rangle$"; "else"; "$\langle E\rangle$" and then drop the initial "if" . If none of these is the case, then the bunch B does not include the remainder of string s , and the assignment reduces it to *null* .

We have now replaced B with r except for the final case $B := null$. The problem is an apparent inadequacy of our chosen representation: there is no representation for the *null* bunch (note: the empty string *nil* is a nonempty bunch). Fortunately we are saved by the occurrence of

$$n := n+1. \quad P$$

which follows the assignment $B := null$. To use it, we must distribute it to the four cases. We get

$$P \Longleftarrow \quad \textbf{if } n = \#s \textbf{ then } q := r = nil$$
$$\textbf{else if } s_n = r_0 \textbf{ then } (r := r_{1;..\#r} . \quad n := n+1. \quad P)$$
$$\textbf{else if } s_n = \text{"x"} \wedge r_0 = \text{"}\langle E\rangle\text{" then } (r := r_{1;..\#r} . \quad n := n+1. \quad P)$$
$$\textbf{else if } s_n = \text{"if"} \wedge r_0 = \text{"}\langle E\rangle\text{" then } (r := \text{"}\langle E\rangle\text{"}; \text{"then"}; \text{"}\langle E\rangle\text{"}; \text{"else"}; r. \; n := n+1. \quad P)$$
$$\textbf{else } (B := null. \quad n := n+1. \quad P)$$

And now

$$B := null. \quad n := n+1. \quad P \quad \Longleftarrow \quad q := \bot$$

We are finished. We can make a minor improvement by changing the representation of E from "$\langle E\rangle$" to "x" ; then one of the cases disappears. We could also notice that variable r behaves as a stack, and replace it by stack operations; that would be "unimplementing" a stack, and there is very little reason to do so. (The only reason for unimplementing something is to be able to reimplement it differently without considering the context of its use.)

Specification by Implementation

A program is a specification of computer behavior. Sometimes (but not always) a program is the clearest kind of specification. Sometimes it is the easiest kind of specification to write. If we write a specification as a program, there is no work to implement it.

A program-tree theory was given earlier. Here is an equivalent way to define it. Let T (for tree) and p (for pointer) be implementer's variables. Then the axioms are

$$node = T@p$$
$$change = \lambda x : X \cdot T := p \rightarrow x \mid T$$
$$goUp = p := p_{0;..\#p-1}$$
$$goLeft = p := p;0$$
$$goRight = p := p;1$$

If strings and the @ operator are implemented, then this theory is already an implementation. If not, it is still a presentation of program-tree theory, and should be compared to the earlier presentation for clarity.

Even though a specification may already be a program, we can, if we like, implement it differently. By saying that T and p are implementer's variables, an implementer reserves the right to change them. In some programming languages, implementer's variables are distinguished by being placed inside a "module" or "object". Perhaps the implementer's variables were chosen to make the specification as clear as possible, but other implementer's variables might be more storage-efficient, or provide faster access on average. Since a theory user has no access to the implementer's variables except through the theory, an implementer is free to change them in any way that provides the same theory to the user. Here's one way.

Data Transformation

Let the user's variables be u , and let the implementer's variables be v (u and v represent any number of variables). Now suppose we want to replace the implementer's variables by new implementer's variables w . We accomplish this transformation by means of a <u>data transformer</u>, which is a boolean expression D relating v and w such that

$$\forall w \cdot \exists v \cdot D$$

Let D' be the same as D but with primes on all the variables. Then each specification S in the theory is transformed to

$$\forall v \cdot D \Rightarrow \exists v' \cdot D' \wedge S$$

Specification S is in variables u and v , and the transformed specification is in variables u and w .

Data transformation is invisible to the user. Although the implementer's variables will be in a state w , the user will be able to suppose they are in a state v related by D because $\forall w \cdot \exists v \cdot D$. When the user makes use of specification S , the implementer's variables will change state from w to w' according to the transformed specification $\forall v \cdot D \Rightarrow \exists v' \cdot D' \wedge S$. This says that whatever related initial state v the user was imagining, there is a related final state v' for the user to imagine as the result of S , and so the fiction is maintained.

In the parsing problem, we replaced variable B with variable r . The data transformer was

$$B = abstract\ r$$

where *abstract* is almost the identity function, except that it maps text "⟨E⟩" to a bunch of strings of texts E .

A better example is Exercise 324(a). The user's variable is u: *bool* and the implementer's variable is v: *nat* . The theory provides three operations, specified by

$$zero \ = \ v := 0$$
$$increase \ = \ v := v+1$$
$$inquire \ = \ u := even \ v$$

Since the only question asked of the implementer's variable is whether it is even, we decide to replace it by a new implementer's variable w: *bool* according to the data transformer $w = even \ v$. The first operation *zero* becomes

$$\forall v \cdot w = even \ v \ \Rightarrow \ \exists v' \cdot w' = even \ v' \ \wedge \ (v := 0)$$

The assignment refers to a state consisting of u and v .

$= \quad \forall v \cdot w = even \ v \ \Rightarrow \ \exists v' \cdot w' = even \ v' \ \wedge \ u' = u \ \wedge \ v' = 0 \quad$ One-Point law
$= \quad \forall v \cdot w = even \ v \ \Rightarrow \ w' = even \ 0 \ \wedge \ u' = u$
$= \quad w' = \top \ \wedge \ u' = u$
$= \quad w := \top$

Operation *increase* becomes

$$\forall v \cdot w = even \ v \ \Rightarrow \ \exists v' \cdot w' = even \ v' \ \wedge \ (v := v+1)$$
$= \quad \forall v \cdot w = even \ v \ \Rightarrow \ \exists v' \cdot w' = even \ v' \ \wedge \ u' = u \ \wedge \ v' = v+1 \quad$ One-Point law
$= \quad \forall v \cdot w = even \ v \ \Rightarrow \ w' = even \ (v+1) \ \wedge \ u' = u$
$= \quad w' = \neg w \ \wedge \ u' = u$
$= \quad w := \neg w$

Operation *inquire* becomes

$$\forall v \cdot w = even \ v \ \Rightarrow \ \exists v' \cdot w' = even \ v' \ \wedge \ (u := even \ v)$$
$= \quad \forall v \cdot w = even \ v \ \Rightarrow \ \exists v' \cdot w' = even \ v' \ \wedge \ u' = even \ v \ \wedge \ v' = v \quad$ One-Point law
$= \quad \forall v \cdot w = even \ v \ \Rightarrow \ w' = even \ v \ \wedge \ u' = even \ v$
$= \quad w' = w \ \wedge \ u' = w$
$= \quad u := w$

In the previous example, we replaced a big state space by a smaller state space. Just to show that it works both ways, here is Exercise 325(a). The user's variable is u: *bool* and the implementer's variable is v: *bool* . The theory provides three operations, specified by

$$set \ = \ v := \top$$
$$flip \ = \ v := \neg v$$
$$ask \ = \ u := v$$

We decide to replace the implementer's variable by a new implementer's variable w: *nat* (perhaps for easier access on some computers) according to the data transformer $v = even \ w$. The first operation *set* becomes

$$\forall v \cdot v = even \ w \ \Rightarrow \ \exists v' \cdot v' = even \ w' \ \wedge \ (v := \top) \quad$$ One-Point law twice
$= \quad even \ w' \ \wedge \ u' = u$
$\Leftarrow \quad w := 0$

Operation *flip* becomes

$$\forall v\cdot\ v = even\ w\ \Rightarrow\ \exists v'\cdot\ v' = even\ w'\ \wedge\ (v:=\neg v)$$

$$=\quad even\ w' \neq even\ w\ \wedge\ u'=u$$

$$\Leftarrow\quad w:= w+1$$

Operation *ask* becomes

$$\forall v\cdot\ v = even\ w\ \Rightarrow\ \exists v'\cdot\ v' = even\ w'\ \wedge\ (u:= v)$$

$$=\quad w'=w\ \wedge\ u' = even\ w$$

$$=\quad u:= even\ w$$

In those two examples, there was one implementer's variable, and we replaced it with one new implementer's variable. In general, we do not have to replace all the implementer's variables, and the number of variables we are replacing does not have to equal the number of variables we are replacing them with.

One more exercise will help to cement the idea of data transformation. Exercise 327 (take a number): Maintain a list of natural numbers standing for those that are "in use". The three operations are:

- make the list empty (for initialization)
- assign to variable n a number not currently in use, and add this number to the list (it is now in use)
- given a number n that is currently in use, remove it from the list (it is now no longer in use, and it can be reused later)

The user's variable is $n: nat$. Although the exercise talks about a list, we see from the operations that the items must always be distinct, that their order is irrelevant, and there is no nested structure; we may as well use a finite bunch B as our implementer's variable. The three operations are

$$start\ =\ B' = null$$

$$take\ =\ \neg\ n': B\ \wedge\ B' = B,\ n'$$

$$give\ =\ n: B\ \Rightarrow\ \neg\ n: B'\ \wedge\ B',\ n = B$$

Here is a data transformation that replaces bunch B with natural m according to the transformer

$$B:\ 0,..m$$

Instead of maintaining the exact bunch of numbers that are in use, we will maintain a possibly larger bunch. We will still be sure never to give out a number that is in use. Then *start* is transformed as follows.

$$\forall B\cdot\ B:\ 0,..m\ \Rightarrow\ \exists B'\cdot\ B':\ 0,..m'\ \wedge\ B' = null$$

$$=\quad \top$$

$$\Leftarrow\quad ok$$

The transformed specification is just $\top$, which is most efficiently refined as ok. Since B is only included in $0,..m$, not necessarily equal to $0,..m$, it does not matter what m is; we may as well leave it alone.

Operation *take* is transformed as follows.

$$\forall B \cdot \; B: 0,..m \; \Rightarrow \; \exists B' \cdot \; B': 0,..m' \; \wedge \; \neg \; n': B \; \wedge \; B' = B, n'$$

$$= \quad m \le n' < m'$$

$$\Leftarrow \quad n := m. \; m := m+1$$

Operation *give* is transformed as follows.

$$\forall B \cdot \; B: 0,..m \; \Rightarrow \; \exists B' \cdot \; B': 0,..m' \; \wedge \; (n: B \; \Rightarrow \neg \; n: B' \; \wedge \; B', n = B)$$

$$= \quad (n+1 = m \Rightarrow n \le m') \wedge (n+1 < m \Rightarrow m \le m')$$

$$\Leftarrow \quad ok$$

Thanks to the data transformation, we have an extremely efficient solution to the problem. One might argue that we have not solved the problem at all, because we do not maintain a list of numbers that are "in use". But who can tell? The only use made of the list is to obtain a number that is not currently in use, and that service is provided.

Our implementation of the "take a number" problem corresponds to the "take a number" machines that are common at busy service centers. Now suppose we want to provide two "take a number" machines that can operate independently. We might try replacing B with two variables i, j: *nat* according to the transformer $B: 0,..max\; i\; j$. Operation *take* becomes

$$\forall B \cdot \; B: 0,..max\; i\; j \; \Rightarrow \; \exists B' \cdot \; B': 0,..max\; i'\; j' \; \wedge \; \neg \; n': B \; \wedge \; B' = B, n'$$

$$= \quad max\; i\; j \le n' < max\; i'\; j'$$

$$\Leftarrow \quad n := max\; i\; j. \; \textbf{if } i \ge j \textbf{ then } i := i+1 \textbf{ else } j := j+1$$

From the program on the last line we see that this data transformation does not provide the independent operation of two machines as we were hoping. Perhaps a different data transformation will work better. Let's put the even numbers on one machine and the odd numbers on the other. The new variables are i: $2 \times nat$ and j: $2 \times nat+1$. The transformer is

$$\forall b: B \cdot \; even\; b \wedge b<i \; \vee \; odd\; b \wedge b<j$$

Now *take* becomes

$$\forall B \cdot \qquad (\forall b: B \cdot \; even\; b \wedge b<i \; \vee \; odd\; b \wedge b<j)$$

$$\Rightarrow \; \exists B' \cdot \; (\forall b: B' \cdot \; even\; b \wedge b<i' \; \vee \; odd\; b \wedge b<j') \; \wedge \; \neg \; n': B \; \wedge \; B' = B, n'$$

$$= \quad even\; n' \; \wedge \; i \le n' < i' \; \vee \; odd\; n' \; \wedge \; j \le n' < j'$$

$$\Leftarrow \quad (n := i. \; i := i+2) \; \vee \; (n := j. \; j := j+2)$$

This is what we want; we can take a number from either machine without disturbing the other. We have a "distributed" solution to the problem.

―――――――――――――――――――――――――――――――――――――――End of Data Transformation

―――――――――――――――――――――――――――――――End of Specification by Implementation

―――――――――――――――――――――――End of Theory Design and Implementation

8 Concurrency

We will define the <u>independent composition</u> ‖ of specifications P and Q so that $P\|Q$ (pronounced " P parallel Q ") is satisfied by a computer that behaves according to P and at the same time, in parallel, according to Q. The operands of ‖ are called <u>processes</u>. The connective ‖ is similar to $\wedge$ (conjunction), but weaker, so that

$$P\|Q \;\;\Leftarrow\;\; P\wedge Q$$

The trouble with conjunction is that it is not always implementable, even when both conjuncts are. For example, in variables x and y ,

$$\begin{aligned} & (x:=x+1) \wedge (y:=y+1) \\ =\;\; & x'=x+1 \;\wedge\; y'=y \;\wedge\; x'=x \;\wedge\; y'=y+1 \\ =\;\; & \bot \end{aligned}$$

We define independent composition so that $P\|Q$ is implementable whenever P and Q are. In particular, we will have

$$x:=x+1 \;\|\; y:=y+1 \;\;=\;\; x'=x+1 \;\wedge\; y'=y+1$$

The program ok will be the identity for independent composition

$$ok\,\|\,P \;\;=\;\; P\,\|\,ok \;\;=\;\; P$$

just as for dependent composition, unlike conjunction.

According to the reflexive and transparent axioms of equality, we can always replace $x=x$ by $\top$. Therefore

$$\begin{aligned} & b:=x{=}x \;\;\|\;\; x:=x+1 \\ =\;\; & b:=\top \;\;\|\;\; x:=x+1 \end{aligned}$$

On the first line, it may seem possible for the process on the right side to increase x between the two evaluations of x in the left process, resulting in the assignment of $\bot$ to b . According to the last line, this does not happen; the state does not change during the evaluation of an expression.

Since $x:=x \;=\; ok$,

$$\begin{aligned} & x:=x \;\;\|\;\; x:=x+1 \\ =\;\; & ok \;\;\|\;\; x:=x+1 \\ =\;\; & x:=x+1 \end{aligned}$$

On the first line of this continued equation we have two processes. Execution of the left process begins by evaluating variable x . Now suppose the right process is executed, increasing x , before the left process has completed the assignment. In that case, the left process will restore the original value of x . According to the last line, this does not happen.

Finally, since

$$x := x+1. \ \ x := x-1 \ = \ ok$$

we have, according to the transparency axiom,

$$(x := x+1. \ \ x := x-1) \parallel y := x$$
$$= \quad ok \parallel y := x$$
$$= \quad y := x$$

According to the first line, it may seem that $y' = x+1$ is a possibility: the right process $y := x$ may be executed in between the two assignments $x := x+1$ and $x := x-1$ in the left process. According to the last line of this continued equation, this does not happen; the final value of y is the initial value of x.

As the three preceding examples show, according to the axioms of equality, no process may see or affect the intermediate states of another process. Intermediate state arises in the definition of dependent composition, which describes sequential execution; it is the means by which information is passed from one program to a sequentially later program. It was not invented for passing information between parallel processes. Our processes will not communicate with each other through shared variables, but through communication channels that do not invalidate our mathematics. We postpone communication to the next chapter, and in this chapter consider non-interacting processes.

Independent Composition

An independent composition can be executed by executing the processes in parallel, but each process makes its assignments to local copies of variables. Then, when both processes are finished, the final value of a variable is determined as follows: if both processes left it unchanged, it is unchanged; if one process changed it and the other left it unchanged, its final value is the changed one; if both processes changed it, its final value is arbitrary. This final rewriting of variables does not require coordination or communication between the processes; each process rewrites those variables it has changed. In the case when both processes have changed a variable, we do not even require that the final value be one of the two changed values; the rewriting may mix the bits.

In a commonly occurring special case, there is no need to copy variables. When both processes are expressed as programs, and neither assigns to any variable appearing in the other, copying and rewriting are unnecessary. For the sake of efficiency, it is tempting to make this case the definition of independent composition. But we must define our connectives for all specifications, not just for programs. We must be able to divide a specification into processes before deciding how each process is refined by a program.

Let the space variables be x, y, ... and the time variable be t. Then

$$P\|Q \;=\; \exists xP, xQ, yP, yQ, ..., tP, tQ\cdot$$

$$\text{(substitute } xP \text{ for } x', \; yP \text{ for } y', \; ..., \; tP \text{ for } t' \text{ in } P)$$

$$\land \text{ (substitute } xQ \text{ for } x', \; yQ \text{ for } y', \; ..., \; tQ \text{ for } t' \text{ in } Q)$$

$$\land (xP{=}x \Rightarrow x'{=}xQ) \land (xQ{=}x \Rightarrow x'{=}xP)$$

$$\land (yP{=}y \Rightarrow y'{=}yQ) \land (yQ{=}y \Rightarrow y'{=}yP)$$

$$\land \; ...$$

$$\land t' = \mathit{max}\ tP\ tQ$$

The final values according to P are renamed xP, yP, ..., tP. The final values according to Q are renamed xQ, yQ, ..., tQ. The final values according to the composition are as follows: if P leaves a variable unchanged, then Q determines its final value; if Q leaves a variable unchanged, then P determines its final value. The execution time of an independent composition is the maximum of the process times. This definition is unfortunately complicated; the best way to use it is to prove some laws, and then use the laws. We'll see some laws in a moment, but first some examples.

Let the state consist of three integer variables x, y, and z (ignore time). Here are two unsurprising examples.

$$x := z \parallel y := z \;=\; x' = y' = z' = z$$

$$x := y \parallel y := x \;=\; x'{=}y \land y'{=}x \land z'{=}z$$

In each example, the right process leaves x unchanged, so the left process determines its value; the left process leaves y unchanged, so the right process determines its value; both processes leave z unchanged, so both processes determine its value. The second example shows us a concise way to express that two variables swap values, or more generally, that several variables permute their values, without introducing any temporary variables.

Normally we do not want different processes to change the same variable, but here is an example to show what can happen if they do.

$$x := y \parallel x := z$$

$$=\quad \exists xP, xQ, yP, yQ, zP, zQ\cdot$$

$$\text{(substitute } xP \text{ for } x', \; yP \text{ for } y', \; zP \text{ for } z' \text{ in } x'{=}y \land y'{=}y \land z'{=}z)$$

$$\land \text{ (substitute } xQ \text{ for } x', \; yQ \text{ for } y', \; zQ \text{ for } z' \text{ in } x'{=}z \land y'{=}y \land z'{=}z)$$

$$\land (xP{=}x \Rightarrow x'{=}xQ) \land (xQ{=}x \Rightarrow x'{=}xP)$$

$$\land (yP{=}y \Rightarrow y'{=}yQ) \land (yQ{=}y \Rightarrow y'{=}yP)$$

$$\land (zP{=}z \Rightarrow z'{=}zQ) \land (zQ{=}z \Rightarrow z'{=}zP)$$

$$= \quad \exists xP,\ xQ,\ yP,\ yQ,\ zP,\ zQ\cdot$$

$\quad xP{=}y \land yP{=}y \land zP{=}z$	use One-Point Law
$\land\, xQ{=}z \land yQ{=}y \land zQ{=}z$	six times
$\land\, (xP{=}x \Rightarrow x'{=}xQ) \land (xQ{=}x \Rightarrow x'{=}xP)$	
$\land\, (yP{=}y \Rightarrow y'{=}yQ) \land (yQ{=}y \Rightarrow y'{=}yP)$	
$\land\, (zP{=}z \Rightarrow z'{=}zQ) \land (zQ{=}z \Rightarrow z'{=}zP)$	

$$
\begin{aligned}
= \quad & (y{=}x \Rightarrow x'{=}z) \land (z{=}x \Rightarrow x'{=}y) \\
& \land (y{=}y \Rightarrow y'{=}y) \land (y{=}y \Rightarrow y'{=}y) \\
& \land (z{=}z \Rightarrow z'{=}z) \land (z{=}z \Rightarrow z'{=}z)
\end{aligned}
$$

$$= \quad (x{=}y \Rightarrow x'{=}z) \land (x{=}z \Rightarrow x'{=}y) \land y'{=}y \land z'{=}z$$

This example illustrates what can happen when two processes assign to the same variable; if initially x differs from both y and z, its final value is undetermined. This example also illustrates why we will avoid this situation.

Laws of Independent Composition

Let x and y be different state variables, let e, f, and b be expressions of the prestate, and let P, Q, R, and S be specifications. Then

$(x{:=}\,e \parallel y{:=}\,f).\ P\ =\ $ (for x substitute e and independently for y substitute f in P)	
	independent substitution
$P \parallel Q = Q \parallel P$	symmetry
$P \parallel (Q \parallel R) = (P \parallel Q) \parallel R$	associativity
$P \parallel ok = ok \parallel P = P$	identity
$P \parallel Q{\lor}R = (P \parallel Q) \lor (P \parallel R)$	distributivity
$P \parallel \textbf{if } b \textbf{ then } Q \textbf{ else } R = \textbf{if } b \textbf{ then } (P \parallel Q) \textbf{ else } (P \parallel R)$ distributivity	
$\textbf{if } b \textbf{ then } (P{\parallel}Q) \textbf{ else } (R{\parallel}S) = \textbf{if } b \textbf{ then } P \textbf{ else } R \parallel \textbf{if } b \textbf{ then } Q \textbf{ else } S$ distributivity	

As an example of the Substitution Law,

$$(x{:=}\,x{+}y \parallel y{:=}\,x{\times}y).\ z' = x{-}y \ = \ z' = (x{+}y) - (x{\times}y)$$

Note that each substitution replaces all and only the original occurrences of its variable. This law generalizes the earlier Substitution Law from one variable to two, and it can be generalized further to any number of variables.

Refinement by Steps works for independent composition:

If $A \Leftarrow B{\parallel}C$ and $B \Leftarrow D$ and $C \Leftarrow E$ are theorems, then $A \Leftarrow D{\parallel}E$ is a theorem.

So does Refinement by Parts:

If $A \Leftarrow B{\parallel}C$ and $D \Leftarrow E{\parallel}F$ are theorems, then $A{\land}D \Leftarrow B{\land}E \parallel C{\land}F$ is a theorem.

───End of Laws of Independent Composition

List Concurrency

We have defined independent composition by considering which process determines the final value of each variable. For finer-grained concurrency, we can extend this same idea to the individual items within list variables. Suppose the variables are x, L, and t, where L is a list. We can define independent composition as follows.

$$P \| Q \;=\; \exists x_P, x_Q, L_P, L_Q, t_P, t_Q \cdot$$
$$\text{(substitute } x_P \text{ for } x', \; L_P \text{ for } L', \; t_P \text{ for } t' \text{ in } P \text{)}$$
$$\wedge \text{ (substitute } x_Q \text{ for } x', \; L_Q \text{ for } L', \; t_Q \text{ for } t' \text{ in } Q \text{)}$$
$$\wedge \; (x_P{=}x \Rightarrow x'{=}x_Q) \wedge (x_Q{=}x \Rightarrow x'{=}x_P)$$
$$\wedge \; (\forall n \cdot (L_P\, n = L\, n \Rightarrow L'\, n = L_Q\, n) \wedge (L_Q\, n = L\, n \Rightarrow L'\, n = L_P\, n))$$
$$\wedge \; t' = max\; t_P\; t_Q$$

As a good example of list concurrency, we do Exercise 121: find the maximum item in a list. The maximum of a list is easily expressed with the MAX quantifier, but we will assume MAX is not implemented. The easiest and simplest solution is probably functional, with parallelism coming from the fact that the arguments of a function (operands of an operator) can always be evaluated in parallel. To use our parallel operator, we present an imperative solution. Let L be the list whose maximum item is sought. If L is an empty list, its maximum is $-\infty$; assume that L is nonempty. Assume further that L is a variable whose value is not wanted after we know its maximum (we'll remove this assumption later). Our specification will be $L' 0 = MAX\, L$; at the end, item 0 of list L will be the maximum of all original items. The first step is to generalize from the maximum of a nonempty list to the maximum of a nonempty segment of a list. So define

$$findmax \;=\; \lambda i, j \cdot i{<}j \Rightarrow L'\, i = MAX\, L\, [i;..j]$$

Our specification is $findmax\; 0\; (\#L)$. We refine as follows.

$$findmax\; i\; j \;\Longleftarrow\; \textbf{if}\; j{-}i = 1\; \textbf{then}\; ok$$
$$\textbf{else}\; (\; (findmax\; i\; (div\; (i{+}j)\; 2) \,\|\, findmax\; (div\; (i{+}j)\; 2)\; j).$$
$$L\; i := max\; (L\; i)\; (L\; (div\; (i{+}j)\; 2))\;)$$

If $j{-}i = 1$ the segment contains one item; to place the maximum item (the only item) at index i requires no change. In the other case, the segment contains more than one item; we divide the segment into two halves, placing the maximum of each half at the beginning of the half. In the parallel composition, the two processes $findmax\; i\; (div\; (i{+}j)\; 2)$ and $findmax\; (div\; (i{+}j)\; 2)\; j$ change disjoint segments of the list. We finish by placing the maximum of the two maximums at the start of the whole segment. The recursive execution time is $ceil\; (log\; (j{-}i))$, exactly the same as for binary search, which this program closely resembles.

If list L must remain constant, we can use a new list M of the same type as L to collect our partial results. We redefine

$$findmax \;=\; \lambda i, j \cdot i{<}j \Rightarrow M'\, i = MAX\, L\, [i;..j]$$

and in the program we change *ok* to $M\,i := L\,i$ and we change the final assignment to

$$M\,i := max\,(M\,i)\,(M\,(div\,(i{+}j)\,2))$$

―――End of List Concurrency
―――――――――――――――――――――――――――――――――End of Independent Composition

Circuit Design

The kind of parallelism we have introduced is exactly what is needed for combinational and sequential circuit design. A combinational circuit can be specified by a program that does not use dependent composition. Thus we reduce the problem of combinational circuit design to programming with a constraint: no sequencing. A circuit can be constructed automatically from such a program, but to reduce the magic, we define <u>circuit normal form</u> as a parallel composition of assignments, one assignment for each state variable. From a program in circuit normal form it is quite obvious how to build a combinational circuit.

A sequential circuit consists of a combinational circuit and some memory connected in a loop.

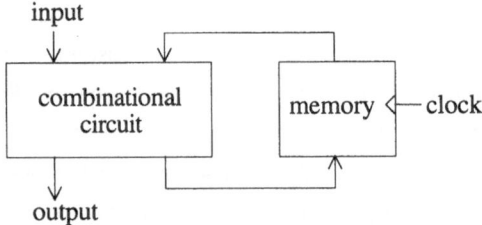

At each pulse of the clock, the memory records its input, and its output is then the new contents of the memory. Between pulses, the output of the combinational circuit becomes a function of its new input, providing a new state for the memory at the next clock pulse. To design a sequential circuit for some purpose, we must choose the number of bits of memory, and design the combinational circuit. We thus separate the sequencing, with its intermediate states, from the rest of the circuit.

Security Switch

Let us try Exercise 340: A security switch has two boolean inputs and one boolean output. The output changes when both inputs have changed. More precisely, the output changes when both inputs differ from what they were the previous time the output changed. For example, suppose at some time the inputs are $\top$ and $\bot$ and the output changes to $\bot$. The output will remain $\bot$ until the first time the inputs become $\bot$ and $\top$, whereupon the output will change to $\top$ and the story will begin again. (For circuit design, we may prefer to pronounce $\top$ and $\bot$ as "high voltage" and "low voltage", or as "power" and "ground".)

Let the inputs be a and b and let the output be x. Our first solution uses three bits of memory: boolean A records the state of input a at last change; boolean B records the state of input b at last change; boolean x records the output at last change (since this bit of memory is always the same as the output, they can have the same name). Let

$$c = a \neq A \land b \neq B$$

so c tells us that both inputs have changed. Then the combinational circuit we want is described by the program

$\textbf{if } c \textbf{ then } (x := \neg x \parallel A := a \parallel B := b) \textbf{ else } ok \quad \text{distribution}$

$= \qquad \textbf{if } c \textbf{ then } x := \neg x \textbf{ else } ok$
$\parallel \quad \textbf{if } c \textbf{ then } A := a \textbf{ else } ok$
$\parallel \quad \textbf{if } c \textbf{ then } B := b \textbf{ else } ok \qquad\qquad\qquad \text{use Functional-Imperative Law}$

$= \qquad x := \textbf{if } c \textbf{ then } \neg x \textbf{ else } x$
$\parallel \quad A := \textbf{if } c \textbf{ then } a \textbf{ else } A \qquad\qquad \text{use } c \Rightarrow a \neq A$
$\parallel \quad B := \textbf{if } c \textbf{ then } b \textbf{ else } B \qquad\qquad \text{and } c \Rightarrow b \neq B$

$= \qquad x := \textbf{if } c \textbf{ then } \neg x \textbf{ else } x$
$\parallel \quad A := \textbf{if } c \textbf{ then } \neg A \textbf{ else } A$
$\parallel \quad B := \textbf{if } c \textbf{ then } \neg B \textbf{ else } B$

$= \quad x := c \neq x \parallel A := c \neq A \parallel B := c \neq B$

Our solution uses three flip-flops (A , B , x), five "exclusive or" gates ($\neq$), and an "and" ($\land$) gate (three of the gates occur in c).

Here is a second solution that uses only one flip-flop (x). Noticing that A and B change whenever x does, we replace variables A and B by variables p and q defined as follows:

$p = (x = A) \qquad\qquad\qquad q = (x = B)$

By the symmetry and assoçiativity of $=$, we can invert this transformation:

$A = (x = p) \qquad\qquad\qquad B = (x = q)$

and thus replace all mention of A and B by p and q . Here is the transformation:

$\qquad x := c \neq x \parallel A := c \neq A \parallel B := c \neq B$

$= \quad x' = (c \neq x) \land A' = (c \neq A) \land B' = (c \neq B) \qquad \text{replace } A , A', B , B'$
$= \quad x' = (c \neq x) \land (x' = p') = (c \neq (x = p)) \land (x' = q') = (c \neq (x = q))$

Using the symmetry and associativity of $=$ and $\neq$, we can rearrange the last two conjuncts so that the first conjunct appears in each.

$= \quad x' = (c \neq x) \land (p' = p) = (x' = (c \neq x)) \land (q' = q) = (x' = (c \neq x))$
$= \quad x' = (c \neq x) \land p' = p \land q' = q$
$= \quad x := c \neq x \qquad\qquad\qquad\qquad \text{replace } c \text{ by its transformed expression}$
$= \quad x := (a \neq (x = p) \land b \neq (x = q)) \neq x$

Thus p and q are actually constants not needing implementation as flip-flops. They are arbitrary constants, and we can get rid of them by choosing values for them. Choosing $\top$ for both, our final solution is

$x := (a \neq x \land b \neq x) \neq x$

At each cycle, x becomes the majority value of a, b, and x.

———End of Security Switch

This section illustrated that circuit design is partly programming. A theory of programming is therefore also helpful in circuit design.

———End of Circuit Design

Found Concurrency

The time for a dependent composition $P.Q$ is the sum of the times for P and Q, and in general that forces the execution to be sequential. In this section, we get rid of the time variable, measuring time informally, in order to investigate when $P.Q$ allows parallel execution. The goal is to be able to write programs without using the $\parallel$ connective, and then let the implementation find the concurrency.

A simple example illustrates the idea.

$$x := y. \ \ x := x+1. \ \ z := y$$
$$= \quad x := y. \ \ (x := x+1 \parallel z := y)$$
$$= \quad (x := y. \ \ x := x+1) \parallel z := y$$

We write the program that appears on the first line. Its execution can be depicted as follows.

start $\longrightarrow$ $x := y$ $\longrightarrow$ $x := x+1$ $\longrightarrow$ $z := y$ $\longrightarrow$ finish

The implementation determines that the first two assignments cannot be executed concurrently, but the last two can, and transforms the program. Execution can now be depicted as

start $\longrightarrow$ $x := y$ $\diagdown$ $\nearrow x := x+1 \searrow$ $\nearrow$ finish $\searrow z := y \nearrow$

Now we have the first and last assignments next to each other, in sequence; they too can be executed concurrently. Execution can be

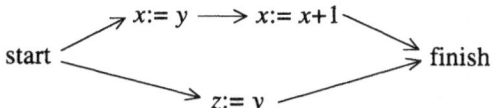

Whenever two programs occur in sequence, and neither assigns to a variable appearing in the other, they can be placed in parallel.

Buffer

Consider two programs, *produce* and *consume* , whose only common variable is b . *produce* assigns to b and *consume* uses the value of b .

> $produce \;=\; \cdots\cdots b{:=}\,e\cdots\cdots$
>
> $consume \;=\; \cdots\cdots b\cdots\cdots$

These two programs are executed alternately, repeatedly, forever.

> $control \;=\; produce.\; consume.\; control$

Using P for *produce* and C for *consume* , execution looks like this:

$$P \longrightarrow C \longrightarrow P \longrightarrow C \longrightarrow P \longrightarrow C \longrightarrow P \longrightarrow C \longrightarrow$$

Many programs have producer and consumer components somewhere in them. Variable b is called a buffer; it may be an entire data structure. As they are, executing *produce* and *consume* concurrently does not achieve the desired result because one assigns to b and the other uses it. We must split b into two variables, bp and bc , as follows.

> $produce \;=\; \cdots\cdots bp{:=}\,e\cdots\cdots$
>
> $consume \;=\; \cdots\cdots bc\cdots\cdots$
>
> $control \;=\; produce.\; bc{:=}\,bp.\; consume.\; control$

Using B for the assignment $bc{:=}\,bp$, execution can be

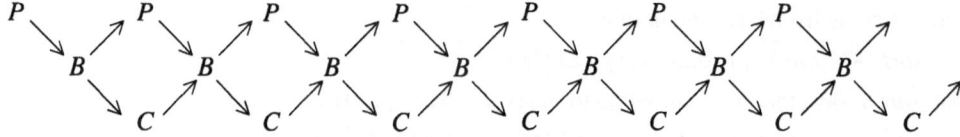

If one of *produce* or *consume* consistently takes longer than the other, this is the best that can be done. If their execution times vary so that in some cycles *produce* takes longer while in others *consume* takes longer, we can improve by splitting the buffer into an infinite list. We need natural variable w to indicate how much *produce* has written into the buffer, and natural variable r to indicate how much *consume* has read from the buffer. We initialize both w and r to 0 . Then

$produce \; = \; \cdots\cdots b{:=}\, w{\to}e \mid b\cdots\cdots$

$consume \; = \; \cdots\cdots b\, r\cdots\cdots$

$control \; = \; produce. \; w{:=}\, w{+}1. \; consume. \; r{:=}\, r{+}1. \; control$

If $w \neq r$ then $produce$ and $consume$ can be executed in parallel. Using W for $w{:=}\,w{+}1$, and R for $r{:=}\,r{+}1$, execution can be as follows.

$$P \longrightarrow W \longrightarrow P \longrightarrow W \longrightarrow P \longrightarrow W \longrightarrow P \longrightarrow W \longrightarrow P \longrightarrow W \longrightarrow$$
$$C \longrightarrow R \longrightarrow C \longrightarrow R \longrightarrow C \longrightarrow R \longrightarrow C \longrightarrow R \longrightarrow C \longrightarrow$$

When the execution of $produce$ is fast, it can get arbitrarily far ahead of the execution of $consume$. When the execution of $consume$ is fast, it can catch up to $produce$ but not pass it; the sequence is retained when $w{=}r$.

If the buffer is a finite list of length n , we can use it in a cyclic fashion with this modification:

$control \; = \; produce. \; w{:=}\, mod\,(w{+}1)\, n. \; consume. \; r{:=}\, mod\,(r{+}1)\, n. \; control$

As before, $consume$ cannot overtake $produce$ because $w{=}r$ when the buffer is empty. But now $produce$ cannot get more than n executions ahead of $consume$ because $w{=}r$ also when the buffer is full. Synchronization is what remains of sequential execution after all opportunities for concurrency have been found.

―――End of Buffer

Programs are sometimes easier to develop and prove when they do not include any mention of concurrency. The burden of finding concurrency can be placed upon a clever implementation.

Insertion Sort

Exercise 150 asks for a program to sort a list in time bounded by the square of the length of the list, assuming that dependent composition is implemented as sequential execution. Here is a solution. Let the list be L , and define

$sort \; = \; \lambda n\cdot \; \forall i, j\colon \; 0,..n\cdot \; i{\leq}j \Rightarrow Li \leq Lj$

so that $sort\, n$ says that L is sorted up to index n . The specification is

$(\, L' \text{ is a permutation of } L \,) \wedge sort'\,(\#L) \wedge t' \leq t + (\#L)^2$

We leave the first conjunct informal, and ensure that it is satisfied by making all changes to L using

$swap \; = \; \lambda i, j\cdot \; L{:=}\, i{\to}Lj \mid j{\to}Li \mid L$

We ignore the third conjunct; found concurrency will give us a linear time solution. The second conjunct is equal to $sort\, 0 \Rightarrow sort'\,(\#L)$ since $sort\, 0$ is a theorem.

$sort\, 0 \Rightarrow sort'\,(\#L) \quad \Longleftarrow \quad \textbf{for } n{:=}\, 0;..\#L \textbf{ do } sort\, n \Rightarrow sort'\,(n{+}1)$

To solve $sort\ n \Rightarrow sort'\ (n+1)$, it may help to refer to an example list.

$$[\ L\,0\ ;L\,1\ ;L\,2\ ;L\,3\ ;L\,4\ ]$$
$$\quad\ 0\quad\ \ 1\quad\ \ 2\quad\ \ 3\quad\ \ 4\quad\ \ 5$$

$sort\ n \Rightarrow sort'\ (n+1)\ \ \Longleftarrow$ **if** $n=0$ **then** ok

          else if $L\ (n{-}1) \leq L\ n$ **then** ok

          else $(swap\ (n{-}1)\ n.\quad sort\ (n{-}1) \Rightarrow sort'\ n)$

If we consider $sort\ n \Rightarrow sort'\ (n+1)$ to be a procedure with parameter n we are finished; the final specification $sort\ (n{-}1) \Rightarrow sort'\ n$ calls the same procedure with argument $n{-}1$. Or, we could let n be a variable instead of a **for**-loop index, and decrease it by 1 just before the final call. We leave this detail, and move on to the possibilities for parallel execution.

Let Cn stand for the comparison $L\ (n{-}1) \leq L\ n$ and let Sn stand for $swap\ (n{-}1)\ n$. For $\#L{=}5$, the worst case sequential execution is shown in the following picture.

If i and j differ by more than 1 , then Si and Sj can be executed concurrently. Under the same condition, Si can be executed and Cj can be evaluated concurrently. And of course, any two expressions such as Ci and Cj can always be evaluated concurrently. Execution becomes

For the ease of writing a square sequential sort, given a clever implementation, we obtain a linear parallel sort.

———————————————————————————————————End of Insertion Sort

———————————————————————————————————End of Found Concurrency

———————————————————————————————————End of Concurrency

9   Communication

Until now, the only input to a computation has been the initial state of the variables, and its only output has been the final state. Now we consider input and output during the course of a computation. We allow any number of named communication <u>channel</u>s through which a computation communicates with its environment, which may be people or other computations running in parallel.

Communication on channel c is described by two infinite lists $\mathcal{M}_c$ and $\mathcal{T}_c$ called the <u>message script</u> and the <u>time script</u>, and two extended natural variables r_c and w_c called the <u>read cursor</u> and the <u>write cursor</u>. The message script is the list of all messages, past, present, and future, that pass along the channel. The time script is the corresponding list of times that the messages were or are or will be sent. The scripts are constants, not state variables. The read cursor is a state variable saying how many messages have been read, or input, on the channel. The write cursor is a state variable saying how many messages have been written, or output, on the channel. During execution, the read and write cursors increase as inputs and outputs occur; more and more of the script items are seen, but the scripts do not vary. At any time, the future messages and the times they are sent on a channel may be unknown, but they can be referred to as items in the scripts. For example, after 2 more reads the next input on channel c will be $\mathcal{M}_c(r_c+2)$, and after 5 more writes the next output will be $\mathcal{M}_c(w_c+5)$ and it will occur at time $\mathcal{T}_c(w_c+5)$. If there is only one channel, or if the channel is known from context, we may omit the subscripts on $\mathcal{M}$, $\mathcal{T}$, r, and w. Omitting subscripts, after 2 more reads the next input will be $\mathcal{M}(r+2)$, and after 5 more writes the next output will be $\mathcal{M}(w+5)$ at time $\mathcal{T}(w+5)$.

$$\mathcal{M} \quad = \quad [\; 6\; ;\; 4\; ;\; 7\; ;\; 1\; ;\; 0\; ;\; 3\; ;\; 8\; ;\; 9\; ;\; 2\; ;\; 5\; ;\; ... \;]$$
$$\mathcal{T} \quad = \quad [\; 3\; ;\; 5\; ;\; 5\; ;20\; ;25\; ;28\; ;31\; ;31\; ;45\; ;48\; ;\; ... \;]$$

$$\qquad\qquad\qquad \uparrow \qquad\quad \uparrow$$
$$\qquad\qquad\qquad r \qquad\quad w$$

The scripts and the cursors are not programming notations, but they allow us to specify any desired communications. Here is an example specification. It says that if the next input on channel c is even, then the next output on channel d will be $\top$, and otherwise it will be $\bot$. Formally, we may write

> **if** $even\,(\mathcal{M}_c r_c)$ **then** $\mathcal{M}_d w_d = \top$ **else** $\mathcal{M}_d w_d = \bot$

or more briefly

> $\mathcal{M}_d w_d \;=\; even\,(\mathcal{M}_c r_c)$

Implementability

Consider computations involving two space variables x and y, a time variable t, and communications on a single channel (no subscripts needed). The state of a computation consists of the values of the space variables, the time variable, and the two cursor variables r and w. During a computation, the space variables can change value in any direction, but time and the cursors can only increase. Once an input has been read, it cannot be unread; once an output has been written, it cannot be unwritten. Every computation satisfies

$$t' \geq t \wedge r' \geq r \wedge w' \geq w$$

An implementable specification can say what the scripts are in the segment written by a computation, that is the segment $\mathcal{M}[w;..w']$ and $\mathcal{T}[w;..w']$ between the initial and final values of the write cursor, but it cannot specify the scripts outside this segment. Furthermore, the time script must be monotonic, and all its values in this segment must be in the range from t to t'.

A specification S (in initial state σ, final state σ', message script $\mathcal{M}$, and time script $\mathcal{T}$) is <u>implementable</u> if and only if

$$\forall \sigma, \mathcal{M}'', \mathcal{T}'' \cdot \exists \sigma', \mathcal{M}, \mathcal{T} \cdot \quad S \wedge t' \geq t \wedge r' \geq r \wedge w' \geq w$$
$$\wedge \ \mathcal{M}[0;..w \ ; \ w';..\infty] = \mathcal{M}''[0;..w \ ; \ w';..\infty]$$
$$\wedge \ \mathcal{T}[0;..w \ ; \ w';..\infty] = \mathcal{T}''[0;..w \ ; \ w';..\infty]$$
$$\wedge \ \forall i, j: w,..w' \cdot i{\leq}j \Rightarrow t \leq \mathcal{T}i \leq \mathcal{T}j \leq t'$$

If we have many channels, we need similar conjuncts for each, appropriately subscripted. If we have no channels, implementability reduces to the definition given in Chapter 4.

———End of Implementability

Input and Output

We provide four programming notations for communication. Let c be a channel. Then $c?$ describes a computation that reads one input on that channel. We use the channel name c to denote the message that was last previously read on the channel. The notation $c! \, e$ describes a computation that writes the output message e on channel c. And $?c$ is a boolean expression meaning "there is unread input available on channel c". Here are the formal definitions (omitting the obvious subscripts).

$c?$	$=$	$r:= r+1$	"c input"
c	$=$	$\mathcal{M}(r{-}1)$	
$c! \, e$	$=$	$\mathcal{M}w = e \wedge \mathcal{T}w = t \wedge (w:= w+1)$	"c output e"
$?c$	$=$	$\mathcal{T}r < t$	"probe c"

Suppose the input channel from a keyboard is named *key* , and the output channel to a screen is named *screen* . Then execution of the program

> **if** *?key*
>
> **then** (*key?*. **if** *key=`y* **then** *screen!* "If you wish." **else** *screen!* "Not if you don't want.")
>
> **else** *screen!* "Well?"

tests if a character of input is available, and if so, reads it and prints some output, which depends on the character read, and if not, prints other output.

Let us refine the specification $\mathcal{M}_d w_d = \textit{even} (\mathcal{M}_c r_c)$ given earlier.

$$\mathcal{M}_d w_d = \textit{even} (\mathcal{M}_c r_c) \impliedby c?. \; d! \; \textit{even } c$$

To prove the refinement, we can rewrite the solution as follows:

$$
\begin{aligned}
& c?. \; d! \; \textit{even } c \\
=\;& r_c := r_c+1. \;\; \mathcal{M}_d w_d = \textit{even} (\mathcal{M}_c(r_c-1)) \, \wedge \, \mathcal{T}_d w_d = t \, \wedge (w_d := w_d+1) \\
=\;& \mathcal{M}_d w_d = \textit{even} (\mathcal{M}_c r_c) \, \wedge \, \mathcal{T}_d w_d = t \, \wedge (w_d := w_d+1)
\end{aligned}
$$

which implies the problem.

A problem specification should be written as clearly, as understandably, as possible. A programmer refines the problem specification to obtain a solution program, which a computer can execute. In our example, the solution seems more understandable than the problem! Whenever that is the case, we should consider using the program as the problem specification, and then there is no need for refinement.

Our next problem is to read numbers from channel c , and write their doubles on channel d . Formally, the specification can be written

$$S \;\; = \;\; \forall n: \textit{nat} \cdot \, \mathcal{M}_d \, (w_d+n) = 2 \times \mathcal{M}_c \, (r_c+n)$$

or more succinctly

$$S \;\; = \;\; \mathcal{M}_d \, [w_d;..\infty] = 2 \times \mathcal{M}_c \, [r_c;..\infty]$$

We cannot assume that the input and output are the first input and output ever on channels c and d . We can only ask that from now on, starting at the initial read cursor r_c and initial write cursor w_d , the outputs will be double the inputs. This specification can be refined as follows.

$$S \impliedby c?. \; d! \; 2 \times c. \; S$$

Ignoring time, the proof is:

$$
\begin{aligned}
& c?. \; d! \; 2 \times c. \; S \\
=\;& r_c := r_c+1. \;\; \mathcal{M}_d w_d = 2 \times \mathcal{M}_c \, (r_c-1) \, \wedge (w_d := w_d+1). \; S \\
=\;& \mathcal{M}_d w_d = 2 \times \mathcal{M}_c r_c \, \wedge \, \mathcal{M}_d \, [w_d+1;..\infty] = 2 \times \mathcal{M}_c \, [r_c+1;..\infty] \\
=\;& \mathcal{M}_d \, [w_d;..\infty] = 2 \times \mathcal{M}_c \, [r_c;..\infty] \\
=\;& S
\end{aligned}
$$

Communication Timing

In the real time measure, we need to know how long output takes, how long communication transit takes, and how long input takes, and we place time increments appropriately. To be independent of these implementation details, we can use the <u>transit time</u> measure, in which we suppose that the acts of input and output take no time at all, and that communication transit takes 1 time unit.

The message to be read next on channel c is the one at index r_c. This message was or is or will be sent at time $\mathcal{T}_c r_c$. Its arrival time, according to the transit time measure, is $\mathcal{T}_c r_c + 1$. So input becomes

$$t := max\ t\ (\mathcal{T}_c r_c + 1).\ \ c?$$

If the input has already arrived, $\mathcal{T}_c r_c + 1 \le t$, and no time is spent waiting for input; otherwise execution of $c?$ is delayed until the input arrives.

In some applications (called "batch processing"), all inputs are available at the start of execution, and we may as well leave out the time assignments for input. In other applications (called "process control"), inputs are provided at regular intervals by a physical sampling device; the time script (but not the message script) is known in advance. In still other applications (called "interactive computing"), a human provides inputs at irregular intervals, and we have no way of saying what the time script is. In this case, we have to leave out the waiting times, and just attach a note to our calculation saying that execution time will be increased by any time spent waiting for input.

Exercise 359(a): Let W be "wait for input on channel c and then read it". Formally,

$$W\ =\ t := max\ t\ (\mathcal{T}r + 1).\ \ c?$$

Prove $W\ \Longleftarrow\ $ **if** $?c$ **then** $r := r+1$ **else** $(t := t+1.\ \ W)$ assuming time is an extended integer. The significance of this exercise is that input is often implemented in just this way, with a test to see if input is available, and a loop if it is not.

Proof: **if** $?c$ **then** $r := r+1$ **else** $(t := t+1.\ \ W)$

$=$ **if** $\mathcal{T}r < t$ **then** $r := r+1$ **else** $(t := t+1.\ \ t := max\ t\ (\mathcal{T}r + 1).\ \ r := r+1)$

$=$ **if** $\mathcal{T}r < t$ **then** $(t := t.\ \ r := r+1)$ **else** $(t := max\ (t+1)\ (\mathcal{T}r + 1).\ \ r := r+1)$

Now if $\mathcal{T}r < t$ and time is an extended integer, then $\mathcal{T}r + 1 \le t$, and $t = max\ t\ (\mathcal{T}r + 1)$. If $\mathcal{T}r \ge t$ then $max\ (t+1)\ (\mathcal{T}r + 1)\ =\ \mathcal{T}r + 1\ =\ max\ t\ (\mathcal{T}r + 1)$.

$=$ **if** $\mathcal{T}r < t$ **then** $(t := max\ t\ (\mathcal{T}r + 1).\ \ r := r+1)$ **else** $(t := max\ t\ (\mathcal{T}r + 1).\ \ r := r+1)$

$=$ W

—————————————————————————End of Communication Timing

—————————————————————————End of Input and Output

The following section is optional, and requires Chapter 6.

Recursively Defined Communication

Define *dbl* by the fixed-point construction (including recursive time but ignoring input waits)

$$dbl \ = \ c?. \ d! \ 2{\times}c. \ t{:=}t{+}1. \ dbl$$

Regarding *dbl* as the unknown, this equation has several solutions. The weakest is

$$\mathcal{M}_d\,[w_{\vec{d}};..\infty] = 2 \times \mathcal{M}_c\,[r_{\vec{c}};..\infty] \ \wedge \ \mathcal{T}_d\,[w_{\vec{d}};..\infty] = [t;..\infty]$$

A strongest implementable solution is

$$\mathcal{M}_d\,[w_{\vec{d}};..\infty] = 2 \times \mathcal{M}_c\,[r_{\vec{c}};..\infty] \ \wedge \ \mathcal{T}_d\,[w_{\vec{d}};..\infty] = [t;..\infty]$$
$$\wedge \ r_c'{=}w_d'{=}t'{=}\infty \ \wedge \ w_c'{=}w_c \ \wedge \ r_d'{=}r_d$$

The strongest solution is $\perp$. If this fixed-point construction is all we know about *dbl* , then we cannot say that it is equal to a particular one of the solutions. But we can say this: it refines the weakest solution

$$\mathcal{M}_d\,[w_{\vec{d}};..\infty] = 2 \times \mathcal{M}_c\,[r_{\vec{c}};..\infty] \ \wedge \ \mathcal{T}_d\,[w_{\vec{d}};..\infty] = [t;..\infty] \ \ \Longleftarrow \ \ dbl$$

and it is refined by the right side of the fixed-point construction

$$dbl \ \ \Longleftarrow \ \ c?. \ d! \ 2{\times}c. \ t{:=}t{+}1. \ dbl$$

Thus we can use it to solve problems, and we can execute it.

If we begin recursive construction with

$$dbl_0 \ = \ \top$$

we find

$$\begin{aligned}
dbl_1 \ &= \ c?. \ d! \ 2{\times}c. \ t{:=}t{+}1. \ dbl_0 \\
&= \ r_c{:=}r_c{+}1. \ \mathcal{M}_d w_d = 2{\times}\mathcal{M}_c(r_c{-}1) \ \wedge \ \mathcal{T}_d w_d = t \ \wedge (w_{\vec{d}}{:=}w_d{+}1). \ t{:=}t{+}1. \ \top \\
&= \ \mathcal{M}_d w_d = 2{\times}\mathcal{M}_c r_c \ \wedge \ \mathcal{T}_d w_d = t \\
dbl_2 \ &= \ c?. \ d! \ 2{\times}c. \ t{:=}t{+}1. \ dbl_1 \\
&= \ r_c{:=}r_c{+}1. \ \mathcal{M}_d w_d = 2{\times}\mathcal{M}_c(r_c{-}1) \ \wedge \ \mathcal{T}_d w_d = t \ \wedge (w_{\vec{d}}{:=}w_d{+}1). \\
&\quad \ t{:=}t{+}1. \ \mathcal{M}_d w_d = 2{\times}\mathcal{M}_c r_c \ \wedge \ \mathcal{T}_d w_d = t \\
&= \ \mathcal{M}_d w_d = 2{\times}\mathcal{M}_c r_c \ \wedge \ \mathcal{T}_d w_d = t \ \wedge \ \mathcal{M}_d(w_d{+}1) = 2{\times}\mathcal{M}_c(r_c{+}1) \ \wedge \ \mathcal{T}_d(w_d{+}1) = t{+}1
\end{aligned}$$

and so on. The result of the construction

$$dbl_\infty \ = \ \mathcal{M}_d\,[w_{\vec{d}};..\infty] = 2 \times \mathcal{M}_c\,[r_{\vec{c}};..\infty] \ \wedge \ \mathcal{T}_d\,[w_{\vec{d}};..\infty] = [t;..\infty]$$

is the weakest solution of the *dbl* fixed-point construction.

———End of Recursively Defined Communication

Input Composition

The <u>input composition</u> operator $\mathbb{I}$ applies to specifications that begin with input. $S\,\mathbb{I}\,R$ can be implemented by a computer that behaves according to either S or R depending on the availability of input. More precisely, $(c?. \ P) \ \mathbb{I} \ (d?. \ Q)$ says: if input is already available on both channels c and d , execute either $(c?. \ P)$ or $(d?. \ Q)$; if input is available on just one channel, execute the corresponding operand; if input is available on neither channel, wait for the first input and execute the corresponding operand (in case of a tie, execute either one).

To define input composition, we will consider a composition of three specifications; it should then be reasonably clear how to compose fewer or more specifications. Let

$$m = min \; (\mathcal{T}_c r_c) \; (\mathcal{T}_d r_d) \; (\mathcal{T}_e r_e)$$

be the time of the earliest unread message on channels c, d, and e (if you allow the use of min with three operands). Then

$$(c?.\; P) \; \mathbb{I} \; (d?.\; Q) \; \mathbb{I} \; (e?.\; R)$$
$$= \quad (?c \; \vee \; \mathcal{T}_c r_c = m) \; \wedge \; (c?.\; P)$$
$$\vee \quad (?d \; \vee \; \mathcal{T}_d r_d = m) \; \wedge \; (d?.\; Q)$$
$$\vee \quad (?e \; \vee \; \mathcal{T}_e r_e = m) \; \wedge \; (e?.\; R)$$

To account for the time spent waiting for input, we should insert $t:= max \; t \; (\mathcal{T}r + 1)$ just before each input operation, as usual. From the definition of $\mathbb{I}$ we see that it is symmetric, associative, and idempotent.

In the subsection on Communication Timing we proved that waiting for input can be implemented recursively. Using the same reasoning, we implement input composition as follows. Let

$$IC \quad = \qquad (t:= max \; t \; (\mathcal{T}_c r_c + 1).\; c?.\; P)$$
$$\mathbb{I} \; (t:= max \; t \; (\mathcal{T}_d r_d + 1).\; d?.\; Q)$$
$$\mathbb{I} \; (t:= max \; t \; (\mathcal{T}_e r_e + 1).\; e?.\; R)$$

Then

$$IC \quad \Longleftarrow \quad \textbf{if } ?c \textbf{ then } (c?.\; P)$$
$$\textbf{else if } ?d \textbf{ then } (d?.\; Q)$$
$$\textbf{else if } ?e \textbf{ then } (e?.\; R)$$
$$\textbf{else } (t:= t+1.\; IC)$$

assuming time is an extended integer.

Merge

A direct application of input composition is Exercise 361(a) (time merge). Merging means reading repeatedly from two or more input channels and writing those inputs onto a third channel. The output is an interleaving of the messages from the input channels. The output must be all and only the messages read from the inputs, and it must preserve the order in which they were read on each channel. Infinite merging can be specified formally as follows. Let the input channels be c and d, and the output channel be e. Then

$$merge \; = \; (c?.\; e!\; c) \vee (d?.\; e!\; d).\; merge$$

This specification does not state any criterion for choosing between the input channels at each step. To write a merge program, we must decide on a criterion for choosing. We might choose between the input channels based on the value of the inputs or on their arrival times. The exercise asks us to choose the first available input, so we define

$$timemerge \; = \; ((c?.\; e!\; c) \; \mathbb{I} \; (d?.\; e!\; d)).\; timemerge$$

—End of Merge

Monitor

For reasons stated in the previous chapter, parallel processes cannot communicate and cooperate via the intermediate states of variables. They must communicate through channels. To obtain the effect of a shared variable, we create a process called a <u>monitor</u> that resolves conflicting uses of the variable. A monitor for variable x receives on channels $x0in$, $x1in$, ... data from other processes to be written to the variable, whereupon it sends an acknowledgment back to the writing process on one of the channels $x0ack$, $x1ack$, ... It receives on channels $x0req$, $x1req$, ... requests from other processes to read the variable, whereupon it sends the value of the variable back to the requesting process on one of the channels $x0out$, $x1out$, ...

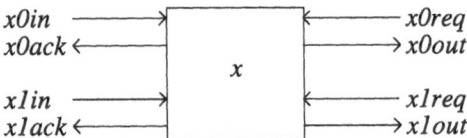

A monitor for variable x with two writing processes and two reading processes can be defined and implemented as follows.

$$monitor \;=\; (\quad (x0in?.\ \ x:= x0in.\ \ x0ack!)$$
$$\amalg\ (x1in?.\ \ x:= x1in.\ \ x1ack!)$$
$$\amalg\ (x0req?.\ \ x0out!\ x)$$
$$\amalg\ (x1req?.\ \ x1out!\ x)\ ).$$
$$monitor$$

The acknowledgment messages have been omitted because they are irrelevant; the acknowledgment is the fact that a message is sent. A monitor for several variables, for several writing processes, and for several reading processes, is similar.

To illustrate the use of variable sharing through a monitor, we do Exercise 365: specify the control of a gas burner. Its inputs are:

•   boolean *heatwanted* , which comes from a thermostat and indicates whether heat is wanted.

•   boolean *flame* , which comes from a flame sensor and indicates whether the gas is burning.

Its outputs are:

•   *gas*! *on* , which turns the gas on.

•   *gas*! *off*, which turns the gas off.

•   *spark*! , which causes a spark for the purpose of igniting the gas.

The spark should be applied to the gas for at least 1 second to give it a chance to ignite and to allow the flame to become stable. But a safety regulation states that the gas must not remain on and unlit for more than 3 seconds. Another regulation says that when the gas is shut off, it must not be turned on again for at least 20 seconds to allow any accumulated gas to clear. And finally, the gas burner must respond to its inputs within 1 second.

Here is a first attempt to write a specification: *GasIsOff* ∨ *GasIsOn* , defined by two mutually recursive equations:

$$GasIsOff \; = \; \textbf{if } heatwanted$$
$$\textbf{then } (gas! \; on. \;\; spark!. \;\; 1 \leq t'\!-\!t \leq 3. \;\; GasIsOn)$$
$$\textbf{else } (t'\!-\!t < 1. \;\; GasIsOff)$$

$$GasIsOn \; = \; \textbf{if } heatwanted \wedge flame$$
$$\textbf{then } (t'\!-\!t < 1. \;\; GasIsOn)$$
$$\textbf{else } (gas! \; off. \;\; 20 \leq t'\!-\!t < 21. \;\; GasIsOff)$$

We are using the time variable to represent real time in seconds. The specification $1 \leq t'\!-\!t \leq 3$ represents the passage of at least 1 second but not more than 3 . The specification $20 \leq t'\!-\!t < 21$ is similar. A specification that a computation be slow enough is always easy to satisfy. A specification that it be fast enough requires us to build fast enough hardware.

One can always argue about whether a formal specification captures the intent of an informal specification. For example, if the gas is off, and *heatwanted* becomes ⊤ , and the ignition sequence begins, and then *heatwanted* becomes ⊥ again, this last input may not be noticed for up to 3 seconds. It may be argued that this is not responding to an input within 1 second, or it may be argued that the entire ignition sequence is the response to the first input, and until its completion no response to further inputs is required. At least the formal specification is unambiguous.

In this specification we are using *heatwanted* and *flame* as shared variables; their values may be changed at any time by another process. Shared variables, like side effects, prevent us from applying any theory; we cannot even replace $x=x$ by ⊤ if x is shared. Our theory tells us that the condition after an **if** can be assumed true in the **then** part and false in the **else** part. But the theory does not apply when there are shared variables. In order to reason, we must replace the shared variables by monitors. Our equations become

$$GasIsOff \; = \; requestheatwanted!. \;\; heatwanted?.$$
$$\textbf{if } heatwanted$$
$$\textbf{then } (gas! \; on. \;\; spark!. \;\; 1 \leq t'\!-\!t \leq 3. \;\; GasIsOn)$$
$$\textbf{else } (t'\!-\!t < 1. \;\; GasIsOff)$$

$$GasIsOn \; = \; requestheatwanted!. \;\; heatwanted?. \;\; requestflame!. \;\; flame?.$$
$$\textbf{if } heatwanted \wedge flame$$
$$\textbf{then } (t'\!-\!t < 1. \;\; GasIsOn)$$
$$\textbf{else } (gas! \; off. \;\; 20 \leq t'\!-\!t < 21. \;\; GasIsOff)$$

It's cluttered with communications, but it obeys all the laws of mathematics and programming.

———End of Monitor

———End of Input Composition

Reaction Controller

Many kinds of reactions are controlled by a feedback loop, as shown in the following picture.

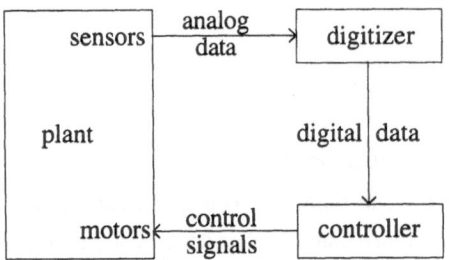

The "plant" could be a chemical reactor, or a nuclear reactor, or even just an assembly plant. The sensors detect concentrations or temperatures or positions in the form of analog data, and feed them to a digitizer. The digitizer converts these data to digital form suitable for the controller. The controller computes what should happen next to control the plant; perhaps some rods should be pushed in farther, or some valves should be opened, or a robot arm should move in some direction. The controller sends signals to the plant to cause the appropriate change.

Here's the problem. The sensors send their data continuously to the digitizer. The digitizer is fast and uniform, sending digital data rapidly to the controller. The time required by the controller to compute its output signals varies according to the input messages; sometimes the computation is trivial and it can keep up with the input; sometimes the computation is more complex and it falls behind. When several inputs have piled up, the controller should not continue to read them and compute outputs in the hope of catching up. Instead, we want all but the latest input to be discarded. It is not essential that control signals be produced as rapidly as digital data. But it is essential that each control signal be based on the latest available data. How can we achieve this?

The solution is to place a synchronizer between the digitizer and controller, as in the following picture.

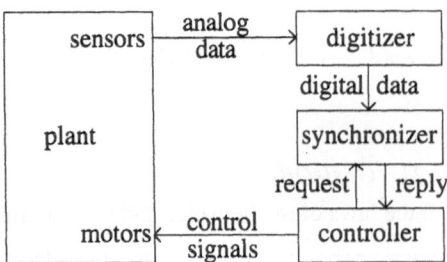

The synchronizer's job is as simple and uniform as the digitizer's; it can easily keep up. It repeatedly reads the data from the digitizer, always keeping only the latest. Whenever the controller requests some data, the synchronizer sends the latest. This is exactly the function of a monitor, and we could implement the synchronizer that way. But a synchronizer is simpler than a monitor in two respects: first, there is only one writing process and one reading process; second, the writing process is uniformly faster than the reading process. Here is its definition.

> *synchronizer* = *digitaldata?* .
>
> **if** *?request* **then** (*request?* ‖ *reply! digitaldata*) **else** *ok* .
>
> *synchronizer*

The message on channel *request* is of no interest; the fact that it is there carries the request. Still, we must read it to get rid of it, so the same request will not be seen again.

―――――――――――――――――――――――――――――――――End of Reaction Controller

Communicating Processes

A channel may just connect two processes, one writing and the other reading. More generally, a channel may connect several processes. Parallel processes can read from the same channel; each process reads the same messages at its own rate. Independent composition gives each process, in effect, its own read cursor. If parallel processes write different things on the same channel, the result is unimplementable. So, for the sake of implementability, at most one process can write to a channel.

Our first example looks like interprocess communication, but it may not be. In one variable x and one channel c,

$$c! 2 \; \| \; (c?. \; x:= c)$$
$$= \quad \mathcal{M}w = 2 \; \wedge (w:= w+1) \; \| \; (r:= r+1. \; x:= \mathcal{M}(r-1))$$
$$= \quad \exists x_P, \, x_Q, \, r_P, \, r_Q, \, w_P, \, w_Q \cdot \quad \mathcal{M}w = 2 \; \wedge \; x_P = x \; \wedge \; r_P = r \; \wedge \; w_P = w+1$$
$$\wedge \; x_Q = \mathcal{M}r \; \wedge \; r_Q = r+1 \; \wedge \; w_Q = w$$
$$\wedge \; (x_P = x \; \Rightarrow \; x' = x_Q) \; \wedge \; (x_Q = x \; \Rightarrow \; x' = x_P)$$
$$\wedge \; (r_P = r \; \Rightarrow \; r' = r_Q) \; \wedge \; (r_Q = r \; \Rightarrow \; r' = r_P)$$
$$\wedge \; (w_P = w \; \Rightarrow \; w' = w_Q) \; \wedge \; (w_Q = w \; \Rightarrow \; w' = w_P)$$
$$= \quad x' = \mathcal{M}r \; \wedge \; \mathcal{M}w = 2 \; \wedge \; r' = r+1 \; \wedge \; w' = w+1$$

We do not know that initially $w=r$, so we cannot conclude that finally $x'=2$. The independent composition may be part of a dependent composition, for example,

$$c! 1. \; (c! 2 \; \| \; (c?. \; x:= c)). \; c?$$

and the final value of x may be the 1 from the earlier output, with the 2 going to the later input. In order to achieve useful communication between processes, we have to introduce a local channel.

Channel Declaration

Channel declaration is similar to variable declaration; it defines a new channel within some local portion of a program or specification. Each language must have rules to say what the scope of the declaration is, or in other words, its precedence. We consider that a channel declaration applies to what follows it, with the same precedence as dependent and independent composition. Here is a syntax and equivalent specification.

$$\textbf{chan } c\text{: } T \cdot P \quad = \quad \exists \mathcal{M}_c\text{: } [\infty * T] \cdot \exists \mathcal{T}_c\text{: } [\infty * xnat] \cdot \textbf{var } r_c, w_c\text{: } xnat := 0 \cdot P$$

The type T says what communications are possible on this new channel. The declaration introduces two scripts, which are infinite lists; they are not state variables, but constants of unknown value (ordinary variables). We have let time be extended natural, but we could let it be extended integer or extended rational or extended real. The channel declaration also introduces a read cursor r_c with initial value 0 to say that initially there has been no input on this channel, and a write cursor w_c with initial value 0 to say that initially there has been no output on this channel.

Here are two processes with a communication between them.

$$\textbf{chan } c\text{: } int \cdot c! 2 \parallel (c?. \ x := c)$$

Use the definition of local channel declaration, and use the previous result for the independent composition

$$= \quad \exists \mathcal{M}\text{: } [\infty * int] \cdot \exists \mathcal{T}\text{: } [\infty * xnat] \cdot \textbf{var } r, w\text{: } xnat := 0 \cdot$$
$$x' = \mathcal{M} r \ \wedge \ \mathcal{M} w = 2 \ \wedge \ r' = r + 1 \ \wedge \ w' = w + 1 \ \wedge \text{ (other variables unchanged)}$$

Now apply the initialization $r := 0$ and $w := 0$ using the Substitution Law

$$= \quad \exists \mathcal{M}\text{: } [\infty * int] \cdot \exists \mathcal{T}\text{: } [\infty * xnat] \cdot \textbf{var } r, w\text{: } xnat \cdot$$
$$x' = \mathcal{M} 0 \ \wedge \ \mathcal{M} 0 = 2 \ \wedge \ r' = 1 \ \wedge \ w' = 1 \ \wedge \text{ (other variables unchanged)}$$
$$= \quad x' = 2 \ \wedge \text{ (other variables unchanged)}$$
$$= \quad x := 2$$

Replacing 2 by an arbitrary expression, we have a general theorem equating communication on a local channel with assignment.

A local channel can also be used without concurrency as a queue, or buffer. For example,

$$\textbf{chan } c\text{: } int \cdot c! 3. \ c! 4. \ c?. \ x := c. \ c?. \ x := x + c$$

assigns 7 to x. Here is the proof, including time.

$$\textbf{chan } c\text{: } int \cdot c! 3. \ c! 4. \ t := max \ t \ (\mathcal{T} r + 1). \ c?. \ x := c. \ t := max \ t \ (\mathcal{T} r + 1). \ c?. \ x := x + c$$

$$= \quad \exists \mathcal{M}\text{: } [\infty * int] \cdot \exists \mathcal{T}\text{: } [\infty * xnat] \cdot \textbf{var } r, w\text{: } xnat := 0 \cdot$$
$$\mathcal{M} w = 3 \ \wedge \ \mathcal{T} w = t \ \wedge \ (w := w + 1).$$
$$\mathcal{M} w = 4 \ \wedge \ \mathcal{T} w = t \ \wedge \ (w := w + 1).$$
$$t := max \ t \ (\mathcal{T} r + 1). \ r := r + 1.$$
$$x := \mathcal{M} \ (r - 1).$$
$$t := max \ t \ (\mathcal{T} r + 1). \ r := r + 1.$$
$$x := x + \mathcal{M} \ (r - 1)$$

now use the Substitution Law several times

$$= \quad \exists \mathcal{M}: [\infty^* int] \cdot \exists \mathcal{T}: [\infty^* xnat] \cdot \exists r, r', w, w': xnat \cdot$$

$$\mathcal{M}0 = 3 \ \wedge \ \mathcal{T}0 = t \ \wedge \ \mathcal{M}1 = 4 \ \wedge \ \mathcal{T}1 = t \ \wedge \ r' = 2 \ \wedge \ w' = 2 \ \wedge \ x' = \mathcal{M}0 + \mathcal{M}1$$

$$\wedge \ \ t' = max \ (max \ t \ (\mathcal{T}0 + 1)) \ (\mathcal{T}1 + 1) \ \wedge \ (\text{other variables unchanged})$$

$$= \quad x' = 7 \ \wedge \ t' = t+1 \ \wedge \ (\text{other variables unchanged})$$

_____End of Channel Declaration

Deadlock

In the previous subsection we saw that a local channel can be used as a buffer. Let's see what happens if we try to read first and write after. Inserting the input wait into

> **chan** c: $int \cdot$ $c?. \ c! \ 5$

gives us

> **chan** c: $int \cdot$ $t := max \ t \ (\mathcal{T}r + 1). \ c?. \ c! \ 5$

$$= \quad \exists \mathcal{M}: [\infty^* int] \cdot \exists \mathcal{T}: [\infty^* xnat] \cdot \ \textbf{var} \ r, w: xnat := 0 \cdot$$

$$t := max \ t \ (\mathcal{T}r + 1). \ r := r+1. \ \mathcal{M}w = 5 \ \wedge \ \mathcal{T}w = t \ \wedge (w := w+1)$$

We'll do this one slowly. First, expand **var** and $w := w+1$, taking r, w, x, and t as the state variables.

$$= \quad \exists \mathcal{M}: [\infty^* int] \cdot \exists \mathcal{T}: [\infty^* xnat] \cdot \exists r, r', w, w': xnat \cdot$$

$$r := 0. \ w := 0. \ t := max \ t \ (\mathcal{T}r + 1). \ r := r+1.$$

$$\mathcal{M}w = 5 \ \wedge \ \mathcal{T}w = t \ \wedge \ r' = r \ \wedge \ w' = w+1 \ \wedge \ x' = x \ \wedge \ t' = t$$

Now use the Substitution Law four times.

$$= \quad \exists \mathcal{M}: [\infty^* int] \cdot \exists \mathcal{T}: [\infty^* xnat] \cdot \exists r, r', w, w': xnat \cdot$$

$$\mathcal{M}0 = 5 \ \wedge \ \mathcal{T}0 = max \ t \ (\mathcal{T}0 + 1) \ \wedge \ r' = 1 \ \wedge \ w' = 1 \ \wedge \ x' = x \ \wedge \ t' = max \ t \ (\mathcal{T}0 + 1)$$

Look at the conjunct $\mathcal{T}0 = max \ t \ (\mathcal{T}0 + 1)$. For any start time $t > -\infty$ it says $\mathcal{T}0 = \infty$.

$$= \quad x' = x \ \wedge \ t' = \infty$$

The theory tells us that execution takes forever because the wait for input is infinite. This is called deadlock.

Our first example of deadlock involved only a single process that waited on itself. Deadlocks can also be indirect, involving several processes that wait on each other. Here is an example with two processes.

> **chan** c, d: $int \cdot$ $(c?. \ d! \ 6) \ \| \ (d?. \ c! \ 7)$

Inserting the input waits, we get

$$\text{\textbf{chan }} c, d\text{: } int\cdot\ (t\text{:= } max\ t\ (T_c r_c + 1).\ c?.\ d!\ 6)\ \|\ (t\text{:= } max\ t\ (T_d r_d + 1).\ d?\ c!\ 7)$$

after a little work we obtain

$$=\quad \exists M_c,\ M_d\text{: } [\infty * int]\cdot\ \exists T_c,\ T_d\text{: } [\infty * xnat]\cdot\ \exists r_c,\ r_c',\ w_c,\ w_c',\ r_d,\ r_d',\ w_d,\ w_d'\text{: } xnat\cdot$$

$$M_d 0 = 6\ \wedge\ T_d 0 = max\ t\ (T_c 0 + 1)\ \wedge\ M_c 0 = 7\ \wedge\ T_c 0 = max\ t\ (T_d 0 + 1)$$

$$\wedge\ \ r_c' = w_c' = r_d' = w_d' = 1\ \wedge\ x'=x\ \wedge\ t' = max\ t\ (T_c r_c + 1)\ (T_d r_d + 1)$$

(using *max* with three arguments for t'). Once again, for start time $t > -\infty$, the conjuncts
$T_d 0 = max\ t\ (T_c 0 + 1)\ \wedge\ T_c 0 = max\ t\ (T_d 0 + 1)$ tell us that $T_d 0 = T_c 0 = \infty$.

$$=\quad x'=x\ \wedge\ t'=\infty$$

──End of Deadlock

──End of Communicating Processes

Power Series Multiplication

Our final exercise combines communicating processes, local channel declaration, and dynamic process generation, in one beautiful little program. It is also a striking example of the importance of good notation and good theory. It has been "solved" before without them, but the "solutions" required many pages, intricate synchronization arguments, lacked proof, and were sometimes wrong.

Exercise 368: Write a program to read from channel a an infinite sequence of coefficients a_0 a_1 a_2 a_3 ... of a power series $a_0 + a_1 x + a_2 x^2 + a_3 x^3 + ...$ and in parallel to read from channel b an infinite sequence of coefficients b_0 b_1 b_2 b_3 ... of a power series $b_0 + b_1 x + b_2 x^2 + b_3 x^3 + ...$ and in parallel to write on channel c the infinite sequence of coefficients c_0 c_1 c_2 c_3 ... of the power series $c_0 + c_1 x + c_2 x^2 + c_3 x^3 + ...$ equal to the product of the two input series. Assume that all inputs are already available; there are no input delays. Produce the outputs one per time unit.

The question provides us with a notation for the coefficients: $a_n = M_a(r_a+n)$, $b_n = M_b(r_b+n)$, and $c_n = M_c(w_c+n)$. Let us use A , B , and C for the power series, so we can express our desired result as

$$C = A \times B$$

$$= (a_0 + a_1 x + a_2 x^2 + a_3 x^3 + ...\ ) \times (b_0 + b_1 x + b_2 x^2 + b_3 x^3 + ...\ )$$

$$= a_0 b_0 + (a_0 b_1 + a_1 b_0)x + (a_0 b_2 + a_1 b_1 + a_2 b_0)x^2 + (a_0 b_3 + a_1 b_2 + a_2 b_1 + a_2 b_0)x^3 + ...$$

from which we see $c_n = \Sigma i: 0,..n+1\cdot a_i b_{n-i}$. The question relieves us from concern with input times, but we are still concerned with output times. The complete specification is

$$C = A \times B\ \wedge\ \forall n\cdot T_c(w_c+n) = t+n$$

Consider the problem: output coefficient n requires $n+1$ multiplications and n additions from $2(n+1)$ input coefficients, and it must be produced 1 time unit after the previous coefficient. To accomplish this requires more and more data storage, and more and more parallelism, as execution progresses.

As usual, let us concentrate on the result first, and leave the time for later. Let

$$A_1 = a_1 + a_2x + a_3x^2 + a_4x^3 + \ldots$$
$$B_1 = b_1 + b_2x + b_3x^2 + b_4x^3 + \ldots$$

be the power series from channels a and b beginning with coefficient 1 . Then

$$A \times B$$
$$= \quad (a_0 + A_1x) \times (b_0 + B_1x)$$
$$= \quad a_0b_0 + (a_0B_1 + A_1b_0)x + A_1B_1x^2$$

In place of the problem $A \times B$ we have five new problems. The first is to read one coefficient from each input channel and output their product; that's easy. The next two, a_0B_1 and A_1b_0 , are multiplying a power series by a constant; that's easier than multiplying two power series, requiring only a loop. The fourth, A_1B_1 , is exactly the problem we started with, but one coefficient farther along; it can be solved by recursion. Finally, we have to add three power series together. Unfortunately, these three power series are not synchronized properly. We must add the leading coefficients of a_0B_1 and A_1b_0 without any coefficient from A_1B_1 , and thereafter add coefficient $n+1$ of a_0B_1 and A_1b_0 to coefficient n of A_1B_1 . To synchronize, we move a_0B_1 and A_1b_0 one coefficient farther along. Let

$$A_2 = a_2 + a_3x + a_4x^2 + a_5x^3 + \ldots$$
$$B_2 = b_2 + b_3x + b_4x^2 + b_5x^3 + \ldots$$

be the power series from channels a and b beginning with coefficient 2 . Continuing the earlier equation,

$$= \quad a_0b_0 + (a_0(b_1 + B_2x) + (a_1 + A_2x)b_0)x + A_1B_1x^2$$
$$= \quad a_0b_0 + (a_0b_1 + a_1b_0)x + (a_0B_2 + A_1B_1 + A_2b_0)x^2$$

From this expansion of the desired product we can almost write a solution directly.

One problem remains. A recursive call will be used to obtain a sequence of coefficients of the product A_1B_1 in order to produce the coefficients of AB . But the output channel for A_1B_1 cannot be channel c , the output channel for the main computation AB . Instead, a local channel must be used for output from A_1B_1 . We need a channel parameter. A channel parameter is really four parameters: one for the message script, one for the time script, one for the read cursor, and one for the write cursor. (The cursors are variables, so their parameters are **var** parameters; see Chapter 5.)

Now we are ready. Define P (for product) to be our specification (ignoring time for a moment) parameterized by output channel.

$P = \lambda\mathbf{chan}\ c: rat \cdot\ C = A \times B$

We refine $P\,c$ as follows.

$\qquad P\,c\ \Longleftarrow\ a?.\ b?.\ c!\ a \times b.$

$\qquad\qquad \mathbf{var}\ a0: rat := a\cdot\ \mathbf{var}\ b0: rat := b\cdot\ \mathbf{chan}\ d: rat\cdot$

$\qquad\qquad P\,d$

$\qquad \parallel\ (\ a?.\ b?.\ c!\ a0 \times b + a \times b0.$

$\qquad\qquad L::\ (a?.\ b?.\ d?.\ c!\ a0 \times b + d + a \times b0.\ L)\ )$

That is the whole program: 5 lines! First, an input is read from each of channels a and b and their product is output on channel c ; that takes care of $a_0 b_0$. We will need these values again, so we declare local variables (really constants) $a0$ and $b0$ to retain their values. Now that we have read one message from each input channel, before we read another, we call $P\,d$ to provide the coefficients of $A_1 B_1$ on local channel d , in parallel with the remainder of the program. $P\,d$ will be reading from channels a and b using its own private read cursors; this reading will not affect the reading in the parallel process. Now we read the next inputs a_1 and b_1 and output the coefficient $a_0 b_1 + a_1 b_0$. Finally we execute loop L , defined as

$\qquad L\ =\ C = a0 \times B + D + A \times b0$

where D is the power series whose coefficients are read from channel d . (Recall that $::$ signifies refinement in place.)

The proof is completely straightforward. Here it is in detail. In the main part, we accept L as defined, without looking at its refinement.

$\qquad\quad a?.\ b?.\ c!\ a \times b.$

$\qquad\quad \mathbf{var}\ a0: rat := a\cdot\ \mathbf{var}\ b0: rat := b\cdot\ \mathbf{chan}\ d: rat\cdot$

$\qquad\qquad P\,d$

$\qquad\quad \parallel\ (\ a?.\ b?.\ c!\ a0 \times b + a \times b0.\ L\ )$

$=\qquad r_a := r_a + 1.\ r_b := r_b + 1.\ \mathcal{M}_c w_c = \mathcal{M}_a(r_a - 1) \times \mathcal{M}_b(r_b - 1)\ \wedge\ (w_c := w_c + 1).$

$\qquad \exists a0,\ a0',\ b0,\ b0',\ \mathcal{M}_d,\ r_d,\ r_d',\ w_d,\ w_d'\cdot$

$\qquad a0 := \mathcal{M}_a(r_a - 1).\ b0 := \mathcal{M}_b(r_b - 1).\ r_d := 0.\ w_d := 0.$

$\qquad\quad (\forall n\cdot\ \mathcal{M}_d(w_d + n) = (\Sigma i:\ 0,..n+1\cdot\ \mathcal{M}_a(r_a + i) \times \mathcal{M}_b(r_b + n - i)))$

$\qquad \wedge\ (r_a := r_a + 1.\ r_b := r_b + 1.\ \mathcal{M}_c w_c = a0 \times \mathcal{M}_b(r_b - 1) + \mathcal{M}_a(r_a - 1) \times b0\ \wedge\ (w_c := w_c + 1).$

$\qquad\quad \forall n\cdot\ \mathcal{M}_c(w_c + n) = a0 \times \mathcal{M}_b(r_b + n) + \mathcal{M}_d(r_d + n) + \mathcal{M}_a(r_a + n) \times b0)$

Make all substitutions indicated by assignments.

$=\qquad \mathcal{M}_c w_c = \mathcal{M}_d r_a \times \mathcal{M}_b r_b$

$\qquad \wedge\ \exists a0,\ a0',\ b0,\ b0',\ \mathcal{M}_d,\ r_d,\ r_d',\ w_d,\ w_d'\cdot$

$\qquad\quad (\forall n\cdot\ \mathcal{M}_d n = \Sigma i:\ 0,..n+1\cdot\ \mathcal{M}_a(r_a + 1 + i) \times \mathcal{M}_b(r_b + 1 + n - i))$

$\qquad \wedge\ \mathcal{M}_c(w_c + 1) = \mathcal{M}_d r_a \times \mathcal{M}_b(r_b + 1) + \mathcal{M}_a(r_a + 1) \times \mathcal{M}_b r_b$

$\qquad \wedge\ (\forall n\cdot\ \mathcal{M}_c(w_c + 2 + n) = \mathcal{M}_d r_a \times \mathcal{M}_b(r_b + 2 + n) + \mathcal{M}_d n + \mathcal{M}_a(r_a + 2 + n) \times \mathcal{M}_b r_b)$

Use the first universal quantification to replace $\mathcal{M}_d n$ in the second. Then throw away the first universal quantification (weakening our expression). Now all existential quantifications are unused, and can be thrown away.

$$\Rightarrow \quad \mathcal{M}_c w_c = \mathcal{M}_d r_a \times \mathcal{M}_b r_b$$
$$\wedge \; \mathcal{M}_c(w_c+1) = \mathcal{M}_d r_a \times \mathcal{M}_b(r_b+1) + \mathcal{M}_a(r_a+1) \times \mathcal{M}_b r_b$$
$$\wedge \; \forall n \cdot \; \mathcal{M}_c(w_c+2+n) = \quad \mathcal{M}_d r_a \times \mathcal{M}_b(r_b+2+n)$$
$$+ \; (\Sigma i \colon 0,..n+1 \cdot \mathcal{M}_a(r_a+1+i) \times \mathcal{M}_b(r_b+1+n-i))$$
$$+ \; \mathcal{M}_a(r_a+2+n) \times \mathcal{M}_b r_b$$

Now put the three conjuncts together.

$$= \quad \forall n \cdot \; \mathcal{M}_c(w_c+n) = \Sigma i \colon 0,..n+1 \cdot \mathcal{M}_a(r_a+i) \times \mathcal{M}_b(r_b+n-i)$$
$$= \quad P\,c$$

We still have to prove the loop refinement.

$$a?. \;\; b?. \;\; d?. \;\; c! \; a0 \times b + d + a \times b0. \;\; L$$

$$= \quad r_a := r_a+1. \;\; r_b := r_b+1. \;\; r_d := r_d+1.$$
$$\mathcal{M}_c w_c = a0 \times \mathcal{M}_b(r_b-1) + \mathcal{M}_d(r_d-1) + \mathcal{M}_a(r_a-1) \times b0 \;\; \wedge \;\; (w_c := w_c+1).$$
$$\forall n \cdot \; \mathcal{M}_c(w_c+n) = a0 \times \mathcal{M}_b(r_b+n) + \mathcal{M}_d(r_d+n) + \mathcal{M}_a(r_a+n) \times b0$$

Make all substitutions indicated by assignments.

$$= \quad \mathcal{M}_c w_c = a0 \times \mathcal{M}_b r_b + \mathcal{M}_d r_d + \mathcal{M}_d r_a \times b0$$
$$\wedge \; \forall n \cdot \; \mathcal{M}_c(w_c+1+n) = a0 \times \mathcal{M}_b(r_b+1+n) + \mathcal{M}_d(r_d+1+n) + \mathcal{M}_a(r_a+1+n) \times b0$$

Put the two conjuncts together.

$$= \quad \forall n \cdot \; \mathcal{M}_c(w_c+n) = a0 \times \mathcal{M}_b(r_b+n) + \mathcal{M}_d(r_d+n) + \mathcal{M}_a(r_a+n) \times b0$$
$$= \quad L$$

According to the recursive measure of time, we must place a time increment before the recursive call $P\,d$ and before the recursive call L. We do not need a time increment before inputs on channels a and b according to information given in the question. We do need a time increment before the input on channel d. Placing only these necessary time increments, output $c_0 = a_0 b_0$ will occur at time $t+0$ as desired, but output $c_1 = a_0 b_1 + a_1 b_0$ will also occur at time $t+0$, which is too soon. In order to make output c_1 occur at time $t+1$ as desired, we must place a time increment between the first two outputs. We can consider this time increment to account for actual computing time, or as a delay (see Chapter 5, "Time Dependence"). Here is the program with time.

$$P\,c \;\; \Longleftarrow \;\; a?. \;\; b?. \;\; c! \; a \times b.$$
$$\textbf{var } a0 \colon rat := a \cdot \;\; \textbf{var } b0 \colon rat := b \cdot \;\; \textbf{chan } d \colon rat \cdot$$
$$(t := t+1. \;\; P\,d)$$
$$\| \;\; (\; a?. \;\; b?. \;\; t := t+1. \;\; c! \; a0 \times b + a \times b0.$$
$$L :: (a?. \;\; b?. \;\; t := \max t \, (\mathcal{T}_d r_d+1). \;\; d?. \;\; c! \; a0 \times b + d + a \times b0. \;\; t := t+1. \;\; L) \,)$$

We could factor the first two occurrences of $t := t+1$ out of the independent composition, but no matter. There is one change we can make to the placement of time increments that matters greatly. Within loop L, the assignment $t := max\ t\ (T_d r_d{+}1)$ represents a delay of 1 time unit the first iteration (because $t = T_d r_d$), and a delay of 0 time units each subsequent iteration (because $t = T_d r_d{+}1$). This makes the proof very ugly. To make the proof pretty, we can replace $t := max\ t\ (T_d r_d{+}1)$ by $t := max\ (t{+}1)\ (T_d r_d{+}1)$ and delete $t := t{+}1$ just before the call to L. These changes together do not change the timing at all; they just make the proof easier. The assignment $t := max\ (t{+}1)\ (T_d r_d{+}1)$ obviously increases the time by at least 1, so the loop includes a time increase without the $t := t{+}1$. The program with time is now

$$P c\ \Longleftarrow\ a?.\ b?.\ c!\ a{\times}b.$$

$$\textbf{var}\ a0{:}\ rat := a \cdot\ \textbf{var}\ b0{:}\ rat := b \cdot\ \textbf{chan}\ d{:}\ rat \cdot$$

$$(t := t{+}1.\ P\ d)$$

$$\|\ (\ a?.\ b?.\ t := t{+}1.\ c!\ a0{\times}b + a{\times}b0.$$

$$L{::}\ (a?.\ b?.\ t := max\ (t{+}1)\ (T_d r_d{+}1).\ d?.\ c!\ a0{\times}b + d + a{\times}b0.\ L)\ )$$

where

$$P c\ =\ \forall n \cdot\ T_c(w_c{+}n) = t{+}n$$

$$P d\ =\ \forall n \cdot\ T_d(w_d{+}n) = t{+}n$$

$$L\ =\ (\forall n \cdot\ T_d(r_d{+}n) = t{+}n)\ \Rightarrow\ (\forall n \cdot\ T_c(w_c{+}n) = t{+}1{+}n)$$

In the main part of the timing proof, we accept L as defined, without looking at its refinement.

$$a?.\ b?.\ c!\ a{\times}b.$$

$$\textbf{var}\ a0{:}\ rat := a \cdot\ \textbf{var}\ b0{:}\ rat := b \cdot\ \textbf{chan}\ d{:}\ rat \cdot$$

$$(t := t{+}1.\ P\ d)$$

$$\|\ (a?.\ b?.\ t := t{+}1.\ c!\ a0{\times}b + a{\times}b0.\ L)$$

We can ignore $a?$ and $b?$ because they have no effect on timing (they are substitutions for variables that do not appear in $P\ d$ and L). We also ignore what messages are output, looking only at their times. We can therefore also ignore variables $a0$ and $b0$.

$$\Rightarrow\quad T_c w_c = t\ \wedge\ (w_c := w_c{+}1).$$

$$\exists T_d,\ r_d,\ r_d',\ w_d,\ w_d' \cdot\ r_d := 0.\ w_d := 0.$$

$$(t := t{+}1.\ \forall n \cdot\ T_d(w_d{+}n) = t{+}n)$$

$$\wedge\ (\ t := t{+}1.\ T_c w_c = t\ \wedge\ (w_c := w_c{+}1).$$

$$(\forall n \cdot\ T_d(r_d{+}n) = t{+}n)\ \Rightarrow\ (\forall n \cdot\ T_c(w_c{+}n) = t{+}1{+}n)\ )$$

Make all substitutions indicated by assignments.

$$=\quad T_c w_c = t$$

$$\wedge\ \exists T_d,\ r_d,\ r_d',\ w_d,\ w_d' \cdot$$

$$(\forall n \cdot\ T_d n = t{+}1{+}n)$$

$$\wedge\ T_c(w_c{+}1) = t{+}1$$

$$\wedge\ ((\forall n \cdot\ T_d n = t{+}1{+}n)\ \Rightarrow\ (\forall n \cdot\ T_c(w_c{+}2{+}n) = t{+}2{+}n))$$

Use the first universal quantification to discharge the antecedent. Then throw away the first universal quantification (weakening our expression). Now all existential quantifications are unused, and can be thrown away.

$\Rightarrow \quad T_c w_c = t \ \wedge \ T_c(w_c+1) = t+1 \ \wedge \ \forall n \cdot \ T_c(w_c+2+n) = t+2+n$

Now put the three conjuncts together.

$= \quad \forall n \cdot \ T_c(w_c+n) = t+n$

$= \quad P\, c$

We still have to prove the loop refinement.

$$(L \ \Leftarrow \ a?. \ b?. \ t := max \ (t+1) \ (T_d r_d + 1). \ d?. \ c! \ a0 \times b + d + a \times b0. \ L)$$

Ignore $a?$ and $b?$ and the output message.

$\Leftarrow \quad ((\forall n \cdot \ T_d(r_d+n) = t+n) \ \Rightarrow \ (\forall n \cdot \ T_c(w_c+n) = t+1+n))$

$\quad \Leftarrow \ (\ t := max \ (t+1) \ (T_d r_d + 1). \ r_d := r_d+1. \ T_c w_c = t \ \wedge \ (w_c := w_c+1).$

$\quad\quad (\forall n \cdot \ T_d(r_d+n) = t+n) \ \Rightarrow \ (\forall n \cdot \ T_c(w_c+n) = t+1+n) \ )$

Use the Law of Portation to move the first antecedent to the right side, where it becomes a conjunct.

$= \quad (\forall n \cdot \ T_c(w_c+n) = t+1+n)$

$\quad \Leftarrow \quad (\forall n \cdot \ T_d(r_d+n) = t+n)$

$\quad\quad \wedge \ (\ t := max \ (t+1) \ (T_d r_d + 1). \ r_d := r_d+1. \ T_c w_c = t \ \wedge \ (w_c := w_c+1).$

$\quad\quad\quad (\forall n \cdot \ T_d(r_d+n) = t+n) \ \Rightarrow \ (\forall n \cdot \ T_c(w_c+n) = t+1+n) \ )$

Specializing $\forall n \cdot \ T_d(r_d+n) = t+n$ to the case $n=0$, we use $T_d r_d = t$ to simplify $max \ (t+1) \ (T_d r_d + 1)$.

$= \quad (\forall n \cdot \ T_c(w_c+n) = t+1+n)$

$\quad \Leftarrow \quad (\forall n \cdot \ T_d(r_d+n) = t+n)$

$\quad\quad \wedge \ (\ t := t+1. \ r_d := r_d+1. \ T_c w_c = t \ \wedge \ (w_c := w_c+1).$

$\quad\quad\quad (\forall n \cdot \ T_d(r_d+n) = t+n) \ \Rightarrow \ (\forall n \cdot \ T_c(w_c+n) = t+1+n) \ )$

Make all substitutions indicated by assignments.

$= \quad (\forall n \cdot \ T_c(w_c+n) = t+1+n)$

$\quad \Leftarrow \quad (\forall n \cdot \ T_d(r_d+n) = t+n)$

$\quad\quad \wedge \ T_c w_c = t+1$

$\quad\quad \wedge \ ((\forall n \cdot \ T_d(r_d+1+n) = t+1+n) \ \Rightarrow \ (\forall n \cdot \ T_c(w_c+1+n) = t+2+n))$

The conjunct $\forall n \cdot \ T_d(r_d+n) = t+n$ discharges the antecedent $\forall n \cdot \ T_d(r_d+1+n) = t+1+n$ which can be dropped.

$\Leftarrow \quad (\forall n \cdot \ T_c(w_c+n) = t+1+n)$

$\quad \Leftarrow \ T_c w_c = t+1 \ \wedge \ (\forall n \cdot \ T_c(w_c+1+n) = t+2+n)$

which is clearly a theorem.

---End of Power Series Multiplication

---End of Communication

10   Exercises

Exercises marked with √ have been done in earlier chapters.

Basic Theories

0   Prove each of the following laws of Boolean Theory using the proof format given in Chapter 1, and any laws listed in Chapter 11. Do not just use the Completion Rule.

(a) $a \land b \Rightarrow a \lor b$

(b) $(a \land b) \lor (b \land c) \lor (a \land c) = (a \lor b) \land (b \lor c) \land (a \lor c)$

(c) $\neg a \Rightarrow (a \Rightarrow b)$

(d) $a = (b \Rightarrow a) = a \lor b$

(e) $a = (a \Rightarrow b) = a \land b$

(f) $(a \Rightarrow c) \land (b \Rightarrow \neg c) \Rightarrow \neg(a \land b)$

(g) $a \land \neg b \Rightarrow a \lor b$

(h) $(a \Rightarrow b) \land (c \Rightarrow d) \land (a \lor c) \Rightarrow (b \lor d)$

(i) $a \land \neg a \Rightarrow b$

(j) $(a \Rightarrow b) \lor (b \Rightarrow a)$

(k) $(a \Rightarrow b) \Rightarrow (a \lor c \Rightarrow b \lor c)$

(l) $(a \Rightarrow b) \Rightarrow (a \land c \Rightarrow b \land c)$

(m) $(a \Rightarrow \neg a) \Rightarrow \neg a$

(n) $(a \Rightarrow b) \land (\neg a \Rightarrow b) = b$

(o) $(a \Rightarrow b) \Rightarrow a = a$

(p) $a = b \lor a = c \lor b = c$

(q) $\neg(a \Rightarrow b) \Rightarrow a$

(r) $a \Rightarrow (b \Rightarrow a)$

(s) $a \Rightarrow a \land b = a \Rightarrow b = a \lor b \Rightarrow b$

(t)   **if** a **then** a **else** $\neg a$

(u)   **if** $b \land c$ **then** P **else** Q = **if** b **then if** c **then** P **else** Q **else** Q

(v)   **if** $b \lor c$ **then** P **else** Q = **if** b **then** P **else if** c **then** P **else** Q

(w)   **if** b **then** P **else if** b **then** Q **else** R = **if** b **then** P **else** R

(x)   **if if** b **then** c **else** d **then** P **else** Q

      =   **if** b **then if** c **then** P **else** Q **else if** d **then** P **else** Q

(y)   **if** b **then if** c **then** P **else** R **else if** c **then** Q **else** R

      =   **if** c **then if** b **then** P **else** Q **else** R

(z)   **if** b **then if** c **then** P **else** R **else if** d **then** Q **else** R

      =   **if if** b **then** c **else** d **then if** b **then** P **else** Q **else** R

1   Express formally and succinctly that exactly one of three statements is true.

2   Truth tables and the Evaluation Rule can be replaced by a new proof rule and some new axioms. The new proof rule says: "A boolean expression does not gain, lose, or change classification when a theorem within it is replaced by another theorem. Similarly, a boolean expression does not gain, lose, or change classification when an antitheorem within it is replaced by another antitheorem.". The truth tables become new axioms; for example, one truth table entry becomes the axiom $\top \vee \top$ and another becomes the axiom $\top \vee \bot$. These two axioms can be reduced to one axiom by the introduction of a variable, giving $\top \vee x$. Write the truth tables as axioms and antiaxioms as succinctly as possible.

3   The Case Analysis Laws equate the ternary operator **if** a **then** b **else** c to expressions using only binary and unary operators. In each, the variable a appears twice. Find an equal expression using only binary and unary operators in which the variable a appears only once. Hint: use continuing operators.

4   Complete the following laws of Boolean Theory
(a) $\top =$
(b) $\bot =$
(c) $\neg a =$
(d) $a \wedge b =$
(e) $a \vee b =$
(f) $a = b =$
(g) $a \neq b =$
(h) $a \Rightarrow b =$
by adding a right side using only the following symbols (in any quantity)
(i) $\neg \wedge a\, b\, (\ )$
(ii) $\neg \vee a\, b\, (\ )$
(iii) $\neg \Rightarrow a\, b\, (\ )$
(iv) $\neq \Rightarrow a\, b\, (\ )$
(v) $\neg$ **if then else** $a\, b\, (\ )$

5   Consider a fully parenthesized expression containing only the symbols $\top \ \bot \ = \ \neq \ (\ )$ in any quantity and any syntactically acceptable order.
(a)   Show that all syntactically acceptable rearrangements are equivalent.
(b)   Show that it is equivalent to any expression obtained from it by making an even number of the following substitutions: $\top$ for $\bot$, $\bot$ for $\top$, $=$ for $\neq$, $\neq$ for $=$.

6   Design symbols for the ten binary boolean operators that are not presented in Chapter 1, and find laws about these operators.

7   (dual) The truth table for $\wedge$ appears below left. If you hold this truth table up to a mirror (hold the page horizontal and the mirror vertical) you obtain the truth table for $\vee$, which appears below right. Similarly the truth table for $\vee$ becomes the truth table for $\wedge$ when reflected in a mirror.

$\wedge$:

$\top\top$	$\top$
$\top\bot$	$\bot$
$\bot\top$	$\bot$
$\bot\bot$	$\bot$

$\vee$:

$\top\top$	$\top$
$\top\bot$	$\top$
$\bot\top$	$\top$
$\bot\bot$	$\bot$

Therefore $\wedge$ and $\vee$ are called "duals".

(a)   Of the 16 binary boolean operators, there are 6 pairs of duals, and 4 operators that are their own duals. Find them.

(b)   The dual of a boolean expression (without variables) is formed as follows: replace each $\top$ with $\bot$ and each $\bot$ with $\top$ (they are duals); leave each $\neg$ alone ($\neg$ is its own dual); replace each binary operator with its dual, adding parentheses if necessary to maintain the precedence; exchange the second and third operands of each **if then else** . Explain why the dual of a theorem is an antitheorem, and vice versa.

(c)   Let P be a boolean expression without variables. From part (b) we know that every boolean expression of the form

  (dual of P) $= \neg P$

is a theorem. Therefore, to find the dual of a boolean expression with variables, we must negate each boolean variable. For example, if a and b are boolean variables, then the dual of $a \wedge b$ is $\neg a \vee \neg b$. And since

  (dual of $a \wedge b$) $= \neg(a \wedge b)$

we have one of the Duality Laws:

  $\neg a \vee \neg b = \neg(a \wedge b)$

The other of the Duality Laws is obtained by equating the dual and negation of $a \vee b$. Obtain five more laws (not necessarily ones appearing in this book) by equating a dual with a negation.

(d)   Design symbols (you may redesign existing symbols where necessary) for the 16 binary boolean operators according to the following criteria.

(i) If $a\ op_0\ b = b\ op_1\ a$ then op_0 and op_1 should have symbols that are horizontal mirror reflections. This implies that symmetric operators have horizontally symmetric symbols, and all others have horizontally asymmetric symbols.

(ii) If $\neg a\ op_0\ \neg b = \neg(a\ op_1\ b)$ then op_0 and op_1 should have symbols that are vertical mirror reflections. This implies that self-dual operators have vertically symmetric symbols, and all others have vertically asymmetric symbols.

8   Let p and q be boolean expressions. Suppose p is both a theorem and an antitheorem (the theory is inconsistent).

(a)   Prove, using the rules of proof presented, that q is both a theorem and an antitheorem.

(b)   What is $q=q$?

9   (tennis) An advertisement for a tennis magazine says "If I'm not playing tennis, I'm watching tennis. And if I'm not watching tennis, I'm reading about tennis.". Assuming the speaker cannot do more than one of these activities at a time,

(a)   prove that the speaker is not reading about tennis.

(b)   what is the speaker doing?

10   (maid and butler) The maid said she saw the butler in the living room. The living room adjoins the kitchen. The shot was fired in the kitchen, and could be heard in all nearby rooms. The butler, who had good hearing, said he did not hear the shot. Given these facts, prove that someone lied. Use the following abbreviations.

mtt =   (the maid told the truth)

btt =   (the butler told the truth)

blr =   (the butler was in the living room)

bnk =   (the butler was near the kitchen)

bhs =   (the butler heard the shot)

11   (knights and knaves) There are three inhabitants of an island, named P, Q, and R. Each is either a knight or a knave. Knights always tell the truth. Knaves always lie. For each of the following, write the given information formally, and then answer the questions, with proof.

(a)   You ask P: "Are you a knight?". P replies: "If I am a knight, I'll eat my hat.". Does P eat his hat?

(b)   P says: "If Q is a knight, then I am a knave.". What are P and Q?

(c)   P says: "There is gold on this island if and only if I am a knight.". Can it be determined whether P is a knight or a knave? Can it be determined whether there is gold on the island?

(d)   P, Q, and R are standing together. You ask P: "Are you a knight or a knave?". P mumbles his reply, and you don't hear it. So you ask Q: "What did P say?". Q replies: "P said that he is a knave.". Then R says: "Don't believe Q, he's lying.". What are Q and R?

(e)   You ask P: "How many of you are knights?". P mumbles. So Q says: "P said there is exactly one knight among us.". R says: "Don't believe Q, he's lying.". What are Q and R?

(f)   P says: "We're all knaves.". Q says: "No, exactly one of us is a knight.". What are P, Q, and R?

12   (caskets) The princess had two caskets, one gold and one silver. Into one she placed her
        portrait and into the other she placed a dagger. On the gold casket she wrote the inscription:
        the portrait is not in here. On the silver casket she wrote the inscription: exactly one of
        these inscriptions is true. She explained to her suitor that each inscription is either true or
        false (not both), but on the basis of the inscriptions he must choose a casket. If he chooses
        the one with the portrait, he can marry her; if he chooses the one with the dagger, he must
        kill himself. Assuming marriage is preferable to death, which casket should he choose?

13   (the unexpected egg) There are two boxes, one red and one blue. One box has an egg in it;
        the other is empty. You are to look first in the red box, then if necessary in the blue box, to
        find the egg. But you will not know which box the egg is in until you open the box and
        see the egg. You reason as follows: "If I look in the red box and find it empty, I'll know
        that the egg is in the blue box without opening it. But I was told that I would not know
        which box the egg is in until I open the box and see the egg. So it can't be in the blue box.
        Now I know it must be in the red box without opening the red box. But again, that's ruled
        out, so it isn't in either box." Having ruled out both boxes, you open them and find the
        egg in one unexpectedly, as originally stated. Formalize the given statements and the
        reasoning, and thus explain the paradox.

14   Prove $-\infty<y<\infty \;\wedge\; y\neq 0 \;\Rightarrow\; (x/y=z \;=\; x=z\times y)$.

15   Show that the number axioms become inconsistent when the axiom
        $$-\infty<y<\infty \;\wedge\; y\neq 0 \;\Rightarrow\; x/y\times y = x$$
        is replaced by the simpler axiom
        $$-\infty<y<\infty \;\Rightarrow\; x/y\times y = x$$

16   Is there any harm in adding the axiom $0/0=5$ to Number Theory?

17   A number can be written as a sequence of decimal digits. For the sake of generality, let us
        consider using the sequence notation with arbitrary expressions, not just digits. For
        example, $1(2+3)4$ could be allowed, and be equal to 154 . (Now we really cannot omit
        multiplication signs.) What changes are needed to the number axioms?

18   (scale) There is a tradition in programming languages to use a scale operator, e , in the
        limited context of digit sequences. Thus $12e3$ is equal to 12×10^3 . For the sake of
        generality, let us consider using the scale notation with arbitrary expressions, not just
        digits. For example, $(6+6)e(5-2)$ could be allowed, and be equal to $12e3$. What
        changes are needed to the number axioms?

19   (circular numbers) Redesign the axioms for the extended number system to make it circular, so that $+\infty = -\infty$. Be careful with the transitivity of $<$.

20   When we defined number expressions, we included complex numbers such as $(-1)^{1/2}$, not because we particularly wanted them, but because it was easier than excluding them. If we were interested in complex numbers, we would find that the number axioms given in Chapter 11 do not allow us to prove many things we might like to prove. For example, we cannot prove $(-1)^{1/2} \times 0 = 0$. How can the axioms be made strong enough to prove things about complex numbers, but weak enough to leave room for ∞ ?

21   Express formally
(a)   the absolute value of a real number x .
(b)   the sign of a real number x , which is -1 , 0 , or $+1$ depending on whether x is negative, zero, or positive.

22   Let $\bullet$ be a binary infix operator (precedence 3) whose operands and result are of some type T . Let $\Diamond$ be a binary infix operator (precedence 7) whose operands are of type T and whose result is boolean, defined by the axiom
$$a \Diamond b \;=\; a \bullet b = a$$
(a)   Prove if $\bullet$ is idempotent then $\Diamond$ is reflexive.
(b)   Prove if $\bullet$ is associative then $\Diamond$ is transitive.
(c)   Prove if $\bullet$ is symmetric then $\Diamond$ is antisymmetric.
(d)   If T is the booleans and $\bullet$ is $\wedge$, what is $\Diamond$?
(e)   If T is the booleans and $\bullet$ is $\vee$, what is $\Diamond$?
(f)   If T is the natural numbers and $\Diamond$ is $\leq$, what is $\bullet$?
(g)   The axiom defines $\Diamond$ in terms of $\bullet$. Invert the definition, so that $\bullet$ is defined in terms of $\Diamond$.

23   (family theory) Design a theory of personal relationships. Invent person expressions such as *Jack* , *Jill* , *father of p* , *mother of p* , *parent of p* , *son of p* , *daughter of p* , *child of p* . Invent boolean expressions that use person expressions, such as *p is male* , *p is female* , *p is married to q* , *p=q* . Invent axioms such as (*p is male*) $\neq$ (*p is female*) . Formulate and prove an interesting theorem.

——End of Basic Theories

Basic Data Structures

24   Simplify
(a) $(1, 7–3) + 4 – (2, 6, 8)$
(b)   *nat×nat*
(c)   *nat–nat*
(d) $(nat+1)×(nat+1)$

25   Prove $\neg\, x: null$ where x is an element.

26   We defined bunch *null* with the axiom *null*: A . Is there any harm in defining bunch *all* with the axiom A: *all* ?

27   Let A be a bunch of booleans such that $A = \neg A$. What is A ?

28   Show that some of the axioms of Bunch Theory listed in Chapter 2 are provable from the other axioms. How many of the axioms can you remove without losing any theorems?

29   A composite number is a natural number with 2 or more (not necessarily distinct) prime factors. Express the composite numbers as simply as you can.

30   For this question only, let # be a binary infix operator (precedence 3) with natural operands and an extended natural result. Informally, *n#m* means "the number of times that n is a factor of m ". It is defined by the following two axioms.
                $m: n{\times}nat \ \lor \ n\#m = 0$
                $n{\neq}0 \ \Rightarrow \ n\#(m{\times}n) = n\#m + 1$
(a)   Make a 3×3 chart of the values of $(0,..3)\#(0,..3)$.
(b)   Show that the axioms become inconsistent if the antecedent of the second axiom is removed.
(c)   How should we change the axioms to allow # to have extended natural operands?

31   Prove $A: B \ \land \ C: D \ \Rightarrow \ A, C: B, D$.

32   For naturals n and m , we can express the statement " n is a factor of m " formally as follows:
                $m: n{\times}nat$
(a)   What are the factors of 0 ?
(b)   What is 0 a factor of?
(c)   What are the factors of 1 ?
(d)   What is 1 a factor of?

33   Let B be a bunch of natural numbers. How many elements are in B^2 ? How many elements are in $B{\times}B$?

34   (hyperbunch) A hyperbunch is like a bunch except that each element can occur a number of times other than just zero times (absent) or one time (present). The order of elements remains insignificant. (A hyperbunch does not have a characteristic predicate, but a characteristic function with numeric result.) Design notations and axioms for each of the following kinds of hyperbunch.

(a)   multibunch: an element can occur any natural number of times. For example, a multibunch can consist of one 2, two 7s, three 5s, and zero of everything else. (Note: the equivalent for sets is called either a multiset or a bag.)

(b)   wholebunch: an element can occur any integer number of times.

(c)   fuzzybunch: an element can occur any real number of times between (including) 0 and 1 .

35   (von Neumann numbers)

(a)   Is there any harm in adding the axioms

$$0 \;=\; \{null\} \qquad\qquad\qquad \text{the empty set}$$
$$n{+}1 \;=\; \{n, \sim\!n\} \qquad\qquad\quad \text{for each natural } n$$

(b)   What correspondence is induced by these axioms between the arithmetic operations and the set operations?

(c)   Is there any harm in adding the axioms

$$0 \;=\; \{null\} \qquad\qquad\qquad \text{the empty set}$$
$$i{+}1 \;=\; \{i, \sim\!i\} \qquad\qquad\quad \text{for each integer } i$$

36   (Cantor's heaven)

(a)   Show that $\$_2 S > \$S$ is not a theorem.

(b)   How must the number axioms be weakened so that the expression in part (a) can be added as an axiom?

37   The strings defined in Chapter 2 are "natural strings" because their lengths and indexes are natural numbers. Invent suitable axioms for

(a)   "extended strings", including both "natural strings" and "infinite strings".

(b)   "integer strings", including both "natural strings" and "negative strings".

38   In Chapter 2 there is a self-describing expression. Make it into a self-printing program. To do so, you need to know that $c!e$ outputs the value of expression e on channel c .

39   Prove the trichotomy for strings of numbers. For strings S and T , prove that exactly one of $S{<}T$, $S{=}T$, $S{>}T$ is a theorem.

40   What is the difference between [0, 1, 2] and [0; 1; 2] ?

41   Simplify
(a)   *null, nil*
(b)   *null; nil*
(c)   **nil*
(d)   [*null*]
(e)   [**null*]

42   The compound axiom says
$$x: A, B \;=\; x: A \;\lor\; x: B$$
There are sixteen binary boolean operators that could sit where $\lor$ sits in this axiom if we
just replace bunch union (,) by a corresponding bunch operator. Which of the sixteen
boolean binary operators correspond to useful bunch operators?

43   (prefix order) Give axioms to define the prefix partial order on strings. String S comes
before string T in this order if and only if S is an initial segment of T .

44   Simplify, assuming i: $0,..\#L$
(a) $i{\rightarrow}Li \mid L$
(b) $L\,[0;..i] + [x] + L\,[i{+}1;..\#L]$

45   Simplify
(a) $0{\rightarrow}1 \mid 1{\rightarrow}2 \mid 2{\rightarrow}3 \mid 3{\rightarrow}4 \mid 4{\rightarrow}5 \mid [0;..5]$
(b) $(4{\rightarrow}2 \mid [{-}3;..3])\ 3$
(c) $((3;2){\rightarrow}[10;..15] \mid 3{\rightarrow}[5;..10] \mid [0;..5])\ 3$
(d) $([0;..5]\ [3;\,4])\ 1$
(e) $(2;2){\rightarrow}`j \mid [\text{"abc"; "de"; "fghi"}]$
(f) $\#[nat]$
(g) $\#[*3]$
(h) $[3;\,4]\!: [3*4*int]$
(i) $[3,\,4;\,5]\!: [2*int]$
(j) $[3;\,4]\!: [3;\,int]$
(k) $[3;\,4]\,{`}\,[3;\,4;\,5]$

46   Let L be a list, and let i and j be indexes of L . Express $i{\rightarrow}Lj \mid j{\rightarrow}Li \mid L$ without using
        $\mid$.

───End of Basic Data Structures

Function Theory

47   In each of the following, replace p by

$\lambda x: int \cdot \ \lambda y: int \cdot \ \lambda z: int \cdot \ x{\geq}0 \land x^2{\leq}y \land \forall z: int \cdot z^2{\leq}y \Rightarrow z{\leq}x$

and simplify, assuming $x, y, z, u, w: int$.

(a) $p\ (x + y)\ (2u + w)\ z$

(b) $p\ (x + y)\ (2u + w)$

(c) $p\ (x + z)\ (y + y)\ (2{+}z)$

48   Express formally that L is a longest sorted sublist of M where

(a)   the sublist must be consecutive items (a segment).

(b)   the sublist must be consecutive and nonempty.

(c)   the sublist contains items in their order of appearance in M , but not necessarily consecutively.

49   Express formally that natural n is the length of a longest palindromic segment in list L . A palindrome is a list that equals its reverse.

50   Using the syntax x **can fool** y **at time** t formalize the statements

(a)   You can fool some of the people all of the time.

(b)   You can fool all of the people some of the time.

(c)   You can't fool all of the people all of the time.

        for each of the following interpretations of the word "You":

(i)   Someone

(ii)   Anyone

(iii)   The person I am talking to

51   (whodunit) Here are some statements.

(i)   Some criminal robbed the Russell mansion.

(ii)   Whoever robbed the Russell mansion either had an accomplice among the servants or had to break in.

(iii)   To break in one would have to either smash the door or pick the lock.

(iv)   Only an expert locksmith could pick the lock.

(v)   Anyone smashing the door would have been heard.

(vi)   Nobody was heard.

(vii)   No one could rob the Russell mansion without fooling the guard.

(viii)   To fool the guard one must be a convincing actor.

(ix)   No criminal could be both an expert locksmith and a convincing actor.

(x)   Some criminal had an accomplice among the servants.

(a)   Choosing good abbreviations, translate each of these statements into formal logic.

(b)   Taking the first nine statements as axioms, prove the tenth.

52   (arity) The arity of a function is the number of variables (parameters) it introduces, and the number of arguments it can be applied to. Write axioms to define αf (arity of f) formally.

53   Each of the quantifiers $\forall$, $\exists$, Σ, and Π is defined by three axioms.

(a)   Show that two of the axioms for $\forall$ are sufficient by proving the other axiom.

(b)   Show that two of the axioms for $\exists$ are sufficient by proving the other axiom.

(c)   Show that all three axioms are necessary to define Σ.

(d)   Show that all three axioms are necessary to define Π.

54   Prove that if v does not appear in x, then $\forall v \cdot x {\Leftarrow} y \;=\; x \Leftarrow \exists v \cdot y$.

55   There are four boolean binary associative symmetric operators with an identity. We used two of them to define quantifiers. What happened to the other two?

56   We have defined several quantifiers by starting with an associative symmetric operator with an identity. Bunch union is also such an operator. Does it yield a quantifier?

57   Which binary operator can be used to define a quantifier to give the range of a function?

58   Express $\forall$ and $\exists$ in terms of $\cancel{\in}$ and $\S$.

59   Express formally that

(a)   natural n is the largest proper (neither 1 nor m) factor of natural m.

(b) g is the greatest common divisor of naturals a and b.

(c) p is a prime number.

(d) n and m are relatively prime numbers.

(e)   there is at least one and at most a finite number of naturals n satisfying predicate p.

(f)   there is no smallest integer.

(g)   between every two rational numbers there is another rational number.

(h)   list L is a longest segment (consecutive items) of list M that does not contain item x.

(i)   the segment of list L from (including) index i to (excluding) index j is a segment whose sum is smallest.

(j) a and b are items of lists A and B (respectively) whose absolute difference is least.

(k) p is the length of a longest plateau (segment of equal items) in a non-empty sorted list L.

(l)   all items that occur in list L occur in a segment of length 10.

(m)   at most one item in list L occurs more than once.

(n)   all items of list L are different (no two items are equal).

(o)   the maximum item in list L occurs m times.

(p)   list L is a permutation of list M.

60   Formalize and disprove the statement "There is a natural number that is not equal to any natural number.".

61   (friends) Formalize and prove the statement "The people you know are those known by all who know all whom you know.".

62   (swapping partners) There is a finite bunch of couples. Each couple consists of a man and a woman. The oldest man and the oldest woman have the same age. If any two couples swap partners, forming two new couples, the younger partners of the two new couples have the same age. Prove that in each couple, the partners have the same age.

63   Simplify
(a) $\Sigma\ (0,..n) \rightarrow m$
(b) $\Pi\ (0,..n) \rightarrow m$

64   Are the boolean expressions
        $$nil{\rightarrow}x\ =\ x$$
        $$(S;T) \rightarrow x\ =\ S{\rightarrow}T{\rightarrow}x$$
(a)   consistent with the theory in Chapters 2 and 3?
(b)   theorems according to the theory in Chapters 2 and 3?

65   (unicorns) The following statements are made.
                All unicorns are white.
                All unicorns are black.
                No unicorn is both white and black.
        Are these statements consistent? What, if anything, can we conclude about unicorns?

66   (Russell's barber) Bertrand Russell stated: "In a small town there is a barber who shaves all and only the people in the town who do not shave themselves.". Then Russell asked: "Does the barber shave himself?". If we say yes, then we can conclude from the statement that he does not, and if we say no, then we can conclude from the statement that he does. Formalize this paradox, and thus explain it.

67   (Russell's paradox) Define $rus\ =\ \lambda f\colon null{\rightarrow}bool\cdot\ \neg f\,f$.
(a)   Prove $rus\ rus\ =\ \neg\ rus\ rus$.
(b)   Is this an inconsistency?
(c)   Can we add the axiom $\neg\ f\colon \Delta f$? Would it help?

68   (Cantor's diagonal) Prove $\neg\exists f\colon nat{\rightarrow}nat{\rightarrow}nat\cdot\ \forall g\colon nat{\rightarrow}nat\cdot\ \exists n\colon nat\cdot\ f\,n = g$.

69   (Gödel/Turing incompleteness) Prove that we cannot consistently and completely define an interpreter. An interpreter is a predicate I that applies to texts; when applied to a text representing a boolean expression, its result is equal to the represented expression. For example,

$$I \text{ "}\forall s: [*char]\cdot \#s \geq 0\text{"} = \forall s: [*char]\cdot \#s \geq 0$$

70   Let f and g be functions from nat to nat. For what f do we have the theorem $g\,f = g$? For what f do we have the theorem $f\,g = g$?

71   What is the difference between $\#[n*T]$ and $\text{¢}\S[n*T]$?

72   Prove
(a) $\exists i\cdot Li \leq m = (MIN\ L) \leq m$
(b) $\forall i\cdot Li \leq m = (MAX\ L) \leq m$

73   (pigeon-hole) Prove $(\Sigma L) > n \times \#L \implies \exists i: \Delta L\cdot Li > n$.

74   If $f: A \rightarrow B$ and $p: B \rightarrow bool$ and f distributes over bunch union, then prove
(a) $\exists b: fA\cdot pb = \exists a: A\cdot pfa$
(b) $\forall b: fA\cdot pb = \forall a: A\cdot pfa$

75   Relation R is transitive if $\forall x, y, z\cdot Rxy \wedge Ryz \implies Rxz$. Express formally that relation R is the transitive closure of relation Q (R is the strongest transitive relation that is implied by Q).

76   Is there any harm in defining relation R with the following axioms?

$\forall x\cdot \exists y\cdot Rxy$	totality
$\forall x\cdot \neg Rxx$	irreflexivity
$\forall x, y, z\cdot Rxy \wedge Ryz \implies Rxz$	transitivity
$\exists u\cdot \forall x\cdot x=u \vee Rxu$	unity

77   This question explores a simpler, more elegant function theory than the one presented in Chapter 3. We separate the notion of local variable introduction from the notion of domain, and we generalize the latter to become local axiom introduction. Variable introduction has the form $\lambda v\cdot b$ where v is a variable and b is any expression (the body; no domain). There is a Renaming Axiom

$$\lambda v\cdot b = \lambda w\cdot (\text{substitute } w \text{ for } v \text{ in } b)$$

and an Application Axiom

$$(\lambda v\cdot b)\, x = (\text{substitute } x \text{ for } v \text{ in } b)$$

Let a be boolean, and let b be any expression. Then $a \triangleright b$ is an expression of the same type as b. The $\triangleright$ operator has precedence level 12 and is right-associating. Its axioms include:

$$\mathsf{T} \triangleright b \;=\; b$$

$$a \triangleright b \triangleright c \;=\; a \wedge b \triangleright c$$

The expression $a \triangleright b$ is a "one-tailed if-expression", or "asserted expression"; it introduces a as a local axiom within b. A function is a variable introduction whose body is an asserted expression in which the assertion has the form $v: D$. In this case, we allow an abbreviation: for example, the function $\lambda n \cdot \; n: nat \; \triangleright \; n{+}1$ can be abbreviated $\lambda n: nat \cdot \; n{+}1$. Applying this function to 3, we find

$$(\lambda n \cdot \; n: nat \; \triangleright \; n{+}1) \; 3$$

$$= \quad 3: nat \; \triangleright \; 3{+}1$$

$$= \quad \mathsf{T} \triangleright 4$$

$$= \quad 4$$

Applying it to -3 we find

$$(\lambda n \cdot \; n: nat \; \triangleright \; n{+}1) \; (-3)$$

$$= \quad -3: nat \; \triangleright \; -3{+}1$$

$$= \quad \bot \triangleright -2$$

and then we are stuck; no further axiom applies. In the example, we have used variable introduction and axiom introduction together to give us back the kind of function we had; but in general, they are independently useful.

(a)   Show how function-valued variables can be introduced in this new theory.

(b)   What expressions in the old theory have no equivalent in the new? How closely can they be approximated?

(c)   What expressions in the new theory have no equivalent in the old? How closely can they be approximated?

──End of Function Theory

Program Theory

78   Prove specification S is satisfiable for prestate σ if and only if $S.\mathsf{T}$ (note: T is the "true" boolean).

79   Let x be an integer state variable. Which of the following specifications are implementable?

(a) $x \geq 0 \;\Rightarrow\; x'^2 = x$

(b) $x' \geq 0 \;\Rightarrow\; x = 0$

(c) $\neg(x \geq 0 \;\wedge\; x' = 0)$

(d) $\neg(x \geq 0 \;\vee\; x' = 0)$

80   A specification is transitive if, for all states a, b, and c, if it allows the state to change from a to b, and it allows the state to change from b to c, then it allows the state to change from a to c. Prove S is transitive if and only if S is refined by $S.S$.

81√   Simplify each of the following (in integer variables x and y).

(a) $x:=y+1$. $y'>x'$

(b) $x:=x+1$. $y'>x \wedge x'>x$

(c) $x:=y+1$. $y'=2x$

(d) $x:=1$. $x{\geq}1 \Rightarrow \exists x \cdot y'=2x$

(e) $x:=y$. $x{\geq}1 \Rightarrow \exists y \cdot y'=x{\times}y$

(f) $x:=1$. ok

(g) $x:=1$. $y:=2$

(h) $x:=1$. P where $P = y:=2$

(i) $x:=1$. $y:=2$. $x:=x+y$

(j) $x:=1$. **if** $y>x$ **then** $x:=x+1$ **else** $x:=y$

(k) $x:=1$. $x'>x$. $x'=x+1$

82   Prove

(a) $x:=x = ok$

(b) $x:=e$. $x:=f\,x = x:=f\,e$

(c)   **if** b **then** $x:=e$ **else** $x:=f = x:=$ **if** b **then** e **else** f

83   Prove or disprove

(a) R. **if** b **then** P **else** $Q = $ **if** b **then** $(R.\ P)$ **else** $(R.\ Q)$

(b)   **if** b **then** $P{\wedge}Q$ **else** $R{\wedge}S = ($ **if** b **then** P **else** $R) \wedge ($ **if** b **then** Q **else** $S)$

(c)   **if** b **then** $(P.\ Q)$ **else** $(R.\ S) = $ **if** b **then** P **else** R. **if** b **then** Q **else** S

84   Prove

(a) P and Q are both refined by R if and only if their conjunction is refined by R .

(b) $P{\Rightarrow}Q$ is refined by R if and only if Q is refined by $P{\wedge}R$.

85   For which kinds of specifications P and Q is the following a theorem:

(a) $\neg(P.\ \neg Q) \Leftarrow P.\ Q$

(b) $P.\ Q \Leftarrow \neg(P.\ \neg Q)$

(c) $P.\ Q = \neg(P.\ \neg Q)$

86   Let x and n be natural variables. Find a specification P such that both the following
      hold:

$$x = x' \times 2^{n'} \Leftarrow n:=0.\ P$$
$$P \Leftarrow \text{ if } even\ x \text{ then } (x:= div\ x\ 2.\ n:=n+1.\ P) \text{ else } ok$$

87   Suppose $S \Leftarrow A.\ A.\ S.\ Z.\ Z$. Can we conclude $S \Leftarrow A.\ S.\ Z$? Can we always roll
      up a loop?

88   (square) Let s and n be natural variables. Find a specification P such that both the following hold:

$$s' = n^2 \iff s := n. \ P$$
$$P \iff \text{if } n=0 \text{ then } ok \text{ else } (n := n-1. \ s := s+n+n. \ P)$$

This program squares using only addition, subtraction, and test for zero.

89   Write a formal specification of the following problem: "Change the value of list variable L so that each item is repeated. For example, if L is $[6; 3; 5; 5; 7]$ then it should be changed to $[6; 6; 3; 3; 5; 5; 5; 5; 7; 7]$.".

90   Let P and Q be specifications. Let C be a precondition and let C' be the corresponding postcondition. Prove the condition law

$$P. \ Q \iff P \wedge C'. \ C \Rightarrow Q$$

91   Let P and Q be specifications. Let C be a precondition and let C' be the corresponding postcondition. Which three of the following condition laws can be turned around, switching the problem and the solution?

$$C \wedge (P. \ Q) \iff C \wedge P. \ Q$$
$$(P.Q) \wedge C' \iff P. \ Q \wedge C'$$
$$C \Rightarrow (P.Q) \iff C \Rightarrow P. \ Q$$
$$P. \ C \wedge Q \iff P \wedge C'. \ Q$$
$$P. \ Q \iff P \wedge C'. \ C \Rightarrow Q$$

92   Let S be a specification. Let C be a precondition and let C' be the corresponding postcondition. How does the exact precondition for C' to be refined by S differ from $(S. \ C)$?

93   We have Refinement by Steps, Refinement by Parts, and Refinement by Cases. In this question we propose Refinement by Alternatives:

If $A \iff \text{if } b \text{ then } C \text{ else } D$ and $E \iff \text{if } b \text{ then } F \text{ else } G$ are theorems,

then $A \vee E \iff \text{if } b \text{ then } C \vee F \text{ else } D \vee G$ is a theorem.

If $A \iff B.C$ and $D \iff E.F$ are theorems, then $A \vee D \iff B \vee E. \ C \vee F$ is a theorem.

If $A \iff B$ and $C \iff D$ are theorems, then $A \vee C \iff B \vee D$ is a theorem.

Discuss the merits and demerits of this proposed law.

94√   In one integer variable x,

(a)   find the exact precondition A for $x'>5$ to be refined by $x := x+1$.

(b)   find the exact postcondition for A to be refined by $x := x+1$, where A is your answer from part (a).

95   Let all variables be natural except L is a list of naturals. What is the exact precondition for

(a) $x'+y' > 8$ to be refined by $x:= 1$

(b) $x'=1$ to be refined by $x:= 1$

(c) $x'=2$ to be refined by $x:= 1$

(d) $x'=y$ to be refined by $y:= 1$

(e) $x' \geq y'$ to be refined by $x:= y+z$

(f) $y'+z' \geq 0$ to be refined by $x:= y+z$

(g) $x' \leq 1 \lor x' \geq 5$ to be refined by $x:= x+1$

(h) $x'<y' \land \exists x \cdot Lx<y'$ to be refined by $x:= 1$

(i) $\exists y \cdot Ly<x'$ to be refined by $x:= y+1$

(j) $L'\,3 = 4$ to be refined by $L:= i \rightarrow 4 \,|\, L$

(k) $x'=a$ to be refined by **if** $a > b$ **then** $x:= a$ **else** ok

(l) $x'=y \land y'=x$ to be refined by $z:= x.\ \ x:= y.\ \ y:= z$

(m) $ax'^{\,2} + bx' + c = 0$ to be refined by $x:= ax + b.\ \ x:= -x/a$

(n) $f' = n'!$ to be refined by $n:= n+1.\ \ f:= f \times n$ where $!$ means factorial.

(o) $7 \leq c' < 28 \land odd\ c'$ to be refined by $a:= b-1.\ \ b:= a+3.\ \ c:= a+b$

(p) $s' = \Sigma\, L\,[0;..i']$ to be refined by $s:= s + Li.\ \ i:= i+1$

96   For what exact precondition and postcondition does the following assignment move integer
      variable x farther from zero?

(a) $x:= x+1$

(b) $x:= abs\,(x+1)$

(c)√ $x:= x^2$

97   For what exact precondition and postcondition does the following assignment move integer
      variable x farther from zero staying on the same side of zero?

(a) $x:= x+1$

(b) $x:= abs\,(x+1)$

(c) $x:= x^2$

98   (weakest prespecification) Given specifications P and Q , find the weakest specification
      S (in terms of P and Q) such that P is refined by $S.Q$.

99   Let a and b be integer variables. Simplify

(a) $b:= a-b.\ \ b:= a-b$

(b) $a:= a+b.\ \ b:= a-b.\ \ a:= a-b$

100   Let x and y be boolean variables. Simplify

(a) $x:= x=y.\ \ x:= x=y$

(b) $x:= x \neq y.\ \ y:= x \neq y.\ \ x:= x \neq y$

101   Let x be an integer variable. Prove the refinement

(a)√ $x'=0 \iff$ if $x=0$ then ok else $(x:=x-1.\ x'=0)$

(b) $P \iff$ if $x=0$ then ok else $(x:=x-1.\ t:=t+1.\ P)$

where $P = x'=0 \land$ if $x\geq0$ then $t' = t+x$ else $t'=\infty$

102   Let x be an integer variable. Prove the refinement

(a) $x'=1 \iff$ if $x=1$ then ok else $(x:= div\ x\ 2.\ x'=1)$

(b)√ $R \iff$ if $x=1$ then ok else $(x:= div\ x\ 2.\ t:=t+1.\ R)$

where $R = x'=1 \land$ if $x\geq1$ then $t' \leq t + log\ x$ else $t'=\infty$

103   Is the refinement

          $P \iff$ if $x=0$ then ok else $(x:=x-1.\ t:=t+1.\ P)$

a theorem when

          $P = x<0 \Rightarrow x'=1 \land t'=\infty$

Is this reasonable? Explain.

104   (factorial) In natural variables n and f prove

          $f:= n! \iff$ if $n=0$ then $f:= 1$ else $(n:= n-1.\ f:= n!.\ n:= n+1.\ f:= f\times n)$

where $n! = 1\times2\times3\times...\times n$.

105   In natural variables n and m prove

          $P \iff n:= n+1.$

                    if $n=10$ then ok

                    else $(m:= m-1.\ P)$

where $P = m:= m+n-9.\ n:= 10$.

106   Let i be an integer variable. Add time according to the recursive measure, and then find the strongest P you can such that

(a) $P \iff$ if $even\ i$ then $i:= i/2$ else $i:= i+1.$

                    if $i=1$ then ok else P

(b) $P \iff$ if $even\ i$ then $i:= i/2$ else $i:= i-3.$

                    if $i=0$ then ok else P

107   Find a finite function f of natural variables i and j to serve as an upper bound on the execution time of the following program, and prove

          $t' \leq t + fij \iff$ if $i=0 \land j=0$ then ok

                    else if $i=0$ then $(i:= j\times j.\ j:= j-1.\ t:= t+1.\ t' \leq t + fij)$

                    else $(i:= i-1.\ t:= t+1.\ t' \leq t + fij)$

108   Let a and b be positive integers. Let x, u, and v be integer variables. Let
$$P = u{\geq}0 \ \wedge \ v{\geq}0 \ \wedge \ x = ua - vb \ \Rightarrow \ x'{=}0$$

(a)   Prove
$$P \ \Longleftarrow \ \textbf{if } x{>}0 \textbf{ then } (x{:=} x{-}a. \ u{:=} u{-}1. \ P)$$
$$\textbf{else if } x{<}0 \textbf{ then } (x{:=} x{+}b. \ v{:=} v{-}1. \ P)$$
$$\textbf{else } ok$$

(b)   Find an upper bound for the execution time of the program in part (a).

109   Let P mean that the final values of natural variables a and b are the largest exponents of 2 and 3 respectively such that both powers divide evenly into the initial value of positive integer x.

(a)   Define P formally.

(b)   Define Q suitably and prove
$$P \ \Longleftarrow \ a{:=} 0. \ b{:=} 0. \ Q$$
$$Q \ \Longleftarrow \ \textbf{if } x{:} \ 2{\times}nat \textbf{ then } (x{:=} x/2. \ a{:=} a{+}1. \ Q)$$
$$\textbf{else if } x{:} \ 3{\times}nat \textbf{ then } (x{:=} x/3. \ b{:=} b{+}1. \ Q)$$
$$\textbf{else } ok$$

(c)   Find an upper bound for the execution time of the program in part (b).

110   Write a program to make a list of the first twenty natural numbers in descending order.

111   Write a program to make a list of the first twenty powers of 2 , in order, without using exponentiation.

112   (cube) Write a program that cubes using only addition, subtraction, and test for zero.

113   (cube test) Write a program to determine if a given natural number is a cube.

114   (running total) Given list variable L and any other variables you need, write a program to convert L into a list of cumulative sums. Formally,

(a) $\forall n{:} \ 0,..\#L{\cdot} \ L'n \ = \ \Sigma \, L \, [0;..n]$

(b) $\forall n{:} \ 0,..\#L{\cdot} \ L'n \ = \ \Sigma \, L \, [0;..n{+}1]$

115   (Zeno) Here is an infinite loop.
$$R \ \Longleftarrow \ x{:=} x{+}1. \ R$$
Suppose that the execution time of the assignment plus the call (one iteration) is 2^{-x}. How much time does the loop require? Prove it.

116   Can we prove the refinement
$$P \ \Longleftarrow \ t{:=} t{+}1. \ P$$
for $P = t'{=}5$? Does this mean that execution will terminate at time 5 ? What is wrong?

117 Let n and r be natural variables in the refinement
$$P \quad \Longleftarrow \quad \text{if } n=1 \text{ then } r:= 0 \text{ else } (n:= \text{div } n\ 2. \quad P. \quad r:= r+1)$$
Suppose the operations div and $+$ each take time 1 and all else is free (even the call is free). Insert appropriate time increments, and find an appropriate P to express the execution time in terms of

(a) the initial values of the state space variables. Prove the refinement for your choice of P.

(b) the final values of the state space variables. Prove the refinement for your choice of P.

118 ($\text{mod } 2$) Let n be a natural variable. The problem to reduce n modulo 2 can be solved as follows:
$$n' = \text{mod } n\ 2 \quad \Longleftarrow \quad \text{if } n<2 \text{ then } ok \text{ else } (n:= n-2. \quad n' = \text{mod } n\ 2)$$
Using the recursive time measure, find and prove an upper time bound. Make it as small as you can.

119 (fast $\text{mod } 2$) Let n and p be natural variables. The problem to reduce n modulo 2 can be solved as follows:
$$n' = \text{mod } n\ 2 \quad \Longleftarrow \quad \text{if } n<2 \text{ then } ok \text{ else } (\text{even } n' = \text{even } n. \quad n' = \text{mod } n\ 2)$$
$$\text{even } n' = \text{even } n \quad \Longleftarrow \quad p:= 2. \quad \text{even } p \ \Rightarrow \ \text{even } p' \wedge \text{even } n' = \text{even } n$$
$$\text{even } p \ \Rightarrow \ \text{even } p' \wedge \text{even } n' = \text{even } n \quad \Longleftarrow$$
$$\qquad n:= n-p. \quad p:= p+p.$$
$$\qquad \text{if } n<p \text{ then } ok \text{ else } \text{even } p \ \Rightarrow \ \text{even } p' \wedge \text{even } n' = \text{even } n$$

(a) Prove these refinements.

(b) Using the recursive time measure, find and prove a sublinear upper time bound. Warning: this problem is hard.

120 With t as time variable, what is the exact precondition for termination of

(a) $\qquad x \geq 0 \ \Rightarrow \ t' \leq t+x$

(b) $\qquad \exists n: nat \cdot \ t' \leq t+n$

(c) $\qquad \exists f: int \rightarrow nat \cdot \ t' \leq t + fx$

121√ (maximum item) Write a program to find the maximum item in a list.

122 (list comparison) Using item comparison but not list comparison, write a program to determine whether one list comes before another in the list order.

123√ (list summation) Write a program to find the sum of a list of numbers.

124 (alternating sum) Write a program to find the alternating sum $L0 - L1 + L2 - L3 + L4 - \ldots$ of a list L of numbers.

125   (combinations) For natural numbers a and b , define
$$a \lozenge b \ = \ (a+b)! \, / \, (a! \ b!)$$
where ! is the factorial function. $a \lozenge b$ is the number of ways to include a things and
exclude b things. If $\lozenge$ is not an implemented operator, we must refine $x:= a \lozenge b$ to make
it a program. Do so, including recursive time.

126   (earliest meeting time) Write a program to find the earliest meeting time acceptable to three
people. Each person is willing to state their possible meeting times by means of a function
that tells, for each time t , the earliest time at or after t that they are available for a meeting.
(Do not confuse this t with the execution time variable. You may ignore execution time
for this problem.)

127   (polynomial) You are given n: nat , c: $[n*rat]$, x: rat and variable y: rat . c is a list of
coefficients of a polynomial ("of degree $n-1$ ") to be evaluated at x . Write a program for
$$y' = \Sigma i: \ 0,..n \cdot \ c_i \times x^i$$

128   (multiplication table) Given n: nat and variable M: $[*[*nat]]$, write a program to assign
to M a multiplication table of size n without using multiplication. For example, if
$n = 4$, then
$$M' = [\ \ [0];$$
$$[0; 1];$$
$$[0; 2; 4];$$
$$[0; 3; 6; 9] \ ]$$

129   (Pascal's triangle) Given n: nat and variable P: $[*[*nat]]$, write a program to assign to
P a Pascal's triangle of size n . For example, if $n = 4$, then
$$P' = [\ \ [1];$$
$$[1; 1];$$
$$[1; 2; 1];$$
$$[1; 3; 3; 1] \ ]$$
The left side and diagonal are all 1s; each interior item is the sum of the item above it and
the item diagonally above and left.

130√   (binary exponentiation) Given natural variables x and y , write a program for $y' = 2^x$
without using exponentiation.

131   Write a program to find the smallest power of 2 that is bigger than or equal to a given
positive integer.

132√   (fast exponentiation) Given rational variables x and z and natural variable y , write a
program for $z' = x^y$ that runs fast without using exponentiation.

133   (sort test) Write a program to assign a boolean variable to indicate whether a given list is sorted.

134√   (linear search) Write a program to find the first occurrence of a given item in a given list. The execution time must be linear in the length of the list.

135√   (binary search) Write a program to find a given item in a given sorted list. The execution time must be logarithmic in the length of the list. The strategy is to identify which half of the list contains the item if it occurs at all, then which quarter, then which eighth, and so on.

136   (ternary search) The problem is the same as binary search. The strategy this time is to identify which third of the list contains the item if it occurs at all, then which ninth, then which twenty-seventh, and so on.

137   (fixed point) Let L be a nonempty sorted list of n different integers. Write a $log\ n$ program to find a fixed-point of L, that is an index i such that $Li = i$, or to report that no such index exists.

138√   (two-dimensional search) Write a program to find a given item in a given 2-dimensional array. The execution time must be linear in the product of the dimensions.

139   (sorted two-dimensional search) Write a program to find a given item in a given 2-dimensional array in which each row is sorted and each column is sorted. The execution time must be linear in the sum of the dimensions.

140   (sorted two-dimensional count) Write a program to count the number of occurrences of a given item in a given 2-dimensional array in which each row is sorted and each column is sorted. The execution time must be linear in the sum of the dimensions.

141   (saddleback search) Write a program to find a given item in a given 2-dimensional array in which each row is sorted in ascending order and each column is sorted in descending order. The execution time must be linear in the sum of the dimensions.

142   (saddleback count) Write a program to count the number of occurrences of a given item in a given 2-dimensional array in which each row is sorted in ascending order and each column is sorted in descending order. The execution time must be linear in the sum of the dimensions.

143   (pattern search) Let *subject* and *pattern* be two texts. Write a program to do the following. If *pattern* occurs somewhere within *subject* , natural variable *h* is assigned to indicate the beginning of its first occurrence

(a)   using any list operators given in Chapter 2.

(b)   using list indexing, but no other list operators.

144   (all present) Given a natural number and a list, write a program to determine if every natural number up to the given number is an item in the list.

145   (missing number) You are given a list of length *n* whose items are the numbers $0,..n+1$ in some order, but with one number missing. Write a program to find the missing number.

146   (Pascal string length) You are given a text (list of characters) that begins with zero or more "ordinary" characters, and then ends with zero or more "padding" characters. A padding character is not an ordinary character. Write a program to find the number of ordinary characters in the text. Execution time should be logarithmic in the text length.

147   (ordered pair search) Given a list of at least two items whose first item is less than or equal to its last item, write a program to find an adjacent pair of items such that the first of the pair is less than or equal to the second of the pair. Execution time should be logarithmic in the length of the list.

148   (convex equal pair) A list of numbers is convex if every item (except the first and last) is less than or equal to the average of its two neighbors. Given a convex list, write a program to determine if it has a consecutive pair of equal items. Execution should be logarithmic in the length of the list.

149   Define a partial order « on pairs of integers as follows:
$$[a; b] \ll [c; d] \;=\; a{<}c \land b{<}d$$
Given *n*: *nat* and *L*: $[n*[int; int]]$ write a program to find the index of a minimal item in *L* . That is, find *j*: $0,..\#L$ such that $\neg\exists i\cdot\ Li \ll Lj$. The execution time should be $n \times log\ n$ or less.

150√   (n^2 sort) Write a program to sort a list. Execution time should be at most n^2 where *n* is the length of the list.

151   (*n log n* sort) Write a program to sort a list. Execution time should be at most $n \times log\ n$ where *n* is the length of the list.

152   (reverse) Write a program to reverse the order of the items of a list.

153   (next sorted list) Given a sorted list of naturals, write a program to find the next (in list order) sorted list having the same sum.

154   (next combination) You are given a sorted list of m different numbers, all in the range $0,..n$. Write a program to find the lexicographically next sorted list of m different numbers, all in the range $0,..n$.

155   (next permutation) You are given a list of the numbers $0,..n$ in some order. Write a program to find the lexicographically next list of the numbers $0,..n$.

156   (permutation inverse) You are given a list variable P of different items in $0,..\#P$. Write a program for $P\,P' = [0;..\#P]$.

157   (permutation cube) You are given a list variable P of different items in $0,..\#P$. Write a program for $P' = P\,P\,P$.

158   (idempotent permutation) You are given a list variable L of items in $0,..\#L$ (not necessarily all different). Write a program to permute the list so that finally $L'\,L' = L'$.

159   (local minimum) You are given a list L of at least 3 numbers such that $L0 \geq L1$ and $L(\#L{-}2) \leq L(\#L{-}1)$. A local minimum is an interior index i: $1,..\#L{-}1$ such that
$$L(i{-}1) \geq Li \leq L(i{+}1)$$
(a)   Prove L has a local minimum.
(b)   Write a program to find a local minimum of L .

160   (natural division) The natural quotient of natural n and positive integer p is the natural number q satisfying
$$q \leq n/p < q{+}1$$
Write a program to find the natural quotient of n and p in $\log n$ time without using any functions (div , mod , $floor$, $ceil$, ...).

161   (remainder) Write a program to find the remainder after integer division, using addition and subtraction (not multiplication or division or mod).

162   (natural binary logarithm) The natural binary logarithm of a positive integer p is the natural number b satisfying
$$2^b \leq p < 2^{b+1}$$
Write a program to find the natural binary logarithm of a given positive integer p in $\log p$ time.

163   (natural square root) The natural square root of a natural number n is the natural number s satisfying

$$s^2 \le n < (s+1)^2$$

(a)   Write a program to find the natural square root of a given natural number n in $log\ n$ time.

(b)   Write a program to find the natural square root of a given natural number n in $log\ n$ time using only addition, subtraction, doubling, halving, and comparisons (no multiplication or division).

164   (factor count) Write a program to find the number of factors (not necessarily prime) of a given natural number.

165   (Fermat's last program) Given natural c, write a program to find the number of unordered pairs of naturals a and b such that $a^2 + b^2 = c^2$ in time proportional to c. (An unordered pair is really a bunch of size 1 or 2. If we have counted the pair a and b, we don't want to count the pair b and a.) Your program may use addition, subtraction, multiplication, division, and comparisons, but not exponentiation or square root.

166   (flatten) Write a program to flatten a list. The result is a new list just like the old one but without the internal structure. For example,

$L = [\ [3; 5]; 2; [5; [7]; [nil]\ ]\ ]$

$L' = [3; 5; 2; 5; 7]$

Your program may employ a test $Li: int$ to see if an item is an integer or a list.

167   (diagonal) Some points are arranged around the perimeter of a circle. The distance from each point to the next point going clockwise is given by a list. Write a program to find two points that are farthest apart.

168√   (minimum sum segment) Given a list of integers, possibly including negatives, write a program to find the minimum sum of any segment (sublist of consecutive items).

169   (segment sum count)

(a)   Write a program to find, in a given list of naturals, the number of segments (consecutive items) whose sum is a given natural.

(b)   Write a program to find, in a given list of positive naturals, the number of segments whose sum is a given natural.

170   (longest plateau) You are given a nonempty sorted list of numbers. A plateau is a segment (sublist of consecutive items) of equal items. Write a program to find

(a)   the length of a longest plateau.

(b)   the number of longest plateaus.

171   (longest smooth segment) In a list of integers, a smooth segment is a sublist of consecutive items in which no two adjacent items differ by more than 1 . Write a program to find a longest smooth segment.

172   (longest balanced segment) Given a list of booleans, write a program to find a longest segment (sublist of consecutive items) having an equal number of $\top$ and $\bot$ items.

173   (longest palindrome) A palindrome is a list that equals its reverse. Write a program to find a longest palindromic segment in a given list.

174   (greatest subsequence) Given a list, write a program to find the sublist that is largest according to list order. (A sublist contains items drawn from the list, in the same order of appearance, but not necessarily consecutively items.)

175   Given a list whose items are all 0 , 1 , or 2 , write a program
(a)   to find the length of a shortest segment (consecutive items) that contains all three numbers in any order.
(b)   to count the number of sublists (not necessarily consecutive items) that are 0 then 1 then 2 in that order.

176   Let L and M be sorted lists of numbers. Write a program to find the number of pairs of indexes i: $0,..\#L$ and j: $0,..\#M$ such that $Li \le Mj$.

177   (heads and tails) Let L be a list of positive integers. Write a program to find the number of pairs of indexes i and j such that
$$\Sigma\, L\, [0;..i] = \Sigma\, L\, [j;..\#L]$$

178   (pivot) You are given a nonempty list of positive numbers. Write a program to find the balance point, or pivot. Each item contributes its value (weight) times its distance from the pivot to its side of the balance. Item i is considered to be located at point $i + 1/2$, and the pivot point may likewise be noninteger.

179   (inversion count) Given a list, write a program to find how many pairs of items (not necessarily consecutive items) are out of order, with the larger item before the smaller item.

180   (minimum difference) Given two nonempty sorted lists of numbers, write a program to find a pair of items, one from each list, whose absolute difference is smallest.

181   (interval union) A collection of intervals along a real number line is given by the list of left ends L and the corresponding list of right ends R. List L is sorted. The intervals might sometimes overlap, and sometimes leave gaps. Write a program to find the total length of the number line that is covered by these intervals.

182   (bit sum) Write a program to find the number of ones in the binary representation of a given natural number.

183   (digit sum) Write a program to find the sum of the digits in the decimal representation of a given natural number.

184   (parity check) Write a program to find whether the number of ones in the binary representation of a given natural number is even or odd.

185   Given two natural numbers s and p, write a program to find four natural numbers a, b, c, and d whose sum is s and product p, in time s^2, if such numbers exists.

186   Given three natural numbers n, s, and p, write a program to find a list of length n of natural numbers whose sum is s and product p, if such a list exists.

187   (transitive closure) A relation R: $(0,..n){\rightarrow}(0,..n){\rightarrow}bool$ can be represented by a square boolean array of size n. Given a relation in the form of a square boolean array, write a program to find
(a)   its transitive closure (the strongest transitive relation that is implied by the given relation).
(b)   its reflexive transitive closure (the strongest reflexive and transitive relation that is implied by the given relation).

188   (reachability) You are given a finite bunch of places; and a successor function S on places that tells, for each place, those places that are directly reachable from it; and a special place named h (for home). Write a program to find all places that are reachable (reflexively, directly, or indirectly) from h.

189   (shortest path) You are given a square extended rational array in which item ij represents the direct distance from place i to place j. If it is not possible to go directly from i to j, then item ij is ∞. Write a program to find the square extended rational array in which item ij represents the shortest, possibly indirect, distance from place i to place j.

190   (approximate search) Given a nonempty sorted list of numbers and a number, write a program to determine the index of an item in the list that is closest in value to the given number.

191   (McCarthy's 91 problem) Let i be an integer variable. Let
$$M \;=\; \textbf{if}\ i{>}100\ \textbf{then}\ i{:=}\ i{-}10\ \textbf{else}\ i{:=}\ 91$$
(a)   Prove $M \;\Longleftarrow\; \textbf{if}\ i{>}100\ \textbf{then}\ i{:=}\ i{-}10\ \textbf{else}\ (i{:=}\ i{+}11.\ M.\ M)$.
(b)   Find the execution time of M as refined in part (a).

192   (Ackermann-Péter) Function ack of two natural variables is defined as follows.
$$ack\ 0\ n \;=\; n{+}1$$
$$ack\ (m{+}1)\ 0 \;=\; ack\ m\ 1$$
$$ack\ (m{+}1)\ (n{+}1) \;=\; ack\ m\ (ack\ (m{+}1)\ n)$$
(Historical note: Ackermann was the first to show a function that is not primitive-recursive. The function defined here, due to Péter, is also not primitive-recursive, and is simpler than the one defined by Ackermann.)
(a)   Suppose that functions and function application are not implemented expressions; in that case $n{:=}\ ack\ m\ n$ is not a program. Refine $n{:=}\ ack\ m\ n$.
(b)   Find a time bound. Hint: you may use function ack in your time bound.

193   Let n be a natural variable. Add time according to the recursive measure, and find a finite upper bound on the execution time of
$$P \;\Longleftarrow\; \textbf{if}\ n \geq 2\ \textbf{then}\ (n{:=}\ n{-}2.\ P.\ n{:=}\ n{+}1.\ P.\ n{:=}\ n{+}1)\ \textbf{else}\ ok$$

194   (roller-coaster) Let n be a natural variable. It is easy to prove
$$n'{=}1 \;\Longleftarrow\; \textbf{if}\ n{=}1\ \textbf{then}\ ok$$
$$\textbf{else}\ \ \textbf{if}\ even\ n\ \textbf{then}\ (n{:=}\ n/2.\ \ n'{=}1)$$
$$\textbf{else}\ (n{:=}\ 3n + 1.\ \ n'{=}1)$$
The problem is to find the execution time. Warning: this problem has never been solved.

195√   (Fibonacci numbers) The Fibonacci numbers fn are defined as follows.
$$f\ 0 = 0$$
$$f\ 1 = 1$$
$$f\ (n{+}2) = f\ n + f\ (n{+}1)$$
Write a program to find fn in time $log\ n$. Hint: see Exercise 267.

196   (Fibolucci numbers) Let a and b be integers. Then the Fibolucci numbers for a and b are
$$f\ 0 = 0$$
$$f\ 1 = 1$$
$$f\ (n{+}2) = a \times f\ n + b \times f\ (n{+}1)$$
(The Fibonacci numbers are Fibolucci numbers for 1 and 1 .) Given natural k , without using any list variables, write a program to compute
$$\Sigma n{:}\ 0,..k\cdot\ fn \times f(k{-}n)$$

197   (item count) Write a program to find the number of occurrences of a given item in a given list.

198   (duplicate count) Write a program to find how many items are duplicates (repeats) of earlier items

(a)   in a given sorted list.

(b)   in a given list.

199   (z-free subtext) Given a text, write a program to find the longest subtext that does not contain the letter `z .

200   (merge) Given two sorted lists, write a program to merge them into one sorted list.

201   (machine multiplication) Given two natural numbers, write a program to find their product using only addition, subtraction, doubling, halving, test for even, and test for zero, but not multiplication or division.

202   (machine division) Given two natural numbers, write a program to find their quotient using only addition, subtraction, doubling, halving, test for even, and test for zero, but not multiplication or division.

203   (machine squaring) Given a natural number, write a program to find its square using only addition, subtraction, doubling, halving, test for even, and test for zero, but not multiplication or division.

204   (longest sorted sublist) Write a program to find the length of a longest sorted sublist of a given list, where

(a)   the sublist must be consecutive items (a segment).

(b)   the sublist consists of items in their order of appearance in the given list, but not necessarily consecutively.

205   (almost sorted segment) An almost sorted list is a list in which at most one adjacent pair of elements is out of order. Write a program to find the length of a longest almost sorted segment of a given list.

206   (edit distance) Given two lists, write a program to find the minimum number of item insertions, item deletions, and item replacements to change one list into the other.

207 (ultimately periodic sequence) Let $f: int \rightarrow int$ be such that the sequence
$$x_0 = 0$$
$$x_{n+1} = f(x_n)$$
is ultimately periodic:
$$\exists p: nat+1 \cdot \exists n: nat \cdot x_n = x_{n+p}$$
The smallest positive p such that $\exists n: nat \cdot x_n = x_{n+p}$ is called the period. Write a program to find the period. Your program should use an amount of storage that is bounded by a constant, and not dependent on f.

208 (partitions) A list of positive integers is called a partition of natural number n if the sum of its items is n. Write a program to find

(a) a list of all partitions of a given natural n. For example, if $n=3$ then an acceptable answer is
$$[[3]; [1; 2]; [2; 1]; [1; 1; 1]]$$

(b) a list of all sorted partitions of a given natural n. For example, if $n=3$ then an acceptable answer is
$$[[3]; [1; 2]; [1; 1; 1]]$$

(c) the sorted list of all partitions of a given natural n. For example, if $n=3$ then the answer is
$$[[1; 1; 1]; [1; 2]; [2; 1]; [3]]$$

(d) the sorted list of all sorted partitions of a given natural n. For example, if $n=3$ then the answer is
$$[[1; 1; 1]; [1; 2]; [3]]$$

209 (largest true square) Write a program to find, within a boolean array, a largest square subarray consisting entirely of items with value $\top$.

210 (arithmetic) Let us represent a natural number as a list of naturals, each in the range $0,..b$ for some natural base $b>1$, in reverse order. For example, if $b=10$, then $[9; 2; 7]$ represents 729. Write programs for each of the following.

(a) Find the list representing a given natural in a given base.

(b) Given a base and two lists representing natural numbers, find the list representing their sum.

(c) Given a base and two lists representing natural numbers, find the list representing their difference. You may assume the first list represents a number greater than or equal to the number represented by the second list. What is the result if this is not so?

(d) Given a base and two lists representing natural numbers, find the list representing their product.

(e) Given a base and two lists representing natural numbers, find the lists representing their quotient and remainder.

211   Given a list of roots of a polynomial, write a program to find the list of coefficients of the polynomial.

212   (*P*-list) Given a non-empty list S of natural numbers, define a *P*-list as a non-empty list P of natural numbers such that each item of P is an index of S , and

$$\forall i: 1,..\#P\cdot\ P\,(i{-}1) < P\,i \le S\,(P\,(i{-}1))$$

Write a program to find the length of a longest *P*-list for a given list S .

213   (*J*-list) For natural number n , a *J*-list of order n is a list of $2n$ naturals in which each m: $0,..n$ occurs twice, and between the two occurrences of m there are m items.
(a)   Write a program that creates a *J*-list of order n if there is one, for given n .
(b)   For which n do *J*-lists exist?

214   (diminished *J*-list) For positive integer n , a diminished *J*-list of order n is a list of $2n{-}1$ naturals in which 0 occurs once and each m: $1,..n$ occurs twice, and between the two occurrences of m there are m items.
(a)   Write a program that creates a diminished *J*-list of order n if there is one, for given n .
(b)   For which n do diminished *J*-lists exist?

215   (greatest common divisor) Given two positive integers, write a program to find their greatest common divisor.

216   (least common multiple) Given two positive integers, write a program to find their least common multiple.

217   Given two integers (not necessarily positive ones) that are not both zero, write a program to find their greatest common divisor.

218   Given three positive integers, write a program to find their greatest common divisor. One method is to find the greatest common divisor of two of them, and then find the greatest common divisor of that and the third, but there is a better way.

219   (longest common prefix) A positive integer can be written as a sequence of decimal digits without leading zeros. Given two positive integers, write a program to find the number that is written as their longest common prefix of digits. For example, given 25621 and 2547 , the result is 25 . Hint: this question is about numbers, not about strings or lists.

220   (squash) Let L be a list variable assigned a non-empty list. Reassign it so that any run of two or more identical items is collapsed to a single item.

221   (museum) You are given natural n , rationals s and f (start and finish), and lists A, D:
        $[n*rat]$ (arrive and depart) such that
                $\forall i\cdot\ s \le Ai \le Di \le f$
        They represent a museum that opens at time s , is visited by n people with person i
        arriving at time Ai and departing at time Di and closes at time f . Write a program to find
        the total amount of time during which at least one person is inside the museum, and the
        average number of people in the museum during the time it is open, in time linear in n , if
(a)   list A is sorted.
(b)   list D is sorted.

222   (common items) Let A be a sorted list of different integers. Let B be another such list.
        Write a program to find the number of integers that occur in both lists.

223   (unique items) Let A be a sorted list of different integers. Let B be another such list.
        Write a program to find the sorted list of integers that occur in exactly one of A or B .

224   (smallest common item) Given two sorted lists having at least one item in common, write a
        program to find the smallest item occurring in both lists.

225   Given three sorted lists having at least one item common to all three, write a program to
        find the smallest item occurring in all three lists.

226   (rotation test) Given two lists, write a program to determine if one list is a rotation of the
        other. You may use item comparisons, but not list comparisons. Execution time should be
        linear in the length of the lists.

227   (smallest rotation) Given a text variable t , write a program to reassign t its alphabetically
        (lexicographically) smallest rotation. You may use character comparisons, but not text
        comparisons.

228   You are given a list variable L assigned a nonempty list. All changes to L must be via
        procedure $swap$, defined as
                $swap\ =\ \lambda i, j\colon\ 0,..\#L\cdot\ L:= i{\rightarrow}Lj\,|\,j{\rightarrow}Li\,|\,L$
(a)   Write a program to reassign L a new list obtained by rotating the old list one place to the
        right (the last item of the old list is the first item of the new).
(b)   (rotate) Given an integer r , write a program to reassign L a new list obtained by rotating
        the old list r places to the right. (If $r{<}0$, rotation is to the left $-r$ places.) Recursive
        execution time must be at most $\#L$.
(c)   (segment swap) Given an index p , swap the initial segment up to p with the final
        segment beginning at p .

229   Let n and p be natural variables. Write a program to solve

$$n{\geq}2 \;\Rightarrow\; p': 2^{2^{nat}} \;\wedge\; n{\leq}p'{<}n^2$$

Include a finite upper bound on the execution time, but it doesn't matter how small.

230   (greatest square under a histogram) You are given a histogram in the form of a list H of natural numbers. Write a program to find the longest segment of H in which the height (each item) is at least as large as the segment length.

231   (long texts) A particular computer has a hardware representation for texts less than n characters long, for some constant n . Longer texts must be represented in software as a list of short texts. (The long text represented is the catenation of the short texts.) A list of short texts is called "packed" if all items except possibly the last have maximum length. Write a program to pack a list of short texts without changing the long text represented.

232   (Knuth, Morris, Pratt)

(a)   Given list P , find list F such that for every index n of list P , Fn is the length of the longest list that is both a proper prefix and a proper suffix of P $[0;..n+1]$. Here is a program to find F .

> $A::$ ($i:= 0$. $F:= [\#P{*}0]$. $j:= 1$.
>> $B::$ **if** $j{\geq}\#P$ **then** ok
>>> **else** ($C::$ **if** $Pi{=}Pj$ **then** $i:= i{+}1$
>>>> **else** **if** $i{=}0$ **then** ok
>>>> **else** $(i:= F\,(i{-}1)$. $C)$.
>>> $F:= j{\rightarrow}i \mid F$.
>>> $j:= j{+}1$. B))

Find specifications A , B , and C so that A is the problem and the three refinements are theorems.

(b)   Given list S (subject), list P (pattern), and list F (as in part (a)), determine if P is a segment of S , and if so, where it occurs. Here is a program.

> $D::$ ($m:= 0$. $n:= 0$.
>> $E::$ **if** $m{=}\#P$ **then** $h:= n{-}\#P$
>>> **else** $F::$ **if** $n{=}\#S$ **then** $h:= \infty$
>>>> **else** **if** $Pm{=}Sn$ **then** $(m:= m{+}1$. $n:= n{+}1$. $E)$
>>>> **else** $G::$ **if** $m{=}0$ **then** $(n:= n{+}1$. $F)$
>>>>> **else** $(m:= F\,(m{-}1)$. $G)$)

Find specifications D , E , F , and G so that D is the problem and the four refinements are theorems.

──End of Program Theory

Programming Language

233   (nondeterministic assignment) Generalize the assignment notation $x:= e$ to allow the expression e to be a bunch, with the meaning that x is assigned an arbitrary element of the bunch. For example, $x:= nat$ assigns x an arbitrary natural number. Show the standard boolean notation for this form of assignment. Show what happens to the Substitution Law.

234   Suppose variable declaration is defined as
$$\textbf{var } x: T \cdot P \quad = \quad \exists x: undefined \cdot \exists x': T \cdot P$$
What are the characteristics of this sort of declaration? Look at the example $\textbf{var } x: int \cdot ok$.

235   What is wrong with defining local variable declaration as follows:
$$\textbf{var } x: T \cdot P \quad = \quad \forall x: T \cdot \exists x': T \cdot P$$

236   Suppose variable declaration with initialization is defined as
$$\textbf{var } x: T := e \quad = \quad \textbf{var } x: T \cdot x:= e$$
In what way does this differ from the definition given in Chapter 5?

237   The program
$$\textbf{var } x: nat \cdot x:= -1$$
introduces a local variable and then assigns it a value that is out of bounds. Is this program implementable? (Proof required.)

238   (frame problem) Suppose there is one global variable x, and we define $P = x'=0$. Can we prove
$$P \quad \Leftarrow \quad \textbf{var } y: nat \cdot y:= 0. \ P. \ x:= y$$
The problem is that y was not part of the state space where P was defined, so does P leave y unchanged? Hint: consider the definition of dependent composition. Is it being used properly?

239   Let the state variables be x, y, and z. Rewrite $\textbf{frame } x \cdot \top$ without using $\textbf{frame}$. Say in words what the final value of x is.

240   In a language with array element assignment, the program
$$x:= i. \ i:= A(i). \ A(i):= x$$
was written with the intention to swap the values of i and $A(i)$. Assume that all variables and array elements are of type nat, and that i has a value that is an index of A.
(a)   State the intended specification formally.
(b)   Find the exact precondition for which the program refines the intended specification.
(c)   Find the exact postcondition for which the program refines the intended specification.

241   In a language with array element assignment, what is the exact precondition for $A'(i')=1$ to be refined by $(A(A(i)):= 0.\ A(i):= 1.\ i:= 2)$?

242   (guarded command) In "Dijkstra's little language" there is a conditional program with the syntax

$$\textbf{if } b \rightarrow P \,[]\, c \rightarrow Q \textbf{ fi}$$

where b and c are boolean and P and Q are programs. It can be executed as follows. If exactly one of b and c is true initially, then the corresponding program is executed; if both b and c are true initially, then either one of P or Q (arbitrary choice) is executed; if neither b nor c is true initially, then execution is completely arbitrary.

(a)   Express this program in the notations of this book as succinctly as possible.

(b)   Refine this program using only the programming notations introduced in Chapter 4.

243   Prove

$$(R \Longleftarrow \textbf{repeat } P \textbf{ until } b) \wedge (W \Longleftarrow \textbf{while } \neg b \textbf{ do } P)$$
$$\Longleftarrow (R \Longleftarrow P.\ W) \wedge (W \Longleftarrow \textbf{if } b \textbf{ then } ok \textbf{ else } R)$$

244   Here is one way that we might consider defining the **for**-loop. Let j, n, k and m be integer expressions, and let i be a fresh name.

        for $i:= nil$ **do** $P \;=\; ok$

        for $i:= j$ **do** $P \;=\;$ (substitute j for i in P)

        for $i:= n;..k\,;\,k;..m$ **do** $P \;=\;$ **for** $i:= n;..k$ **do** $P.$ **for** $i:= k;..m$ **do** P

(a)   From this definition, what can we prove about **for** $i:= 0;..n$ **do** $n:= n+1$ where n is an integer variable?

(b)   What kinds of **for**-loop are in the programming languages you know?

245   (majority vote) The problem is to find, in a given list, the majority item (the item that occurs in more than half the places) if there is one. Letting L be the list and m be a variable whose final value is the majority item, prove that the following program solves the problem.

(a)   **var** e: $nat := 0 \cdot$

        for $i:= 0;..\#L$ **do**

            if $m = L\,i$ **then** $e:= e+1$

            else if $i = 2{\times}e$ **then** $(m:= L\,i.\ e:= e+1)$

            else ok

(b)   **var** s: $nat := 0 \cdot$

        for $i:= 0;..\#L$ **do**

            if $m = L\,i$ **then** ok

            else if $i = 2{\times}s$ **then** $m:= L\,i$

            else $s:= s+1$

246 We defined the programmed expression P **result** e with the axiom

$$x' = (P \textbf{ result } e) \;=\; P. \; x'{=}e$$

Why don't we define it instead with the axiom

$$x' = (P \textbf{ result } e) \;=\; P \Rightarrow x'{=}e'$$

247 Let a and b be rational variables. Define procedure P as

$$P \;=\; \lambda x, y\colon rat\cdot \textbf{ if } x{=}0 \textbf{ then } a{:=}x \textbf{ else } (a{:=}x{\times}y.\; a{:=}a{\times}y)$$

(a)   What is the exact precondition for $a'{=}b'$ to be refined by $P\,a\,(1/b)$?

(b)   Discuss the difference between "eager" and "lazy" evaluation of arguments as they affect both the theory of programming and programming language implementation.

248 Here is a procedure applied to an argument.

$$(\lambda x\colon int\cdot a{:=}x.\; b{:=}x)\,(a{+}1)$$

Suppose, by mistake, we replace both occurrences of x in the body with the argument. What do we get? What should we get? (This mistake is known as "call-by-name".)

249 "Call-by-value-result" describes a parameter that gets its initial value from an argument, is then a local variable, and gives its final value back to the argument, which therefore must be a variable. Define "call-by-value-result" formally. Discuss its merits and demerits.

250 We defined **wait until** $w \;=\; t{:=}\,max\,t\,w$ where t is an extended integer time variable, and w is an integer expression.

(a)$\surd$ Prove **wait until** $w \;\Longleftarrow\; \textbf{if } t{\geq}w \textbf{ then } ok \textbf{ else } (t{:=}t{+}1.\; \textbf{wait until } w)$

(b)   Now suppose that t is an extended rational time variable, and w is an extended rational expression. Redefine **wait until** w appropriately, and refine it using the recursive time measure.

251 The specification **wait** w where w is a length of time, not an instant of time, describes a delay in execution of time w . Formalize and implement it using the recursive time measure and

(a)   an extended integer time variable.

(b)   an extended rational time variable.

252 We propose to define a new programming connective $P \blacklozenge Q$. What properties of $\blacklozenge$ are essential? Why?

——————————————————————————————————End of Programming Language

Recursive Definition

253   Prove $\neg -1: nat$. Hint: You will need induction.

254   Prove that the square of an odd natural number is odd, and the square of an even natural
        number is even.

255   Prove $\forall n: nat \cdot Pn = \forall n: nat \cdot \forall m: 0,..n \cdot Pm$

256   Prove that if n is an odd natural number, then its square is $8m + 1$ for some natural m .

257   (stamps) You have an unlimited supply of 3¢ stamps and 5¢ stamps. Prove that you can
        compose any amount of postage of 8¢ or more.

258   Prove that every positive integer is a product of primes. By "product" we mean the result
        of multiplying together any natural number of (not necessarily distinct) numbers.

259   Here is an argument to "prove" that in any group of people, all the people are the same age.
        The "proof" is by induction on the size of groups. The induction base is that in any group
        of size 1 , clearly all the people are the same age. Or we could equally well use groups of
        size 0 as the induction base. The induction hypothesis is, of course, to assume that in any
        group of size n , all the people are the same age. Now consider a group of size $n+1$. Let
        its people be p_0, p_1, ..., p_n . By the induction hypothesis, in the subgroup p_0, p_1, ...,
        p_{n-1} of size n , all the people are the same age; to be specific, they are all the same age as
        p_1 . And in the subgroup p_1, p_2, ..., p_n of size n , all the people are the same age;
        again, they are the same age as p_1 . Hence all $n+1$ people are the same age. Formalize
        this argument and find the flaw.

260   Chapter 6 gives four predicate versions of *nat* induction. Prove that they are equivalent.

261   Give axioms for *nat* construction and induction in which the constructors are 0 , 1 , and
        addition.

262   Here are a construction axiom and an induction axiom for bunch *bad* .
                $(\S n: nat \cdot \neg n: bad) : bad$
                $(\S n: nat \cdot \neg n: B) : B \implies bad: B$
(a)   Are these axioms consistent?
(b)   Can the fixed-point equation
                $bad = \S n: nat \cdot \neg n: bad$
        be proven from them?

263   Prove the following; quantifications are over *nat* .

(a) $\neg\exists i, j \cdot j \neq 0 \wedge 2^{1/2} = i/j$ The square root of 2 is irrational.

(b) $\forall n \cdot (\Sigma i: 0,..n \cdot 1) = n$

(c) $\forall n \cdot (\Sigma i: 0,..n \cdot i) = n \times (n-1)/2$

(d) $\forall n \cdot (\Sigma i: 0,..n \cdot i^3) = (\Sigma i: 0,..n \cdot i)^2$

(e) $\forall n \cdot (\Sigma i: 0,..n \cdot 2^i) + 1 = 2^n$

(f) $\forall n \cdot (\Sigma i: 0,..n \cdot (-2)^i) = (1 - (-2)^n)/3$

(g) $\forall n \cdot n \geq 10 \Rightarrow 2^n > n^3$

(h) $\forall a, d \cdot \exists q, r \cdot d \neq 0 \Rightarrow r < d \wedge a = qd + r$

264   Prove $nat = 0,..\infty$.

265   (rulers) Rulers are formed as follows. A vertical stroke | is a ruler. If you append a horizontal stroke — and then a vertical stroke | to a ruler you get another ruler. Thus the first few rulers are |, |—|, |—|—|, |—|—|—| , and so on. No two rulers formed this way are equal. There are no other rulers. What axioms are needed to define bunch *ruler* consisting of all and only the rulers?

266   Function f is called monotonic if $i \leq j \Rightarrow fi \leq fj$.

(a)   Prove f is monotonic if and only if $fi < fj \Rightarrow i < j$.

(b)   Let $f: int \rightarrow int$. Prove f is monotonic if and only if $fi \leq f(i+1)$.

(c)   Let $f: nat \rightarrow nat$ be such that $\forall n \cdot ffn < f(n+1)$. Prove f is the identity function. Hints: First prove $\forall n \cdot n \leq fn$. Then prove f is monotonic. Then prove $\forall n \cdot fn \leq n$.

267   The Fibonacci numbers $f n$ are defined as follows.

$$f0 = 0$$
$$f1 = 1$$
$$f(n+2) = fn + f(n+1)$$

Prove

(a) $f(gcd\ n\ m) = gcd\ (f\ n)\ (f\ m)$

where *gcd* is the greatest common divisor.

(b) $f n \times f(n+2) = f(n+1)^2 - (-1)^n$

(c) $f(n+m+1) = fn \times fm + f(n+1) \times f(m+1)$

(d) $f(n+m+2) = fn \times f(m+1) + f(n+1) \times fm + f(n+1) \times f(m+1)$

(e) $f(2n+1) = fn^2 + f(n+1)^2$

(f) $f(2n+2) = 2 \times fn \times f(n+1) + f(n+1)^2$

268   What is the smallest bunch satisfying

(a) $B = 0, 2B + 1$

(b) $B = 2, B \times B$

269   What elements can be proven in P from the axiom $P = 1, x, -P, P+P, P{\times}P$? Prove
            $2x^2-1: P$

270   Bunch *this* is defined by the construction and induction axioms
            $2, 2{\times}this:\ this$
            $2, 2{\times}B:\ B\ \Rightarrow\ this: B$
        Bunch *that* is defined by the construction and induction axioms
            $2, that{\times}that:\ that$
            $2, B{\times}B:\ B\ \Rightarrow\ that: B$
        Prove *this = that* .

271   Express the bunch containing the integer powers of 2 , that is 2^{int} , without using
        exponentiation.

272   Let n be a natural number. From the fixed-point equation
            $ply = n,\ ply+ply$
        we obtain a sequence of bunches ply_i by recursive construction.
(a)   State ply_i formally (no proof needed).
(b)   State ply_i in English.
(c)   What is ply_∞ ?

273   For each of the following fixed-point equations, what does recursive construction yield?
        Does it satisfy the fixed-point equation?
(a) $M = [*int], [*M]$
(b) $T = [nil], [T; int; T]$
(c) $A = bool, rat, char, [*A]$

274   Let $A{\rightarrow}B$ be the difference between bunch A and bunch B defined by the axiom
            $x: A{\rightarrow}B\ =\ x: A\ \wedge\neg\, x: B$
        For each of the following fixed-point equations, what does recursive construction yield?
        Does it satisfy the fixed-point equation?
(a) $Q = nat{\rightarrow}(Q+3)$
(b) $D = 0, (D+1){\rightarrow}(D-1)$

275   For each of the following fixed-point equations, what does recursive construction yield?
        Does it satisfy the fixed-point equation?
(a) $P = \S n: nat\cdot\ n=0 \wedge P=null \vee n: P+1$
(b) $Q = \S x: xnat\cdot\ x=0 \wedge Q=null \vee x: Q+1$

276   Here is a pair of mutually recursive equations.

$$even \;=\; 0,\, odd{+}1$$
$$odd \;=\; even{+}1$$

(a)   What does recursive construction yield? Show the construction.

(b)   Are further axioms needed to ensure that *even* consists of only the even naturals, and *odd* consists of only the odd naturals? If so, what axioms?

277   Here is a strange way to define the even natural numbers.

$$even \;=\; \S n\!: nat\cdot \,\neg\, n\!: even{+}1$$

(a)   What does recursive construction yield?

(b)   Is an induction axiom needed to ensure that *even* consists of only the even naturals?

278   What elements are constructed by the axiom 0, 1–*few*: *few* ?

279   Investigate the fixed-point equation

$$strange \;=\; \S n\!: nat\cdot \,\forall m\!: strange\cdot \,\neg\, m{+}1\!: n{\times}nat$$

280   Here are the construction and induction axioms for lists of items of type T .

$$[nil],\ [T],\ list{+}list\!: list$$
$$[nil],\ [T],\ L{+}L\!: L \;\Longrightarrow\; list\!: L$$

Prove $list = [*T]$.

281   Let R be a relation of naturals $R\!: nat{\to}nat{\to}bool$ that is monotonic in its second parameter

$$\forall i, j\cdot\ R\,i\,j \Rightarrow R\,i\,(j{+}1)$$

Prove

$$\exists i\cdot\ \forall j\cdot\ R\,i\,j \;=\; \forall j\cdot\ \exists i\cdot\ R\,i\,j$$

282   (decimal-point numbers) Using recursive data definition, define the bunch of all decimal-point numbers. These are the rationals that can be expressed as a finite string of decimal digits containing a decimal point.   Note: you are defining a bunch of numbers, not a bunch of texts.

283   Let *truer* be a bunch of strings of booleans defined by the construction and induction axioms

$$\top,\ \bot;truer;truer\!:\ truer$$
$$\top,\ \bot;B;B\!:\ B \;\Rightarrow\; truer\!: B$$

Given a string of booleans, write a program to determine if the string is in *truer* .

284   (Backus-Naur Form) Backus-Naur Form is a grammatical formalism in which grammatical
        rules are written as in the following example.

        $\langle exp \rangle ::= \langle exp \rangle + \langle exp \rangle \mid \langle exp \rangle \times \langle exp \rangle \mid 0 \mid 1$

        In our formalism, it would be written

        $exp = exp; "+"; exp, \ exp; "\times"; exp, \ "0", \ "1"$

        In a similar fashion, write axioms to define each of the following.

(a)   palindromes: texts that read the same forward and backward. Use a two-symbol alphabet.

(b)   palindromes of odd length.

(c)   all texts consisting of "a"s followed by the same number of "b"s.

(d)   all texts consisting of "a"s followed by at least as many "b"s.

285   Chapter 6 defines program zap by the fixed-point equation

        $zap = \textbf{if } x=0 \textbf{ then } y:= 0 \textbf{ else } (x:= x-1. \ t:= t+1. \ zap)$

(a)   Prove $zap \implies x \geq 0 \implies x'=y'=0 \wedge t' = t+x$.

(b)   Prove $x \geq 0 \wedge x'=y'=0 \wedge t' = t+x \implies zap$.

(c)   What axiom is needed to make zap the weakest fixed-point?

(d)   What axiom is needed to make zap the strongest fixed-point?

(e)   Chapter 6 gives six solutions to this equation. Find more solutions. Hint: strange things
        can happen at time ∞ .

286   Let all variables be integer. Add recursive time and find a fixed-point of

(a) $run = \textbf{if } i \geq 0 \textbf{ then } (i:= i-1. \ run. \ i:= i+1) \textbf{ else } ok$

(b) $walk = \textbf{if } i \geq 0 \textbf{ then } (i:= i-2. \ walk. \ i:= i+1. \ walk. \ i:= i+1) \textbf{ else } ok$

(c) $crawl = \textbf{if } i \geq 0 \textbf{ then } (i:= i-1. \ crawl. \ i:= i+2. \ crawl. \ i:= i-1) \textbf{ else } ok$

(d) $inc = ok \vee (i:= i+1. \ inc)$

(e) $what = \textbf{if } even \ i \textbf{ then } i:= i/2 \textbf{ else } i:= i+1.$
            $\textbf{if } i=1 \textbf{ then } ok \textbf{ else } what$

(f) $sqr = \textbf{if } i=0 \textbf{ then } ok \textbf{ else } (s:= s + 2i - 1. \ i:= i-1. \ sqr)$

(g) $fac = \textbf{if } i=0 \textbf{ then } f:= 1 \textbf{ else } (i:= i-1. \ fac. \ i:= i+1. \ f:= f \times i)$

(h) $chs = \textbf{if } a=b \textbf{ then } c:= 1 \textbf{ else } (a:= a-1. \ chs. \ a:= a+1. \ c:= c \times a/(a-b) \ )$

287   Investigate how recursive construction is affected when we start with

(a) $t' = \infty$

(b) $t:= \infty$

288   Let x be an integer variable. Using the recursive time measure, add time and then find the
        strongest implementable specifications P and Q that you can find for which

        $P \impliedby x' \geq 0. \ Q$

        $Q \impliedby \textbf{if } x=0 \textbf{ then } ok \textbf{ else } (x:= x-1. \ Q)$

        Assume that $x' \geq 0$ takes no time.

289   Let x be an integer variable.

(a)   Using the recursive time measure, add time and then find the strongest implementable specification S that you can find for which

$$S \quad \Longleftarrow \quad \textbf{if } x=0 \textbf{ then } ok$$
$$\textbf{else if } x>0 \textbf{ then } (x:=x-1. \;\; S)$$
$$\textbf{else } (x' \geq 0. \;\; S)$$

Assume that $x' \geq 0$ takes no time.

(b)   What do we get from recursive construction starting with $t' \geq t$?

290   Prove the laws of Refinement by Steps and Refinement by Parts for **while**-loops.

291   Prove

(a) $\textbf{repeat } P \textbf{ until } b \;\; = \;\; P. \;\; \textbf{while } \neg b \textbf{ do } P$

(b) $\textbf{while } b \textbf{ do } P \;\; = \;\; \textbf{if } b \textbf{ then repeat } P \textbf{ until } \neg b \textbf{ else } ok$

(c) $(\forall \sigma, \sigma' \cdot (R = \textbf{repeat } P \textbf{ until } b)) \wedge (\forall \sigma, \sigma' \cdot (W = \textbf{while } \neg b \textbf{ do } P))$
             $= \;\; (\forall \sigma, \sigma' \cdot (R = P. \;\; W)) \wedge (\forall \sigma, \sigma' \cdot (W = \textbf{if } b \textbf{ then } ok \textbf{ else } R))$

292   Let P: $nat{\rightarrow}bool$.

(a)   Define quantifier $FIRST$ so that $FIRST \; m$: $nat \cdot Pm$ is the smallest natural m such that Pm , and ∞ if there is none.

(b)   Prove $n:= FIRST \; m$: $nat \cdot Pm \quad \Longleftarrow \quad n:= 0. \;\; \textbf{while } \neg Pn \textbf{ do } n:= n+1$.

293   In real variable x , consider the equation

$$P \;\; = \;\; P. \;\; x:= x^2$$

(a)   Find 7 distinct solutions for P .

(b)   Which solution does recursive construction give starting from $\top$? Is it the weakest solution?

(c)   If we add a time variable, which solution does recursive construction give starting from $t' \geq t$? Is it a strongest implementable solution?

(d)   Now let x be an integer variable, and redo the question.

294   Let the state consist of boolean variables b and c . Let

$$W \;\; = \;\; \textbf{if } b \textbf{ then } (P. \;\; W) \textbf{ else } ok$$
$$X \;\; = \;\; \textbf{if } b \vee c \textbf{ then } (P. \;\; X) \textbf{ else } ok$$

(a)   Find a counterexample to $W. \;\; X \;\; = \;\; X$.

(b)   Now let W and X be the weakest solutions of those equations, and prove $W. \;\; X \;\; = \;\; X$.

295   Show that we can define *nat* by fixed-point construction together with

(a) $\forall n: nat \cdot \ 0 \le n < n{+}1$

(b) $\exists m: nat \cdot \ \forall n: nat \cdot \ m \le n < n{+}1$

296√   Suppose we define *nat* by ordinary construction and induction.

            0, *nat*+1: *nat*

            0, *B*+1: *B* $\Rightarrow$ *nat*: *B*

    Prove that fixed-point construction and induction

            nat = 0, *nat*+1

            B = 0, *B*+1 $\Rightarrow$ *nat*: *B*

    are theorems.

297   (fixed-point induction theorem) Suppose we define *nat* by fixed-point construction and induction.

            nat = 0, *nat*+1

            B = 0, *B*+1 $\Rightarrow$ *nat*: *B*

    Prove that ordinary construction and induction

            0, *nat*+1: *nat*

            (0, *B*+1: *B*) $\Rightarrow$ (*nat*: *B*)

    are theorems. Warning: this is hard, and requires the use of limits.

298   Suppose we define **while** *b* **do** *P* by ordinary construction and induction.

            if *b* **then** (*P*. **while** *b* **do** *P*) **else** *ok* $\Longleftarrow$ **while** *b* **do** *P*

            $\forall \sigma, \sigma' \cdot$(**if** *b* **then** (*P*. *W*) **else** *ok* $\Longleftarrow$ *W*) $\Longrightarrow$ $\forall \sigma, \sigma' \cdot$(**while** *b* **do** *P* $\Longleftarrow$ *W*)

    Prove that fixed-point construction and induction

            while *b* **do** *P* = **if** *b* **then** (*P*. **while** *b* **do** *P*) **else** *ok*

            $\forall \sigma, \sigma' \cdot$ (*W* = **if** *b* **then** (*P*. *W*) **else** *ok*) $\Longrightarrow$ $\forall \sigma, \sigma' \cdot$ (**while** *b* **do** *P* $\Longleftarrow$ *W*)

    are theorems.

299   Suppose we define **while** *b* **do** *P* by fixed-point construction and induction.

            while *b* **do** *P* = **if** *b* **then** (*P*. **while** *b* **do** *P*) **else** *ok*

            $\forall \sigma, \sigma' \cdot$ (*W* = **if** *b* **then** (*P*. *W*) **else** *ok*) $\Longrightarrow$ $\forall \sigma, \sigma' \cdot$ (**while** *b* **do** *P* $\Longleftarrow$ *W*)

    Prove that ordinary construction and induction

            if *b* **then** (*P*. **while** *b* **do** *P*) **else** *ok* $\Longleftarrow$ **while** *b* **do** *P*

            $\forall \sigma, \sigma' \cdot$(**if** *b* **then** (*P*. *W*) **else** *ok* $\Longleftarrow$ *W*) $\Longrightarrow$ $\forall \sigma, \sigma' \cdot$(**while** *b* **do** *P* $\Longleftarrow$ *W*)

    are theorems. Warning: this is hard, and requires the use of limits.

    ──End of Recursive Definition

Theory Design and Implementation

300   Implement data-stack theory to make the two boolean expressions
        pop empty = empty
        top empty = 0
antitheorems.

301   Prove that the following definitions implement the simple data-stack theory.
        stack = [*nil*], [*stack*; *X*]
        push = λ*s*: *stack*· λ*x*: *X*· [*s*; *x*]
        pop = λ*s*: *stack*· *s* 0
        top = λ*s*: *stack*· *s* 1

302   (weak data-stack) In Chapter 7 we designed a program-stack theory so weak that we could
       add axioms to count pushes and pops without inconsistency. Design a similarly weak data-
       stack theory.

303   (data-queue implementation) Implement the data-queue theory presented in Chapter 7.

304   (slip) The slip data structure introduces the names *end* and *slip* with the following
       axioms:
        end: *slip*
        slip = [*T*; *slip*]
       where *T* is some given type. Can you implement it?

305   Prove that the program-stack implementation given in Chapter 7 satisfies the program-stack
       axioms.

306   Implement weak program-stack theory as follows: the implementer's variable is a list that
       grows and never shrinks. A popped item must be marked as garbage.

307   You are given a program-stack. Can you write a program composed from the programs
        push `A    *push* `B   *push* `C    *push* `D   *push* `E
       in that order, with the programs *print top* and *pop* interspersed wherever needed as many
       times as needed, to obtain the following output?
(a)   B D E C A
(b)   B C D E A
(c)   C A D E B
(d)   A B E C D
(e)   A B C D E

308   (brackets) You are given a text t of characters drawn from the alphabet `x, `(, `), `[, `] .
       Write a program to determine if t is well-bracketed, with the brackets properly paired and
       nested.

309   (limited-stack) A stack, according to our axioms, has an unlimited capacity to have items
       pushed onto it. A limited-stack is a similar but different data structure with a limited
       capacity to have items pushed onto it. It has the same names as stack theory, plus two
       more: *limit*: *nat* and *full* (like *empty*) or *isfull* (like *isempty*).
(a)   Design axioms for a limited-data-stack.
(b)   Design axioms for a limited-program-stack.
(c)   Can the *limit* be 0 ?

310   (limited-queue) A queue, according to our axioms, has an unlimited capacity to have items
       joined onto it. A limited-queue is a similar but different data structure with a limited
       capacity to have items joined onto it. It has the same names as queue theory, plus two
       more: *limitq*: *nat* and *fullq* (like *emptyq*) or *isfullq* (like *isemptyq*).
(a)   Design axioms for a limited-data-queue.
(b)   Design axioms for a limited-program-queue.
(c)   Can the *limit* be 0 ?

311   You are given a program-queue. Can you write a program composed from the programs
                join `A    *join* `B   *join* `C    *join* `D   *join* `E
       in that order, with the programs *print front* and *leave* interspersed wherever needed as
       many times as needed, to obtain the following output?
(a)   B D E C A
(b)   B C D E A
(c)   C A D E B
(d)   A B E C D
(e)   A B C D E

312   Each of the program theories provides a single, anonymous instance of a data structure.
       How can a program theory be made to provide many instances of a data structure, like data
       theories do?

313   (circular list) Design axioms for a circular list. There should be operations to create an
       empty list, to move along one position in the list (the first item comes after the last, in
       circular fashion), to insert an item at the current position, to delete the current item, and to
       give the current item.

314   (resettable variable) A resettable variable is defined as follows. There are three new names: *value* (of type X), *set* (a procedure with one parameter of type X), and *reset* (a program). Here are the axioms:

$$value'=x \Leftarrow set\ x$$
$$value'=value \Leftarrow set\ x.\ reset$$
$$reset.\ reset = reset$$

Implement this data structure, with proof.

315   A particular program-list has the following operations:
- the operation *mkempty* makes the list empty
- the operation *extend x* catenates item x to the end of the list
- the operation *swap i j* swaps the items at indexes i and j
- the expression *length* tells the length of the list
- the expression *item i* tells the item at index i

(a)   Write axioms to define this program-list.

(b)   Implement this program-list, with proof.

316   (linear algebra) Design a theory of linear algebra. It should include scalar, vector, and matrix sums, products, and inner products. Implement the theory, with proof.

317   (leafy tree) A leafy tree is a tree with information residing only at the leaves. Design appropriate axioms for a binary leafy data-tree.

318   A tree can be implemented by listing its items in breadth order.

(a)   Represent a binary tree by a list of its items such that the root is at index 0 and the left and right subtrees of an item at index n are rooted at indexes $2n+1$ and $2n+2$.

(b)   Generalize this implementation to trees in which each item can have at most k branches for arbitrary (but fixed) k .

319   (hybrid-tree) Chapter 7 presented data-tree theory and program-tree theory. Design a hybrid-tree theory in which there is only one tree structure, so it can be an implementer's variable with program operations on it, but there can be many pointers into the tree, so they are data-pointers (they may be data-stacks).

320   (heap) A heap is a tree with the property that the root is the largest item and the subtrees are heaps.

(a)   Specify the heap property formally.

(b)   Write a function *heapgraft* that makes a heap from two given heaps and a new item. It may make use of *graft* , and may rearrange the items as necessary to produce a heap.

321   (leaf count) Write a program to count the number of leaves in a tree.

322   (binary search tree) A binary search tree is a binary tree with the property that all items in
        the left subtree are less than the root item, all items in the right subtree are greater than the
        root item, and the subtrees are also binary search trees.
(a)   Specify the binary search tree property formally.
(b)   How many binary search trees are there with three items?
(c)   How many binary search trees are there with three distinct items?
(d)   Write a program to find an item in a binary search tree.
(e)   Write a program to add an item to a binary search tree as a new leaf.
(f)   Write a program to make a list of the items in a binary search tree in order.
(g)   Write a program to determine whether two binary search trees have the same items.

323   (insertion list) An insertion list is a data structure similar to a list, but with an associated
        insertion point.

$$[...; \; 4 \;\; ; 7 \; ; 1 \; ; 0 \; ; 3 \; ; 8 \; ; 9 \; ; 2 \; ; 5 \; ; ...]$$
$$\uparrow$$
insertion point

        insert puts an item at the insertion point (between two existing items), leaving the insertion
        point at its right. *erase* removes the item to the left of the insertion point, closing up the
        list. *item* gives the item to the left of the insertion point. *forward* moves the insertion
        point one item to the right. *back* moves the insertion point one item to the left.
(a)   Design axioms for a doubly-infinite data-insertion list.
(b)   Design axioms for a doubly-infinite program-insertion list.
(c)   Design axioms for a finite data-insertion list.
(d)   Design axioms for a finite program-insertion list.

324   A theory provides three names: *zero* , *increase* , and *inquire* . It is presented by an
        implementation. Let u: *bool* be the user's variable, and let v: *nat* be the implementer's
        variable. The axioms are

            zero $=$ $v := 0$
            increase $=$ $v := v+1$
            inquire $=$ $u := even \; v$

        Use data transformation to replace v with w: *bool* according to the transformer
(a)√ $w \; = \; even \; v$
(b) $\top$
(c) $\bot$ (this isn't a data transformer, since $\forall w \cdot \; \exists v \cdot \; \bot$ isn't a theorem, but apply it
        anyway to see what happens)

325   A theory provides three names: *set* , *flip* , and *ask* . It is presented by an implementation. Let *u*: *bool* be the user's variable, and let *v*: *bool* be the implementer's variable. The axioms are

$$set \;=\; v:= \top$$
$$flip \;=\; v:= \neg v$$
$$ask \;=\; u:= v$$

(a)√   Replace *v* with *w*: *nat* according to the data transformer *v* = *even w* .

(b)   Replace *v* with *w*: *nat* according to the data transformer $(w=0 \Rightarrow v) \land (w=1 \Rightarrow \neg v)$. Is anything wrong?

(c)   Replace *v* with *w*: *nat* according to $(v \Rightarrow w=0) \land (\neg v \Rightarrow w=1)$. Is anything wrong?

326   Maintain a natural variable on which the following requests are made:
• make it equal to a given natural *n*
• assign to boolean variable *p* to say whether it is prime
If we let *m* be the natural variable, we can specify the two problems, and solve them, very easily as follows:

$$m:= n$$
$$p:= prime\ m$$

assuming *prime* is suitably defined. If *prime* is an expensive operation and requests to know whether *m* is prime are more frequent than requests to change the value of *m* , we can improve the solution. Using data transformation, find a better solution. Show the transformation formally.

327√   (take a number) Maintain a list of natural numbers standing for those that are "in use". The three operations are:
• make the list empty (for initialization)
• assign to variable *n* a number not currently in use, and add this number to the list (it is now in use)
• given a number *n* that is currently in use, remove it from the list (it is now no longer in use, and it can be reused later)

328√   (parsing) Define *E* as a bunch of strings of texts satisfying the fixed-point equation

$$E \;=\; \text{"x"}, \ \text{"if"};\ E;\ \text{"then"};\ E;\ \text{"else"};\ E$$

Given a string *s* of texts, write a program to determine if *s*: *E* .

329   (sparse array) An array *A*: [*[*rat*]] is said to be sparse if many of its items are 0 . We can represent such an array compactly as a list of triples [*i*; *j*; *x*] of all nonzero items $A\ i\ j = x \neq 0$. Using this idea, find a data transformer and transform the programs

(a) $A:= [100*[100*0]]$

(b) $i:= A\ i\ j$

(c) $A:= (i;j)\!\rightarrow\!j\ |\ A$

Concurrency

330   Redefine $P\|Q$ so that if P and Q agree on a changed value for a variable, then it has that final value, and if they disagree on a changed value for a variable, then its final value is

(a)   arbitrary.

(b)   one of the two changed values.

331   Prove $x:=y \| x:=z \;=\; \textbf{if } x=y \textbf{ then } x:=z \textbf{ else } \textbf{ if } x=z \textbf{ then } x:=y \textbf{ else } (x:=y \| x:=z)$

332   Prove $x:=x+1 \| x:=x-1 \;=\; \textbf{var } y \cdot \; x:=y$

333   Let x, y, and z be boolean variables. Simplify
$$x:=x \wedge z \;\|\; y:=y \wedge \neg z \;\|\; x:=x \wedge \neg z \;\|\; y:=y \wedge z$$

334   Let x and y be integer variables. Without using $\|$, express
$$x:=x+1 \;\|\; \textbf{if } x=0 \textbf{ then } y:=1 \textbf{ else } ok$$

335   Let b be a boolean variable. Define
$$loop \;=\; \textbf{if } b \textbf{ then } loop \textbf{ else } ok$$
Add a time variable, and then without using $\|$, express
$$b:=\bot \;\|\; loop$$

336   Let $w: 0,..4$ and $z: 0, 1$ be variables. Without using $\|$, express
$$w:= 2 \times max\,(div\ w\ 2)\ z \;+\; max\,(mod\ w\ 2)\ (1-z)$$
$$\| \qquad w:= 2 \times max\,(div\ w\ 2)\ (1-z) \;+\; max\,(mod\ w\ 2)\ z$$

337   Consider a language having both array element assignment and list concurrency. Express
$$Ai:= x \;\|\; Aj:= y$$
without using array element assignment or independent composition. Cases to consider: $i=j$, $Ai=x$, $Aj=y$.

338   (n-switch) An n-switch has n boolean inputs and one boolean output. The output changes whenever an odd number of inputs change. Design a circuit.

339   (double-up switch) A double-up switch has two boolean inputs and one boolean output. The output changes whenever the inputs become both $\top$. (Note: the output does not change if the inputs remain both $\top$; at least one input must change for the output to change.) Design a circuit.

340√ (security switch) A security switch has two boolean inputs and one boolean output. The output changes when both inputs have changed. More precisely, the output changes when both inputs differ from what they were the previous time the output changed. Design a circuit.

341   (double-change switch) A double-change switch has two boolean inputs and one boolean output. The output changes when both inputs have changed at least once each since the last time the output changed. (Note: one of the inputs may have changed back to its previous value when the other input changes for the first time.) Design a circuit.

342   (digital watch) A digital watch circuit has two boolean inputs: the mode button M , and the advance button A . It has one integer output: the display D . (In a real watch the display is a list of bits to control the line segments in the digits, and the digits form several integers, but for simplicity we will consider the output to be a single integer.) There are two modes, and we change between them by pressing the mode button. In time-mode, each cycle of the internal clock (a quartz crystal) adds 1 to the display, and pressing the advance button does nothing. In set-mode, each press of the advance button adds 1 to the display. (This method of setting a watch is obviously inadequate, but again we are keeping the question simple.) Design a circuit.

343   If we ignore time, then
$$x := 3. \ y := 4 \ = \ x := 3 \parallel y := 4$$
Some dependent compositions could be executed in parallel if we ignore time. But the time for $P.Q$ is the sum of the times for P and Q , and that forces the execution to be sequential.
$$t := t+1. \ t := t+2 \ = \ t := t+3$$
Likewise some independent compositions could be executed sequentially, ignoring time. But the time for $P \parallel Q$ is the maximum of the times for P and Q , and that forces the execution to be parallel.
$$t := t+1 \parallel t := t+2 \ = \ t := t+2$$
Invent another form of composition, intermediate between dependent and independent composition, whose execution is sequential to the extent necessary, and parallel to the extent possible. Warning: this is a research question.

344   The following program searches for the first number h: $0,..n$ with property p .
$$h := n.$$
for $i := 0;..n$ **do if** $p \ i \wedge i{<}h$ **then** $h := i$ **else** ok
Show how all the $p \ i$ can be evaluated concurrently.

345   (sieve) Given variable p: $[n*bool]$:= $[\bot; \bot; (n-2)*\top]$, the following program is the seive
       of Eratosthenes for determining if a number is prime.

>   **for** i:= $2;..ceil\ (n^{1/2})$ **do**
>
>> **if** $p\ i$ **then for** j:= $i;..ceil\ (n/i)$ **do** p:= $(j{\times}i){\to}\bot\ |\ p$
>>
>> **else** ok

(a)   Find all the concurrency you can in this program. State your answer by drawing the
       execution pattern.

(b)   What is the execution time, as a function of n, with maximum concurrency?
                                                                        ——End of Concurrency

Communication

346   Many programming languages require a variable for input, with a syntax such as **read** x.
       Define this form of input formally. When is it more convenient than the input described in
       Chapter 9? When is it less convenient?

347   Simplify $c!\ 2\ \|\ c!\ 3$.

348   Write a program to print the sequence of natural numbers, one per time unit.

349   Write a program to repeatedly print the current time, up until some given time.

350   (T-lists) Let us call a list L: $[*({`}a, {`}b, {`}c)]$ a T-list if no two adjacent nonempty segments
       are identical:

$$\neg\exists i, j, k\cdot\ 0{\leq}i{<}j{<}k{\leq}\#L\ \wedge\ L\ [i;..j] = L\ [j;..k]$$

       Write a program to output all T-lists in alphabetical order. (The mathematician Thue proved
       that there are infinitely many T-lists.)

351   (reformat) Write a program to read, reformat, and write a sequence of characters. The
       input includes a line-break character at arbitrary places; the output should include a line-
       break character just after each semicolon. Whenever the input includes two consecutive
       stars, or two stars separated only by line-breaks, the output should replace the two stars by
       an up-arrow. Other than that, the output should be identical to the input. Both input and
       output end with a special end-character.

352   According to the definition of programmed data given in Chapter 5, what happens to any
       output that occurs in the program part of programmed data? Can input be read and used?
       What happens to it?

353   (Huffman code) You are given a finite set of messages, and for each message, the probability of its occurrence.

(a)   Write a program to find a code consisting of a sequence of 0s and 1s for each message. It must be possible to unambiguously decode any sequence of 0s and 1s into a sequence of messages, and the average code length (according to message frequency) must be minimum.

(b)   Write the accompanying program to produce the decoder for the codes produced in part (a).

354   (matrix multiplication) Write a program to multiply two $n \times n$ matrices that uses n^2 processes, with $2n^2$ local channels, with execution time n.

355   (coin weights) You are given some coins, all of which have a standard weight except possibly for one of them, which may be lighter or heavier than the standard. You are also given a balance scale, and as many more standard coins as you need. Write a program to determine whether there is a nonstandard coin, and if so which, and whether it is light or heavy, in the minimum number of weighings.

356   How should "deterministic" and "nondeterministic" be defined in the presence of channels?

357   From the fixed-point equation
$$twos \;=\; c!\,2.\ t\!:=\!t\!+\!1.\ twos$$
use recursive construction to find

(a)   the weakest fixed-point.

(b)   a strongest implementable fixed-point.

(c)   the strongest fixed-point.

358   Here are two definitions.

A = **if** $?c \wedge ?d$ **then** $c? \vee d?$
        else if $?c$ **then** $c?$
        else if $?d$ **then** $d?$
        else if $T_c r_c < T_d r_d$ **then** $(t\!:=\!T_c r_c + 1.\ c?)$
        else if $T_d r_d < T_c r_c$ **then** $(t\!:=\!T_d r_d + 1.\ d?)$
        else $(t\!:=\!T_c r_c + 1.\ c? \vee d?)$

B = **if** $?c \wedge ?d$ **then** $c? \vee d?$
        else if $?c$ **then** $c?$
        else if $?d$ **then** $d?$
        else $(t\!:=\!t\!+\!1.\ B)$

Letting time be an extended integer, prove $A = B$.

359   (input implementation) Let W be "wait for input on channel c and then read it".

(a)√   Formally,
$$W = t:= \max t \, (\mathcal{T}r + 1). \ c?$$
Prove $W \ \Longleftarrow \ $ **if** $?c$ **then** $r:= r+1$ **else** $(t:= t+1. \ W)$ assuming time is an extended integer.

(b)   Now let time be an extended real, redefine W appropriately, and reprove the refinement.

360   Define relation *partmerge*: $nat \rightarrow nat \rightarrow bool$ as follows:
$$partmerge \ 0 \ 0$$
$$partmerge \ (m+1) \ 0 \ = \ partmerge \ m \ 0 \ \wedge \ \mathcal{M}_c(w_c+m) = \mathcal{M}_a(r_a+m)$$
$$partmerge \ 0 \ (n+1) \ = \ partmerge \ 0 \ n \ \wedge \ \mathcal{M}_c(w_c+n) = \mathcal{M}_b(r_b+n)$$
$$partmerge \ (m+1) \ (n+1) \ = \ \quad partmerge \ m \ (n+1) \ \wedge \ \mathcal{M}_c(w_c+m+n+1) = \mathcal{M}_a(r_a+m)$$
$$\vee \ partmerge \ (m+1) \ n \ \wedge \ \mathcal{M}_c(w_c+m+n+1) = \mathcal{M}_b(r_b+n)$$
Now *partmerge m n* says that the first $m+n$ outputs on channel c are a merge of m inputs from channel a and n inputs from channel b. Define *merge* as
$$merge \ = \ (a?. \ c! \ a) \vee (b?. \ c! \ b). \ merge$$
Prove $merge \ = \ (\forall m \cdot \exists n \cdot partmerge \ m \ n) \vee (\forall n \cdot \exists m \cdot partmerge \ m \ n)$

361   (time merge) We want to repeatedly read an input on either channel c or channel d, whichever comes first, and write it on channel e. At each reading, if input is available on both channels, read either one; if it is available on just one channel, read that one; if it is available on neither channel, wait for the first one and read that one (in case of a tie, read either one).

(a)√   Write the specification formally, and then write a program.

(b)   Prove
$$\mathcal{T}_e w_e = \max t \, (\min (\mathcal{T}_c r_c) (\mathcal{T}_d r_d) + 1)$$
$$\forall m, n \cdot \mathcal{T}_e(w_e+m+n+1) \leq \max (\max (\mathcal{T}_c(r_c+m)) (\mathcal{T}_d(r_d+n))) (\mathcal{T}_e(w_e+m+n)) + 1$$

362   (fairer time merge) This question is the same as the time merge, but if input is available on both channels, the choice must be made the opposite way from the previous read. If, after waiting for an input, inputs arrive on both channels at the same time, the choice must be made the opposite way from the previous read.

363   In the reaction controller in Chapter 9, it is supposed that the synchronizer receives digital data from the digitizer faster than requests from the controller. Now suppose that the controller is sometimes faster than the digitizer. Modify the synchronizer so that if two or more requests arrive in a row (before new digital data arrives), the same digital data will be sent in reply to each request.

364   (Brock-Ackermann) The following picture shows a network of communicating processes.

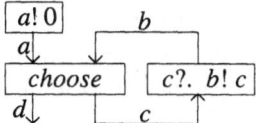

The formal description of this network is

chan $a, b, c \cdot a! 0 \parallel choose \parallel (c?. b! c)$

Add transit time and state the output message and time if

(a) $choose = (a?.\ c!\ 0.\ d!\ 0) \vee (b?.\ c!\ 1.\ d!\ 1)$

choose either reads from a and outputs a 0 on c and d, or reads from b and outputs a 1 on c and d. The choice is made freely.

(b) $choose = (a?.\ c!\ 0.\ d!\ 0)\ \text{II}\ (b?.\ c!\ 1.\ d!\ 1)$

As in part (a), *choose* either reads from a and outputs a 0 on c and d, or reads from b and outputs a 1 on c and d. But this time the choice is not made freely; *choose* reads from the channel whose input is available first (if there's a tie, then take either one).

365√   (gas burner) Specify the control of a gas burner. Its inputs are:
•   boolean *heatwanted*, which comes from a thermostat and indicates whether heat is wanted.
•   boolean *flame*, which comes from a flame sensor and indicates whether the gas is burning.

Its outputs are:
•   *gas*! *on*, which turns the gas on.
•   *gas*! *off*, which turns the gas off.
•   *spark*!, which causes a spark for the purpose of igniting the gas.

The spark should be applied to the gas for at least 1 second to give it a chance to ignite and to allow the flame to become stable. But a safety regulation states that the gas must not remain on and unlit for more than 3 seconds. Another regulation says that when the gas is shut off, it must not be turned on again for at least 20 seconds to allow any accumulated gas to clear. And finally, the gas burner must respond to its inputs within 1 second.

366   (telephone) Specify the control of a simple telephone. Its inputs are those actions you can perform: picking up the phone, dialing a digit, and putting down (hanging up) the phone. Its output is a list of digits (the number dialed). The end of dialing is indicated by 5 seconds during which no further digit is dialed. If the phone is put down without waiting 5 seconds, then there is no output. But, if the phone is put down and then picked up again within 1 second, this is considered to be an accident, and it does not affect the output.

367   (consensus) Some parallel processes are connected in a ring. Each process has a local integer variable with an initial value. These initial values may differ, but otherwise the processes are identical. Execution of all processes must terminate in time linear in the number of processes, and in the end the values of these local variables must all be the same, and equal to one of the initial values. Write the processes.

368√ (power series multiplication) Write a program to read from channel a an infinite sequence of coefficients $a_0 \ a_1 \ a_2 \ a_3 \ ...$ of a power series $a_0 + a_1 x + a_2 x^2 + a_3 x^3 + ...$ and in parallel to read from channel b an infinite sequence of coefficients $b_0 \ b_1 \ b_2 \ b_3 \ ...$ of a power series $b_0 + b_1 x + b_2 x^2 + b_3 x^3 + ...$ and in parallel to write on channel c the infinite sequence of coefficients $c_0 \ c_1 \ c_2 \ c_3 \ ...$ of the power series $c_0 + c_1 x + c_2 x^2 + c_3 x^3 + ...$ equal to the product of the two input series. Assume that all inputs are already available; there are no input delays. Produce the outputs one per time unit.

369 (repetition) Write a program to read an infinite sequence, and after every even number of inputs, to output a boolean saying whether the second half of the input sequence is a repetition of the first half.

370 (sequential file update) A master file of records and a transaction file of records are to be read, one record at a time, and a new file of records is to be written, one record at a time. A record consists of two text fields: a "key" field and an "info" field. The master file is kept in order of its keys, without duplicate keys, and with a final record having a sentinel key "zzzzz" guaranteed to be larger than all other keys. The transaction file is also sorted in order of its keys, with the same final sentinel key, but it may have duplicate keys. The new file is like the master file, but with changes as signified by the transaction file. If the transaction file contains a record with a key that does not appear in the master file, that record is to be added. If the transaction file contains a record with a key that does appear in the master file, that record is a change of the "info" field, unless the "info" text is the empty text, in which case it signifies record deletion. Whenever the transaction file contains a repeated key, the last record for each key determines the result.

371 (mutual exclusion) Process P is an endless repetition of a "non-critical section" NP and a "critical section" CP. Process Q is similar.
　　　　$P \ = \ NP. \ CP. \ P$
　　　　$Q \ = \ NQ. \ CQ. \ Q$
They are executed in parallel $(P \parallel Q)$. Specify formally that the two critical sections are never executed at the same time. Hint: You may insert into P and Q outputs on channels that are never read, but help to specify the mutual exclusion of the critical sections.

372 (synchronous communication) Design a theory of synchronous communication. A communication happens when the sender is ready to send and the receiver(s) is(are) ready to receive. Those that are ready must wait for those that are not. For each channel, you will need only one cursor, but two (or more) time scripts. An output, as well as an input, increases the time to the maximum of the time scripts for the current message. Show how it works in some examples, including a deadlock example. Show an example that is not a deadlock with asynchronous communication, but becomes a deadlock with synchronous communication.

——End of Communication
——End of Exercises

11   Reference

Justifications

This section explains some of the decisions made in choosing and presenting the material in this book. It is probably not of interest to a student whose concern is to learn the material, but it may be of interest to a teacher or researcher.

Notation

This book does not always use the best notations. For example, to express the maximum of two numbers x and y , a function max is applied: $max\ x\ y$. Since maximum is symmetric and associative, it would be better to introduce a symmetric symbol like $\uparrow$ as an infix operator: $x \uparrow y$. I always do so privately, but in this book I have chosen to keep the symbols few in number and reasonably traditional. Most people seeing $max\ x\ y$ will know what is meant without prior explanation; most people seeing $x \uparrow y$ would not.

A precedence scheme is chosen on two criteria: to minimize the need for parentheses, and to be easily remembered. The latter is helped by sticking to tradition, by placing related symbols together, and by having as few levels as possible. The two criteria are sometimes conflicting, traditions are sometimes conflicting, and the three suggestions for helping memory are sometimes conflicting. In the end, one makes a decision and lives with it. Extra parentheses can always be used, and should be used whenever structural similarities would be obscured by the precedence scheme. The scheme in this book has more levels than I would like. In the first draft, I placed $\neg$ with unary $-$, $\wedge$ with $\times$, $\vee$ with binary $+$, and $\Rightarrow$ and $\Leftarrow$ with $=$ and $\ne$, as in Pascal. This saves four levels, but is against mathematical tradition and costs a lot of parentheses. The use of large symbols $=\ \Longleftarrow\ \Longrightarrow$ with large precedence level is a novelty; I hope it is both readable and writable. Do not judge it until you have used it awhile; it saves an enormous number of parentheses. One can immediately see generalizations of this convention to all symbols and many sizes (a slippery slope).

———————————————————————————————————End of Notation

Boolean Theory

Boolean Theory sometimes goes by other names: Boolean Algebra, Propositional Calculus, Sentential Logic. Its expressions are sometimes called "propositions" or "sentences". Sometimes a distinction is made between "terms", which are said to denote values, and "propositions", which are said not to denote values but instead to be true or false. A similar distinction is made between "functions", which apply to arguments to produce values, and "predicates", which are instantiated to become true or false. But slowly, the subject of logic is emerging from its confused, philosophical past. I consider that propositions are just boolean expressions and treat them on a par with number expressions and expressions of other types. I consider that predicates are just boolean functions. I use the same equal sign for booleans as for numbers, characters, sets, and functions. Perhaps in the future we won't feel the need to imagine abstract objects for expressions to denote; we will justify them by their practical applications. We will explain our formalisms by the rules for their use, not by their philosophy.

Why bother with "antiaxioms" and "antitheorems"? They are not traditional (in fact, I made up the words). As stated in Chapter 1, thanks to the negation operator and the Consistency Rule, we don't need to bother with them. Instead of saying that *expression* is an antitheorem, we can say that $\neg$*expression* is a theorem. Why bother with $\bot$? We could instead write $\neg\top$. One reason is just that it is shorter to say "antitheorem" than to say "negation of a theorem". Another reason is to help make clear the important difference between "disprovable" and "not provable". Another reason is that some logics do not use the negation operator and the Consistency Rule. The logic in this book is "classical logic"; "constructive logic" omits the Completion Rule; "evaluation logic" omits both the Consistency Rule and the Completion Rule.

Some books present proof rules (and axioms) with the aid of a formal notation. In this book, there is no formal metalanguage; the metalanguage is English. A formal metalanguage is helpful for the presentation and comparison of a variety of competing formalisms, and necessary for proving theorems about formalisms. But in this book, only one formalism is presented. The burden of learning another formalism first, for the purpose of presenting the main formalism, is unnecessary. A formal metanotation for substitution would allow me to write the function application rule as

$$(\lambda v \cdot b)\, a = b[a/v]$$

but then I would have to explain that $b[a/v]$ means "substitute a for v in b". I may as well say directly

$$(\lambda v \cdot b)\, a = (\text{substitute } a \text{ for } v \text{ in } b)$$

A proof syntax (formalizing the "hints") would be necessary if we were using an automated prover, but in this book it is unnecessary and I have not introduced one.

Some authors may distinguish "axiom" from "axiom schema", the latter having variables which can be instantiated to produce axioms; I have used the term "axiom" for both. I have also used the term "law" as a synonym for "theorem" (I would prefer to reduce my vocabulary, but both words are well established). Other books may distinguish them by the presence or absence of variables, or they may use "law" to mean "we would like it to be a theorem but we haven't yet designed an appropriate theory".

I have taken a few liberties with the names of some axioms and laws. What I have called "transparency" is often called "substitution of equals for equals", which is longer and doesn't quite make sense. Each of my Laws of Portation is historically two laws, one an implication in one direction, and the other an implication in the other direction. One was called "Importation", and the other "Exportation", but I can never remember which was which. The name "Confutation" is new.

──End of Boolean Theory

Bunch Theory

Why bother with bunches? Don't sets work just as well? Aren't bunches really just sets but using a peculiar notation and terminology? The answer is no, but let's take it slowly. Suppose we just present sets. We want to be able to write $\{1, 3, 7\}$ and similar expressions, and we might describe these set expressions with a little grammar like this:

set = "{" $contents$ "}"

$contents$ = $number$,

    set ,

    $contents$ "," $contents$

We will want to say that the order of elements in a set is irrelevant so that $\{1, 2\} = \{2, 1\}$; the best way to say it is formally: $A,B = B,A$ (comma is symmetric, or commutative). Next, we want to say that repetitions of elements in a set are irrelevant so that $\{3, 3\} = \{3\}$; the best way to say that is $A,A = A$ (comma is idempotent). What we are doing here is inventing bunches, but calling them "contents" of a set. And note that the grammar is equating bunches; the catenations (denoted by juxtaposition) distribute over the elements of their operands, and the alternations (the commas that are not in quotes) are bunch unions.

When a child first learns about sets, there is often an initial hurdle: that a set with one element is not the same as the element. How much easier it would be if a set were presented as packaging: a bag with an apple in it is obviously not the same as the apple. Just as $\{2\}$ and 2 differ, so $\{2,7\}$ and $2,7$ differ. Bunch Theory tells us about aggregation; Set Theory tells us about packaging. The two are independent.

We could define sets without relying on bunches (as has been done for many years), and we could use sets wherever I have used bunches. In that sense, bunches are unnecessary. Similarly we could define lists without relying on sets (as I did in this book), and we could always use lists in place of sets. In that sense, sets are unnecessary. But sets are a beautiful data structure that introduces one idea (packaging), and I prefer to keep them. Similarly bunches are a beautiful data structure that introduces one idea (aggregation), and I prefer to keep them. I always prefer to use the simplest structure that is adequate for its purpose.

The subject of functional programming has suffered from an inability to express nondeterminism conveniently. To say something about a value, but not pin it down completely, one can express the set of possible values. Unfortunately, sets do not reduce properly to the deterministic case; in this context it is again a problem that a set containing one element is not equal to the element. What is wanted is bunches. One can always regard a bunch as a "nondeterministic value".

Bunches have also been used in this book as a "type theory". Surely it is discouraging to others, as it is to me, to see type theory duplicating all the operators of its value space: for each operation on values, there is a corresponding operation on type spaces. By using bunches, this duplication is eliminated.

Many mathematicians consider that curly brackets and commas are just syntax, and syntax is annoying and unimportant, though necessary. I have treated them as operators, with algebraic properties (in the section on Set Theory, we see that curly brackets have an inverse). This continues a very long, historical trend. For example, = was at first just a syntax for the statement that two things are (in some way) the same, but now it is an operator with algebraic properties.

——End of Bunch Theory

String Theory

In many papers there is a little apology as the author explains that the notation for catenation of lists will be abused by sometimes catenating a list and an item. Or perhaps there are three catenation notations: one to catenate two lists, one to prepend an item to a list, and one to append an item to a list. The poor author has to fight with unwanted packaging provided by lists in order to get the sequencing. I offer these authors strings: sequencing without packaging. (Of course, they can be packaged into lists whenever wanted. I am not taking away lists.)

——End of String Theory

Function Theory

The tradition in logic, which I have not followed, is to begin with all possible variables (infinitely many of them) already "existing". The function notation (λ) is said to "bind" variables, and any variable that is not bound remains "free". For example,

$(\lambda x: int \cdot x+3)\, y$

has bound variable x , free variable y , and infinitely many other free variables. In this book, variables do not automatically "exist"; they are introduced (rather than bound) either formally using the function notation, or informally by saying in English what they are.

——End of Function Theory

Program Theory

Since the design of Algol-60, sequential execution has often been represented by a semi-colon. The semi-colon is unavailable to me for this purpose because I used it for string catenation. Dependent composition is a kind of product, so I hope a period will be an acceptable symbol. I considered switching the two, using semi-colon for dependent composition and a period for string catenation, but the latter did not work well.

Refinement is implication, universally quantified. In some books, refinement is called "reification", but "refinement" is the more usual term. Even though refinement is the central notion in this book, I have not given it a symbol. The most common symbol for refinement is $\sqsubseteq$, but it suggests implication in the wrong direction. Some authors use the reversed symbol. I used $\cdot:$ in the first draft of this book, but I removed it. There is an equal need for a symbol for specification equality (mutual refinement), and I could not justify having a special inequality (refinement) symbol without a special equality symbol. Also, the first step in any proof of refinement is always to replace it with a universal implication; by not having a refinement symbol, I save a step in every proof. An alternative that I find unattractive is to have a lot of laws about refinement that exactly duplicate laws about implication.

In English, the word "precondition" means "something that is necessary beforehand". In many programming books, the word "precondition" is used to mean "something that is sufficient beforehand". In those books, "weakest precondition" means "necessary and sufficient", which I have called "exact precondition".

In the well-known theory by Hoare, we specify that variable x is to be increased as follows:
$$\S S \cdot \ \forall X \cdot \ \{x = X\} \ S \ \{x > X\}$$
(The quantifications are formally necessary, but usually omitted.) In Dijkstra's theory of weakest preconditions, it is similar:
$$\S S \cdot \ \forall X \cdot \ x{=}X \ \Rightarrow \ wp \ S \ (x{>}X)$$
There are two problems with these notations. One is that they do not provide any way of referring to both the prestate and the poststate, hence the introduction of X . This is solved in the Vienna Development Method, in which the same specification is
$$\S S \cdot \ \{\top\} \ S \ \{x' > x\}$$
The other problem is that the programming language and specification language are disjoint, hence the introduction of S . In my theory, the programming language is a sublanguage of the specification language. The specification that x is to be increased is
$$x' > x$$
The same single-expression double-state specifications are used in Z, but refinement is rather complicated. In Z, P is refined by S if and only if

$$\forall \sigma \cdot (\exists \sigma' \cdot P) \Rightarrow (\exists \sigma' \cdot S) \wedge (\forall \sigma' \cdot P \Leftarrow S)$$

In Hoare's theory, $\S S \cdot \{P\}\, S\, \{Q\}$ is refined by $\S S \cdot \{R\}\, S\, \{U\}$ if and only if

$$\forall \sigma \cdot P \Rightarrow R \wedge (Q \Leftarrow U)$$

In my theory, P is refined by S if and only if

$$\forall \sigma, \sigma' \cdot P \Leftarrow S$$

Since refinement is what we must prove when programming, it is best to make refinement as simple as possible.

One might suppose that any type of mathematical expression can be used as a specification: whatever works. A specification of something, whether cars or computations, distinguishes those things that satisfy it from those that don't. Observation of something provides values for certain variables, and on the basis of those values we must be able to determine whether the something satisfies the specification. Thus we have a specification, some values for variables, and two possible outcomes. That is exactly the job of a boolean expression: a specification (of anything) really is a boolean expression. If instead we use a pair of predicates, or a function from predicates to predicates, or anything else, we make our specifications in an indirect way, and we make the task of determining satisfaction more difficult.

One might suppose that any boolean expression can be used to specify any computer behavior: whatever correspondence works. In Z, the expression $\top$ is used to specify (describe) terminating computations, and $\bot$ is used to specify (describe) nonterminating computations. The reasoning is something like this: $\bot$ is the specification for which there is no satisfactory final state; an infinite computation is behavior for which there is no final state; hence $\bot$ represents infinite computation. Although we cannot observe a "final" state of an infinite computation, we can observe, simply by waiting 10 time units, that it satisfies $t' \geq t+10$, and it does not satisfy $t' < t+10$. Thus it ought to satisfy any specification implied by $t' \geq t+10$, including $\top$, and it ought not to satisfy any specification that implies $t' < t+10$, including $\bot$. Since $\bot$ is not true of anything, it does not (truly) describe anything. A specification is a description, and $\bot$ is not satisfiable, not even by nonterminating computations. Since $\top$ is true of everything, it (truly) describes everything, even nonterminating computations. To say that P refines Q is to say that all behavior satisfying P also satisfies Q, which is just implication. The correspondence between specifications and computer behavior is not arbitrary.

As pointed out in Chapter 4, specifications such as $x'=2 \wedge t'=\infty$ that talk about the "final" values of variables at time infinity are strange. I could change the theory to prevent any mention of results at time infinity, but I do not for two reasons: it would make the theory more complicated, and I need to distinguish among infinite loops when I introduce communications (Chapter 9).

——End of Program Theory

Programming Language

The form of variable declaration given in Chapter 5 assigns the new local variable an arbitrary value of its type. Thus, for example, if y and z are integer variables, then

var x: $nat\cdot$ y:= x $=$ y': nat $\land$ z'=z

For ease of implementation and speed of execution, this is much better than initialization with "the undefined value". For error detection, it is no worse, assuming that we prove all our refinements. Furthermore, there are circumstances in which arbitrary initialization is exactly what's wanted (see Exercise 245 (majority vote)). However, if we do not prove all our refinements, initialization with *undefined* provides a measure of protection. If we allow the generic operators ($=$, $\neq$, **if then else**) to apply to *undefined* , then we can prove trivialities like *undefined* = *undefined* . If not, then we can prove nothing at all about *undefined* . Some programming languages seek to eliminate the error of using an uninitialized variable by initializing each variable to a standard value of its type. Such languages achieve the worst of all worlds: they are not as efficient as arbitrary initialization; and they eliminate only the error detection, not the error.

The most widely known and used rule for **while**-loops is the Method of Invariants and Variants. Let I be a precondition (called the "invariant") and let I' be the corresponding postcondition. Let v be an integer expression (called the "variant" or "bound function") and let v' be the corresponding expression with primes on all the variables. The Rule of Invariants and Variants says:

If $\forall V\cdot$ $(I \land 0{\le}v{=}V \land b \implies I' \land 0{\le}v'{<}V \impliedby P)$ is a theorem,

then $I \land 0{\le}v \implies I' \land \neg b' \impliedby$ **while** b **do** P is a theorem.

The rule says, very roughly, that if the body of the loop maintains the invariant and decreases the variant but not below zero, then the loop maintains the invariant and negates the loop condition. For example, to prove

$s' = s + \Sigma L [n;..\#L] \impliedby$ **while** $n{\neq}\#L$ **do** $(s{:=} s + Ln.\ \ n{:=} n{+}1)$

we must invent an invariant

$s + \Sigma L [n;..\#L] = \Sigma L$

and a variant

$\#L - n$

and prove both

$s' = s + \Sigma L [n;..\#L] \impliedby$

$\quad s + \Sigma L [n;..\#L] = \Sigma L \land 0 \le \#L - n \implies s' + \Sigma L [n';..\#L] = \Sigma L \land n'{=}\#L$

and

$\forall V\cdot$ ($\quad\quad s + \Sigma L [n;..\#L] = \Sigma L \land 0 \le \#L - n = V \land n{\neq}\#L$

$\quad\quad \implies s' + \Sigma L [n';..\#L] = \Sigma L \land 0 \le \#L - n' < V$

$\quad\quad \impliedby s{:=} s + Ln.\ \ n{:=} n{+}1$)

The proof method given in Chapter 5 is far easier and more information (time) is obtained.

The subject of programming has often been mistaken for the learning of a large number of programming language "features". This mistake has been made of both imperative and functional programming. Of course, each fancy operator provided in a programming language makes the solution of some problems easy. In functional programming, an operator called "reduce" is often presented; it is a useful generalization of some quantifiers. Its symbol might be / and it takes as left operand a binary associative operator like $\wedge$, $\vee$, $+$, and $\times$, and as right operand a list. The list summation problem is solved as $+/L$. The search problem could similarly be solved by the use of an appropriate search operator, and it would be a most useful exercise to design and implement such an operator. This exercise cannot be undertaken by someone whose only programming ability is to find an already implemented operator and apply it. The purpose of this book is to teach the necessary programming skills.

As our examples illustrate, functional programming and imperative programming are essentially the same: the same problem in the two styles requires the same steps in its solution. They have been thought to be different for the following reasons: imperative programmers adhere to clumsy loop notations, complicating proofs; functional programmers adhere to equality, rather than refinement, making nondeterminism difficult.

——————————————————————————————————————End of Programming Language

Recursive Definition

The combination of construction and induction is so beautiful and useful that it has a name (generation) and a notation (::=). To keep terminology and notation to a minimum, I have not used them.

——————————————————————————————————————End of Recursive Definition

Theory Design and Implementation

I used the term "data transformation" instead of the term "data refinement" used by others. I don't see any reason to consider one space more "abstract" and another more "concrete". The method of data transformation I have used is sound, but incomplete; there are legitimate transformations that cannot be accomplished this way.

——————————————————————————————————————End of Theory Design and Implementation

Concurrency

In FORTRAN (prior to 1977) we could have a sequential composition of **if**-statements, but we could not have an **if**-statement containing a sequential composition. In ALGOL the syntax was fully recursive; sequential and conditional compositions could be nested, each within the other. Did we learn a lesson? Apparently we did not learn a very general one: we now seem happy to have a parallel composition of sequential compositions, but very reluctant to have a sequential composition of parallel compositions. Suppose, for example, that we decide to have two processes, as follows.

$$(x:= x+y. \ x:= x{\times}y)$$
$$\| \quad (y:= x-y. \ y:= x/y)$$

The first modifies x twice, and the second modifies y twice. But we want to synchronize the two processes at their mid-points, between the two assignments, forcing the faster process to wait for the slower one, and then to allow the two processes to continue with the new, updated values of x and y. The solution seen all too frequently is to invent synchronization primitives. Synchronization is sequencing, and we already have an adequate sequencing primitive. The solution should be

$$(x:= x+y \ \| \ y:= x-y). \ (x:= x{\times}y \ \| \ y:= x/y)$$
$$= \quad x' = (x+y){\times}(x-y) \ \wedge \ y' = (x+y)/(x-y)$$

———End of Concurrency

Communication

In the formula for implementability, there is no conjunct $r' \le w'$ saying that the read cursor must not get ahead of the write cursor. In the subsection on Deadlock we see that it can indeed happen. Of course, it takes infinite time to do so.

The input composition operator Π needs a pronunciation.

In the deadlock examples, we can prove that the time is infinite. But there is a mild weakness in the theory. Consider this example.

$$\textbf{chan } c{\cdot} \ t:= max \ t \ (\mathcal{T}r + 1). \ c?$$
$$= \quad \exists \mathcal{M}, \ \mathcal{T}, \ r, \ r', \ w, \ w'{\cdot} \ t = max \ t \ (\mathcal{T}r + 1) \ \wedge \ r'{=}1 \ \wedge \ w'{=}0$$
$$= \quad t' \ge t$$

We might like to prove $t'{=}\infty$. To get this answer, we must strengthen the definition of local channel declaration by adding the conjunct $\mathcal{T}w' \ge t'$. I prefer the simpler, weaker theory.

We could talk about a structure of channels, and about indexed processes. We could talk about a parallel **for**-loop. There is always something more to say, but we have to stop somewhere.

———End of Communication
———End of Justifications

Sources

Ideas do not come out of nowhere. They are the result of one's education, one's culture, and one's interactions with acquaintances. I would like to acknowledge all those people who have influenced me and enabled me to write this book. I will probably fail to mention people who have influenced me indirectly, even though the influence may be strong. I may fail to thank people who gave me good ideas on a bad day, when I was not ready to understand. I will fail to give credit to people who worked independently, whose ideas may be the same as or better than those that happened to reach my eyes and ears. To all such people, I apologize. I do not believe anyone can really take credit for an idea. Ideally, our research should be done for the good of everyone, perhaps also for the pleasure of it, but not for the personal glory. Still, it is disappointing to be missed. Here then is the best accounting of my sources that I can provide.

The early work in this subject is due to Alan Turing (1949), Peter Naur (1966), Robert Floyd (1967), Tony Hoare (1969), Rod Burstall (1969), and Dana Scott and Christopher Strachey (1970). (See the Bibliography, which follows.) My own introduction to the subject was a book by Edsger Dijkstra (1976); after reading it I took my first steps toward formalizing refinement (1976). Further steps in that same direction were taken by Ralph Back (1978), though I did not learn of them until 1984. The first textbooks on the subject began to appear, including one by me (1984). That work was based on Dijkstra's weakest precondition predicate transformer, and work continues today on that same basis.

In the meantime, Tony Hoare (1978, 1981) was developing communicating sequential processes. During a term at Oxford in 1981 I realized that they could be described as predicates, and published a predicate model (1981, 1983). It soon became apparent that the same sort of description, a single boolean expression, could be used for any kind of computation, and indeed for anything else; in retrospect, it should have been obvious from the start. The result was a series of papers (1984, 1986, 1988, 1989, 1990) leading to the present book.

My wording of the Consistency Rule was corrected by Theo Norvell. The importance of format in expressions and proofs was made clear to me by Netty van Gasteren (1990). The symbols ¢ and $ for bunch and set cardinality were suggested by Chris Lengauer. The word "confutation" was suggested by Brian Parkinson. The value of indexing from 0 was taught to me by Edsger Dijkstra. The word "apposition" and the idea to which it applies come from Lambert Meertens (1986). My Refinement by Parts law was made more general by Theo Norvell. I learned the use of a timing variable from Chris Lengauer (1981), who credits Mary Shaw; we were using weakest preconditions then, so our time variables ran down instead of up. The recursive measure of time is inspired by the work of Paul Caspi, Nicolas Halbwachs, Daniel Pilaud, and John Plaice (1987); in their language LUSTRE, each iteration of a loop takes time 1 , and all else is free. I learned to discount termination by itself, with no time bound, in discussions with Andrew Malton, and from an example of Hendrik Boom (1982). Theo Norvell provided the exact precondition for termination. I was told the logarithmic solution to the Fibonacci number problem by Wlad Turski, who learned it while visiting the University of Guelph. My incorrect version of local variable declaration was corrected by Andrew Malton. Local variable suspension is adapted from Carroll Morgan (1990). The backtracking implementation of unimplementable specifications comes from Greg Nelson (1989). The use of bunches for nondeterminism in functional programming and for function refinement is joint work with Theo Norvell (1992). Alan Rosenthal suggested that I stop worrying about when limits "exist", and just write the axioms describing them. The style of data-type theories (data-stack, data-queue, data-tree) comes from John Guttag and Jim Horning (1978). The implementation of data-trees was influenced by Tony Hoare (1975). Some details of the program-tree theory are due to Theo Norvell. I learned about data transformation from He Jifeng and Carroll Morgan, based on earlier work by Tony Hoare (1972); the formulation here is my own, but I checked it for equivalence with those in Wei Chen and Jan Tijmen Udding (1989). Theo Norvell provided the criterion for data transformers. The second data transformation example (take a number) is adapted from a resource allocation example of Carroll Morgan (1990). I published various formulations of independent (parallel) composition (1981, 1984, 1990), but the current version is better, and is due to Theo Norvell. The section on found concurrency is joint work with Chris Lengauer (1981); he has since made great advances in the automatic production of highly parallel, systolic computations from ordinary sequential, imperative programs. The form of communication was influenced by Gilles Kahn (1974). Time scripts were suggested by Theo Norvell. The probe is an invention of Alain Martin (1985). Monitors were invented by Tony Hoare (1974). The gas burner example is a simplification and adaptation of a similar example due to Anders Ravn, Erling Sørensen, and Hans Rischel (1990). The power series multiplication is from Doug McIlroy (1990), who credits Gilles Kahn. Many of the exercises were given to me by Wim Feijen for my earlier book (1984); they were developed by Edsger Dijkstra, Wim Feijen, Netty van Gasteren, and Martin Rem for examinations at the Technical University of Eindhoven; they have since appeared in a book by Edsger Dijkstra and Wim Feijen (1988). Some exercises come from a series of journal articles by Martin Rem (1983,..1991). Other exercises were taken from a great variety of sources too numerous to mention.

———End of Sources

Bibliography

R.-J.R.Back: "on the Correctness of Refinement in Program Development", University of Helsinki, Department of Computer Science, Report A-1978-4, 1978.

R.-J.R.Back: "a Calculus of Refinement for Program Derivations", *Acta Informatica*, volume 25, pages 593,..625, 1988.

H.J.Boom: "a Weaker Precondition for Loops", *ACM Transactions on Programming Languages and Systems*, volume 4, number 4, pages 668,..678, 1982.

R.Burstall: "Proving Properties of Programs by Structural Induction", University of Edinburgh, Report 17 DMIP, 1968; also *Computer Journal*, volume 12, number 1, pages 41,..49, 1969.

P.Caspi, N.Halbwachs, D.Pilaud, J.A.Plaice: "LUSTRE: a Declarative Language for Programming Synchronous Systems", *fourteenth annual ACM Symposium on Principles of Programming Languages*, pages 178,..189, Munich, 1987.

K.M.Chandy, J.Misra: *Parallel Program Design: a Foundation*, Addison-Wesley, 1988.

W.Chen, J.T.Udding: "Toward a Calculus of Data Refinement", J.L.A.van de Snepscheut (editor): *Mathematics of Program Construction*, Springer-Verlag, Lecture Notes in Computer Science, volume 375, pages 197,..219, 1989.

E.W.Dijkstra: "Guarded Commands, Nondeterminacy, and Formal Derivation of Programs", *Communications ACM*, volume 18, number 8, pages 453,..458, 1975 August.

E.W.Dijkstra: *a Discipline of Programming*, Prentice-Hall, 1976.

E.W.Dijkstra, W.H.J.Feijen: *a Method of Programming*, Addison-Wesley, 1988.

R.W.Floyd: "Assigning Meanings to Programs", *Proceedings of the American Society, Symposium on Applied Mathematics*, volume 19, pages 19,..32, 1967.

A.J.M.van Gasteren: "on the Shape of Mathematical Arguments", Springer-Verlag Lecture Notes in Computer Science, 1990.

J.V.Guttag, J.J.Horning: "the Algebraic Specification of Abstract Data Types", *Acta Informatica*, volume 10, pages 27,..53, 1978.

E.C.R.Hehner: "**do** considered **od**: a Contribution to the Programming Calculus", University of Toronto, Technical Report CSRG-75, 1976 November; also *Acta Informatica*, volume 11, pages 287,..305, 1979.

E.C.R.Hehner: "Bunch Theory: a Simple Set Theory for Computer Science", University of Toronto, Technical Report CSRG-102, 1979 July; also *Information Processing Letters*, volume 12, number 1, pages 26,..31, 1981 February.

E.C.R.Hehner, C.A.R.Hoare: "a More Complete Model of Communicating Processes", University of Toronto, Technical Report CSRG-134, 1981 September; also *Theoretical Computer Science*, volume 26, numbers 1 and 2, pages 105,..121, 1983 September.

E.C.R.Hehner: "Predicative Programming", *Communications ACM*, volume 27, number 2, pages 134,..152, 1984 February.

E.C.R.Hehner: *the Logic of Programming*, Prentice-Hall International, 1984.

E.C.R.Hehner, L.E.Gupta, A.J.Malton: "Predicative Methodology", *Acta Informatica*, volume 23, number 5, pages 487,..506, 1986.

E.C.R.Hehner, A.J.Malton: "Termination Conventions and Comparative Semantics", *Acta Informatica*, volume 25, number 1, pages 1,..15, 1988 January.

E.C.R.Hehner: "Termination is Timing", International Conference on Mathematics of Program Construction, The Netherlands, Enschede, 1989 June; also J.L.A.van de Snepscheut (editor): *Mathematics of Program Construction*, Springer-Verlag, Lecture Notes in Computer Science volume 375, pages 36,..48, 1989.

E.C.R.Hehner: "a Practical Theory of Programming", *Science of Computer Programming*, volume 14, numbers 2 and 3, pages 133,..159, 1990.

C.A.R.Hoare: "an Axiomatic Basis for Computer Programming", *Communications ACM*, volume 12, number 10, pages 576,..581, 583, 1969 October.

C.A.R.Hoare: "Proof of Correctness of Data Representations", *Acta Informatica*, volume 1, number 4, pages 271,..282, 1972.

C.A.R.Hoare: "Monitors: an Operating System Structuring Concept", *Communications ACM*, volume 17, number 10, pages 549,..558, 1974 October.

C.A.R.Hoare: "Recursive Data Structures", *International Journal of Computer and Information Sciences*, volume 4, number 2, pages 105,..133, 1975 June.

C.A.R.Hoare: "Communicating Sequential Processes", *Communications ACM*, volume 21, number 8, pages 666,..678, 1978 August.

C.A.R.Hoare: "a Calculus of Total Correctness for Communicating Processes", *Science of Computer Programming*, volume 1, numbers 1 and 2, pages 49,..73, 1981 October.

C.A.R.Hoare: "Programs are Predicates", in C.A.R.Hoare, J.C.Shepherdson (editors): *Mathematical Logic and Programming Languages*, Prentice-Hall Intenational, pages 141,..155, 1985.

C.A.R.Hoare, I.J.Hayes, J.He, C.C.Morgan, A.W.Roscoe, J.W.Sanders, I.H.Sørensen, J.M.Spivey, B.A.Sufrin: "the Laws of Programming", *Communications ACM*, volume 30, number 8, pages 672,..688, 1987 August.

C.B.Jones: *Software Development: a Rigorous Approach*, Prentice-Hall International, 1980.

C.B.Jones: *Systematic Software Development using VDM*, Prentice-Hall International, 1986 and 1990.

G.Kahn: "the Semantics of a Simple Language for Parallel Programming, *Information Processing 74*, North-Holland, Proceeding of IFIP Congress, 1974.

C.Lengauer, E.C.R.Hehner: "a Methodology for Programming with Concurrency", CONPAR 81, Nürnberg, 1981 June 10,..13; also Springer-Verlag, Lecture Notes in Computer Science volume 111, 1981 June, pages 259,..271; also *Science of Computer Programming*, volume 2, 1982, pages 1,..53.

A.J.Martin: "the Probe: an Addition to Communication Primitives", *Information Processing Letters*, volume 20, number 3, pages 125,..131, 1985.

J.McCarthy: "a Basis for a Mathematical Theory of Computation", *Proceedings of the Western Joint Computer Conference*, pages 225,..239, Los Angeles, 1961 May; also Computer Programming and Formal Systems, North-Holland, pages 33,..71, 1963.

M.D.McIlroy: "Squinting at Power Series", *Software Practice and Experience*, volume 20, number 7, pages 661,..684, 1990 July.

L.G.L.T.Meertens: "Algorithmics — towards Programming as a Mathematical Activity", Proceedings of CWI Symposium on Mathematics and Computer Science, North-Holland, *CWI Monographs*, volume 1, pages 289,..335, 1986.

C.C.Morgan: "the Specification Statement", *ACM Transactions on Programming Languages and Systems*, volume 10, number 3, pages 403,..420, 1988 July.

C.C.Morgan: *Programming from Specifications*, Prentice-Hall International, 1990.

J.M.Morris: "a Theoretical Basis for Stepwise Refinement and the Programming Calculus", *Science of Computer Programming*, volume 9, pages 287,..307, 1987.

P.Naur: "Proof of Algorithms by General Snapshots", *BIT*, volume 6, number 4, pages 310,..317, 1966.

G.Nelson: "a Generalization of Dijkstra's Calculus", *ACM Transactions on Programming Languages and Systems*, volume 11, number 4, pages 517,..562, 1989 October.

T.S.Norvell, E.C.R.Hehner: "Logical Specifications for Functional Programs", International Conference on Mathematics of Program Construction, Oxford, 1992 June.

A.P.Ravn, E.V.Sørensen, H.Rischel: "Control Program for a Gas Burner", Technical University of Denmark, Department of Computer Scence, 1990 March.

M.Rem: "Small Programming Exercises", articles in *Science of Computer Programming*, 1983,..1991.

D.S.Scott, C.Strachey: "Outline of a Mathematical Theory of Computation", Oxford University Report PRG-2, 1970; also *Proceedings of the fourth annual Princeton Conference on Information Sciences and Systems*, pages 169,..177, 1970.

J.M.Spivey: *the Z Notation – a Reference Manual*, Prentice-Hall International, 1989.

A.M.Turing: "Checking a Large Routine", Cambridge University, Report on a Conference on High Speed Automatic Calculating Machines, pages 67,..70, 1949.

———End of Bibliography

Index

Axioms and Laws

Booleans

Let a, b, c, d, and e be boolean.

Boolean Axioms

$\top$

$\neg\bot$

Law of Excluded Middle (Tertium non Datur)

$a \vee \neg a$

Law of Contradiction

$\neg(a \wedge \neg a)$

Base Laws

$\neg(a \wedge \bot)$

$a \vee \top$

$a \Rightarrow \top$

$\bot \Rightarrow a$

Identity Laws

$\top \wedge a = a$

$\bot \vee a = a$

$\top \Rightarrow a = a$

$\top = a = a$

Idempotent Laws

$a \wedge a = a$

$a \vee a = a$

Reflexive Laws

$a \Rightarrow a$

$a = a$

Laws of Indirect Proof

$\neg a \Rightarrow \bot = a$ (Reductio ad Absurdum)

$\neg a \Rightarrow a = a$

Law of Double Negation

$\neg\neg a = a$

Duality Laws (deMorgan)

$\neg(a \wedge b) = \neg a \vee \neg b$

$\neg(a \vee b) = \neg a \wedge \neg b$

Laws of Exclusion

$a \Rightarrow \neg b = b \Rightarrow \neg a$

$a = \neg b = b = \neg a$

Laws of Inclusion

$a \Rightarrow b = \neg a \vee b$ (Material Implication)

$a \Rightarrow b = (a \wedge b = a)$

$a \Rightarrow b = (a \vee b = b)$

Laws of Direct Proof

$(a \Rightarrow b) \wedge a \Rightarrow b$ (Modus Ponens)

$(a \Rightarrow b) \wedge \neg b \Rightarrow \neg a$ (Modus Tollens)

$(a \vee b) \wedge \neg a \Rightarrow b$ (Disjunctive Syllogism)

Associative Laws

$a \wedge (b \wedge c) = (a \wedge b) \wedge c$

$a \vee (b \vee c) = (a \vee b) \vee c$

$a = (b = c) = (a = b) = c$

$a \ne (b \ne c) = (a \ne b) \ne c$

$a = (b \ne c) = (a = b) \ne c$

Transitive Laws

$(a \wedge b) \wedge (b \wedge c) \Rightarrow (a \wedge c)$

$(a \Rightarrow b) \wedge (b \Rightarrow c) \Rightarrow (a \Rightarrow c)$

$(a = b) \wedge (b = c) \Rightarrow (a = c)$

$(a \Rightarrow b) \wedge (b = c) \Rightarrow (a \Rightarrow c)$

$(a = b) \wedge (b \Rightarrow c) \Rightarrow (a \Rightarrow c)$

Law of Specialization

$$a \wedge b \Rightarrow a$$

Law of Generalization

$$a \Rightarrow a \vee b$$

Absorption Laws

$$a \wedge (a \vee b) = a$$
$$a \vee (a \wedge b) = a$$

Symmetry Laws (Commutative Laws)

$$a \wedge b = b \wedge a$$
$$a \vee b = b \vee a$$
$$a = b = b = a$$
$$a \neq b = b \neq a$$

Antisymmetry Law (Double Implication)

$$(a \Rightarrow b) \wedge (b \Rightarrow a) = a = b$$

Laws of Discharge

$$a \wedge (a \Rightarrow b) = a \wedge b$$
$$a \Rightarrow (a \wedge b) = a \Rightarrow b$$

Antimonotonic Law

$$a \Rightarrow b \implies (b \Rightarrow c) \Rightarrow (a \Rightarrow c)$$

Contrapositive Law

$$a \Rightarrow b = \neg b \Rightarrow \neg a$$

Case Base Laws

if $\top$ **then** a **else** $b = a$
if $\bot$ **then** a **else** $b = b$

One Case Laws

if a **then** b **else** $\top = a \Rightarrow b$
if a **then** b **else** $\bot = a \wedge b$

Case Reversal Law

if a **then** b **else** c
$= $ **if** $\neg a$ **then** c **else** b

Distributive Laws (Factoring)

$$a \wedge (b \wedge c) = (a \wedge b) \wedge (a \wedge c)$$
$$a \wedge (b \vee c) = (a \wedge b) \vee (a \wedge c)$$
$$a \vee (b \wedge c) = (a \vee b) \wedge (a \vee c)$$
$$a \vee (b \vee c) = (a \vee b) \vee (a \vee c)$$
$$a \vee (b \Rightarrow c) = (a \vee b) \Rightarrow (a \vee c)$$
$$a \vee (b = c) = (a \vee b) = (a \vee c)$$
$$a \Rightarrow (b \wedge c) = (a \Rightarrow b) \wedge (a \Rightarrow c)$$
$$a \Rightarrow (b \vee c) = (a \Rightarrow b) \vee (a \Rightarrow c)$$
$$a \Rightarrow (b \Rightarrow c) = (a \Rightarrow b) \Rightarrow (a \Rightarrow c)$$
$$a \Rightarrow (b = c) = (a \Rightarrow b) = (a \Rightarrow c)$$

Antidistributive Laws

$$a \wedge b \Rightarrow c = (a \Rightarrow c) \vee (b \Rightarrow c)$$
$$a \vee b \Rightarrow c = (a \Rightarrow c) \wedge (b \Rightarrow c)$$

Laws of Portation

$$a \wedge b \Rightarrow c = a \Rightarrow (b \Rightarrow c)$$
$$a \wedge b \Rightarrow c = a \Rightarrow \neg b \vee c$$

Laws of Confutation

$$(a \Rightarrow b) \wedge (c \Rightarrow d) \implies a \wedge c \Rightarrow b \wedge d$$
$$(a \Rightarrow b) \wedge (c \Rightarrow d) \implies a \vee c \Rightarrow b \vee d$$

Monotonic Laws

$$a \Rightarrow b \implies c \wedge a \Rightarrow c \wedge b$$
$$a \Rightarrow b \implies c \vee a \Rightarrow c \vee b$$
$$a \Rightarrow b \implies (c \Rightarrow a) \Rightarrow (c \Rightarrow b)$$

Case Analysis Laws

if a **then** b **else** $c = (a \wedge b) \vee (\neg a \wedge c)$
if a **then** b **else** $c = (a \Rightarrow b) \wedge (\neg a \Rightarrow c)$

Case Creation Laws

$a = $ **if** b **then** $b \Rightarrow a$ **else** $\neg b \Rightarrow a$
$a = $ **if** b **then** $b \wedge a$ **else** $\neg b \wedge a$
$a = $ **if** b **then** $b = a$ **else** $b \neq a$

Case Idempotent Law

if a **then** b **else** $b = b$

Case Absorption Laws

$\textbf{if } a \textbf{ then } b \textbf{ else } c \;=\; \textbf{if } a \textbf{ then } a{\wedge}b \textbf{ else } c$

$\textbf{if } a \textbf{ then } b \textbf{ else } c \;=\; \textbf{if } a \textbf{ then } a \Rightarrow b \textbf{ else } c$

$\textbf{if } a \textbf{ then } b \textbf{ else } c \;=\; \textbf{if } a \textbf{ then } a{=}b \textbf{ else } c$

$\textbf{if } a \textbf{ then } b \textbf{ else } c \;=\; \textbf{if } a \textbf{ then } b \textbf{ else } \neg a \wedge c$

$\textbf{if } a \textbf{ then } b \textbf{ else } c \;=\; \textbf{if } a \textbf{ then } b \textbf{ else } a \vee c$

$\textbf{if } a \textbf{ then } b \textbf{ else } c \;=\; \textbf{if } a \textbf{ then } b \textbf{ else } a \neq c$

Case Distributive Laws (Case Factoring)

$\neg \textbf{ if } a \textbf{ then } b \textbf{ else } c \;=\; \textbf{if } a \textbf{ then } \neg b \textbf{ else } \neg c$

$(\textbf{if } a \textbf{ then } b \textbf{ else } c) \wedge d \;=\; \textbf{if } a \textbf{ then } b \wedge d \textbf{ else } c \wedge d$

and similarly all operators distribute over the second and third operands of **if**

$\textbf{if } a \textbf{ then } b \wedge c \textbf{ else } d \wedge e \;=\; (\textbf{if } a \textbf{ then } b \textbf{ else } d) \wedge (\textbf{if } a \textbf{ then } c \textbf{ else } e)$

and similarly replacing $\wedge$ by any other operator

———End of Booleans

Generic

The operators $= \neq \textbf{ if } \textbf{ then } \textbf{ else }$ apply to every type of expression, with the axioms

$x = x$	reflexivity
$x{=}y \;=\; y{=}x$	symmetry
$x{=}y \wedge y{=}z \Rightarrow x{=}z$	transitivity
$x{=}y \Rightarrow (\cdots x \cdots) = (\cdots y \cdots)$	transparency
$(x{\neq}y) \neq (x{=}y)$	
$\textbf{if } \top \textbf{ then } x \textbf{ else } y \;=\; x$	
$\textbf{if } \bot \textbf{ then } x \textbf{ else } y \;=\; y$	

Note: in the transparency axiom, the context of x (denoted by dots around x) must be the same as the context of y (denoted by dots around y).

The operators $< \leq > \geq$ apply to numbers, characters, strings, and lists, with the axioms

$\neg\; x{<}x$	irreflexivity
$\neg(x{<}y \wedge y{<}x)$	antisymmetry
$x{<}y \wedge y{<}z \Rightarrow x{<}z$	transitivity
$\neg(x{<}y \wedge x{=}y)$	
$x{\leq}y \;=\; x{<}y \vee x{=}y$	
$x{>}y \;=\; y{<}x$	
$x{\geq}y \;=\; y{\leq}x$	
$x{<}y \vee x{=}y \vee x{>}y$	totality, trichotomy

———End of Generic

Numbers

Let d be a sequence of (zero or more) digits, let x, y, and z be numbers, and let a be boolean. Then the following are the axioms of Number Theory.

$d0+1 = d1$	counting
$d1+1 = d2$	counting
$d2+1 = d3$	counting
$d3+1 = d4$	counting
$d4+1 = d5$	counting
$d5+1 = d6$	counting
$d6+1 = d7$	counting
$d7+1 = d8$	counting
$d8+1 = d9$	counting
$d9+1 = (d+1)0$	counting (see Exercise 17)
$+x = x$	identity
$x+0 = x$	identity
$x+y = y+x$	symmetry
$x+(y+z) = (x+y)+z$	associativity
$-\infty<x<\infty \Rightarrow (x+y = x+z \;\equiv\; y=z)$	cancellation
$--x = x$	self-inverse
$-(x+y) = -x + -y$	distributivity
$-(x\times y) = -x \times y$	semi-distributivity
$x-y = x + -y$	
$-\infty<x<\infty \Rightarrow x-x = 0$	inverse
$-\infty<y<\infty \Rightarrow x - y + y = x$	inverse
$-\infty<x<\infty \Rightarrow x\times 0 = 0$	base
$x\times 1 = x$	identity
$x\times y = y\times x$	symmetry
$x\times(y+z) = x\times y + x\times z$	distributivity
$x\times(y\times z) = (x\times y)\times z$	associativity
$-\infty<x<\infty \wedge x\neq 0 \Rightarrow (x\times y = x\times z \;\equiv\; y=z)$	cancellation
$-\infty<y<\infty \wedge y\neq 0 \Rightarrow x/y\times y = x$	inverse
$-\infty<x<\infty \Rightarrow x^0 = 1$	base
$x^1 = x$	identity
$x^{y+z} = x^y \times x^z$	
$x^{y\times z} = (x^y)^z$	
$0<1<\infty$	direction
$-\infty<x<\infty \Rightarrow (x+y < x+z \;\equiv\; y<z)$	cancellation, translation
$0<x<\infty \Rightarrow (x\times y < x\times z \;\equiv\; y<z)$	cancellation, scale

$$x<y \;=\; -y<-x$$ reflection

$$-\infty \leq x \leq \infty$$ extremes

$$\infty+1 = \infty$$ additive absorption

$$0<x \;\Rightarrow\; x\times\infty = \infty$$ multiplicative absorption

$$0<x \;\Rightarrow\; x/0 = \infty$$

$$-\infty<x<\infty \;\Rightarrow\; x/\infty = 0$$

———End of Numbers

Bunches

Let x and y be elements (booleans, numbers, characters, sets).

$$x\!:\!y \;=\; x=y$$ elementary axiom

$$x\!:\!A,B \;=\; x\!:\!A \;\vee\; x\!:\!B$$ compound axiom

$$A,A = A$$ idempotence

$$A,B = B,A$$ symmetry

$$A,(B,C) = (A,B),C$$ associativity

$$A`A = A$$ idempotence

$$A`B = B`A$$ symmetry

$$A`(B`C) = (A`B)`C$$ associativity

$$A,B\!:\!C \;=\; A\!:\!C \;\wedge\; B\!:\!C$$

$$A\!:\!B`C \;=\; A\!:\!B \;\wedge\; A\!:\!C$$

$$A\!:\!A,B$$ generalization

$$A`B\!:\!A$$ specialization

$$A\!:\!A$$ reflexivity

$$A\!:\!B \;\wedge\; B\!:\!A \;=\; A=B$$ antisymmetry

$$A\!:\!B \;\wedge\; B\!:\!C \;\Rightarrow\; A\!:\!C$$ transitivity

$$\text{¢}x = 1$$

$$\text{¢}(A, B) + \text{¢}(A`B) = \text{¢}A + \text{¢}B$$

$$\neg\, x\!:\!A \;\Rightarrow\; \text{¢}(A`x) = 0$$

$$A\!:\!B \;\Rightarrow\; \text{¢}A \leq \text{¢}B$$

$$A,(A`B) = A$$ absorption

$$A`(A,B) = A$$ absorption

$$A\!:\!B \;=\; A,B = B \;=\; A = A`B$$ inclusion

$$A,(B,C) = (A,B),(A,C)$$ distributivity

$$A,(B`C) = (A,B)`(A,C)$$ distributivity

$$A`(B,C) = (A`B), (A`C)$$ distributivity

$$A`(B`C) = (A`B)`(A`C)$$ distributivity

$$A\!:\!B \;\wedge\; C\!:\!D \;\Rightarrow\; A,C\!:\!B,D$$ confutation, monotonicity

$$A\!:\!B \;\wedge\; C\!:\!D \;\Rightarrow\; A`C\!:\!B`D$$ confutation, monotonicity

$null$: A induction

A, $null = A$ identity

A ' $null = null$ base

$¢ null = 0$ base

$¢A = 0$ $=$ $A = null$

$i: x, ..y$ $=$ $x \le i < y$ (for extended integers i, x, y, $x \le y$)

$¢(x, ..y) = y - x$ (for extended integers x, y, $x \le y$)

$-null = null$ distribution

$-(A, B) = -A, -B$ distribution

$(A, B) + null = null$ distribution

$(A, B) + C = A + C, B + C$ distribution

$(A, B) + (C, D) = A + C, A + D, B + C, B + D$ distribution

and similarly for many other operators (see the final page of the book).

———End of Bunches

Sets

$\{A\} \ne A$ $\${A\} = ¢A$

$\sim\{A\} = A$ $\{A\} \cup \{B\} = \{A, B\}$

$A \in \{B\}$ $=$ $A: B$ $\{A\} \cap \{B\} = \{A \text{ ' } B\}$

$\{A\} \subseteq \{B\}$ $=$ $A: B$ $\{A\} = \{B\}$ $=$ $A = B$

$\{A\} \in {}_2\{B\}$ $=$ $A: B$ $\{A\} \ne \{B\}$ $=$ $A \ne B$

———End of Sets

Strings

Let S, T, and U be strings; let i and j be items (booleans, numbers, characters, sets, lists, functions); let n be natural; let x, y, and z be integers.

$nil; S = S; nil = S$ $S; (T; U) = (S; T); U$

$\#nil = 0$ $\#i = 1$

$\#(S; T) = \#S + \#T$ $S_{nil} = nil$

$(S; i; T)_{\#S} = i$ $S_{T; U} = S_T; S_U$

$S_{(T_U)} = (S_T)_U$ $0*S = nil$

$(n+1)*S = n*S; S$ $i = j$ $=$ $S; i; T = S; j; T$

$i < j \Rightarrow S; i; T < S; j; U$ $nil \le S < S; i; T$

$x; ..x = nil$ $x; ..x+1 = x$

$(x; ..y) ; (y; ..z) = x; ..z$ $\#(x; ..y) = y - x$

———End of Strings

Lists

Let S and T be strings; let n be a natural number; let i and j be items (booleans, numbers, characters, sets, lists, functions).

$$\#[S] = \#S \qquad\qquad\qquad [S]^+[T] = [S; T]$$
$$[S]\, n = S_n \qquad\qquad\qquad [S]\, [T] = [S_T]$$
$$(\#S) \to i\,|\,[S; j; T] = [S; i; T] \qquad\qquad [S] = [T] \; \Longrightarrow \; S = T$$
$$[S] < [T] \; \Longrightarrow \; S < T \qquad\qquad [S; T]: [S]$$

Let L, M, and N be lists and n be natural.

$$(L\, M)\, n = L\, (M\, n) \qquad\qquad\qquad (L\, M)\, N = L\, (M\, N)$$
$$L\, (M^+N) = L\, M + L\, N$$

$$L\, null = null \qquad\qquad\qquad L\, (A,\, B) = L\, A,\, L\, B$$
$$L\, \{A\} = \{L\, A\} \qquad\qquad\qquad L\, nil = nil$$
$$L\, (S; T) = L\, S; L\, T \qquad\qquad\qquad L\, [S] = [L\, S]$$

$$L@nil = L \qquad\qquad\qquad L@i = L\, i$$
$$L@(S; T) = L@S@T \qquad\qquad\qquad nil \to i\,|\,L = i$$
$$(S; T) \to i\,|\,L = S \to (T \to i\,|\,L@S)\,|\,L$$

———End of Lists

Functions

Renaming Axiom — If v and w do not appear in D and w does not appear in b

$$\lambda v: D \cdot b \; = \; \lambda w: D \cdot (\text{substitute } w \text{ for } v \text{ in } b)$$

Application Axiom: If element $x: D$ Law of Extension

$$(\lambda v: D \cdot b)\, x = (\text{substitute } x \text{ for } v \text{ in } b) \qquad f = \lambda v: \Delta f \cdot f\, v$$

Axioms of Selective Union   Composition Axioms: If $\neg f: \Delta g$

$$\Delta(f\,|\,g) = \Delta f,\, \Delta g \qquad\qquad \Delta(g\, f) = \S x: \Delta f \cdot f x: \Delta g$$
$$(f\,|\,g)\, x = \textbf{if } x: \Delta f \textbf{ then } f\, x \textbf{ else } g\, x \qquad\qquad (g\, f)\, x = g\, (f\, x)$$

Function Inclusion Axiom   Function Equality Law

$$f: g \; = \; \Delta g: \Delta f \wedge \forall x: \Delta g \cdot f x: g x \qquad\qquad f = g \; = \; \Delta f = \Delta g \wedge \forall x: \Delta f \cdot f x = g x$$

Arrow Laws

$f: null \rightarrow A$

$(D \rightarrow A), (D \rightarrow B) = D \rightarrow A, B$

$A \rightarrow B: A`C \rightarrow B, D$

$f: A \rightarrow B = A: \Delta f \land \forall a: A \cdot fa: B$

Laws of Selective Union

$f | f = f$

$(g | h) f = g f | h f$

$(\lambda v: A \cdot x) | (\lambda v: B \cdot y) = \lambda v: A, B \cdot \textbf{if } v: A \textbf{ then } x \textbf{ else } y$

Distributive Laws

$(f, g) x = fx, gx$

$f (\textbf{if } b \textbf{ then } x \textbf{ else } y) = \textbf{if } b \textbf{ then } fx \textbf{ else } fy$

$(\textbf{if } b \textbf{ then } f \textbf{ else } g) x = \textbf{if } b \textbf{ then } fx \textbf{ else } gx$

Associative Laws

$f (g \ h) = (f \ g) \ h \quad \text{composition}$

$f | (g | h) = (f | g) | h$

Domain Axiom

$\Delta \lambda v: D \cdot b = D$

Cardinality Axiom

$\cent A = \Sigma A \rightarrow 1$

——————————————————————————————————End of Functions

Quantifiers

Let x be an element.

$\forall v: null \cdot b$

$\forall v: x \cdot b = (\lambda v: x \cdot b) x$

$\forall v: A, B \cdot b = (\forall v: A \cdot b) \land (\forall v: B \cdot b)$

$\forall v: (\S v: D \cdot b) \cdot c = \forall v: D \cdot b \Rightarrow c$

$\neg \exists v: null \cdot b$

$\exists v: x \cdot b = (\lambda v: x \cdot b) x$

$\exists v: A, B \cdot b = (\exists v: A \cdot b) \lor (\exists v: B \cdot b)$

$\exists v: (\S v: D \cdot b) \cdot c = \exists v: D \cdot b \land c$

$\Sigma v: null \cdot n = 0$

$\Sigma v: x \cdot n = (\lambda v: x \cdot n) x$

$(\Sigma v: A, B \cdot n) + (\Sigma v: A`B \cdot n) = (\Sigma v: A \cdot n) + (\Sigma v: B \cdot n)$

$\Sigma v: (\S v: D \cdot b) \cdot n = \Sigma v: D \cdot \textbf{if } b \textbf{ then } n \textbf{ else } 0$

$\Pi v: null \cdot n = 1$

$\Pi v: x \cdot n = (\lambda v: x \cdot n) x$

$(\Pi v: A, B \cdot n) \times (\Pi v: A`B \cdot n) = (\Pi v: A \cdot n) \times (\Pi v: B \cdot n)$

$\Pi v: (\S v: D \cdot b) \cdot n = \Pi v: D \cdot \textbf{if } b \textbf{ then } n \textbf{ else } 1$

$MIN \ v: null \cdot n = \infty$

$MIN \ v: x \cdot n = (\lambda v: x \cdot n) x$

$MIN \ v: A, B \cdot n = min (MIN \ v: A \cdot n) (MIN \ v: B \cdot n)$

$MIN \ v: (\S v: D \cdot b) \cdot n = MIN \ v: D \cdot \textbf{if } b \textbf{ then } n \textbf{ else } \infty$

$MAX \ v: null \cdot n = -\infty$

$MAX \ v: x \cdot n = (\lambda v: x \cdot n) x$

$MAX \ v: A, B \cdot n = max (MAX \ v: A \cdot n) (MAX \ v: B \cdot n)$

$MAX \ v: (\S v: D \cdot b) \cdot n = MAX \ v: D \cdot \textbf{if } b \textbf{ then } n \textbf{ else } -\infty$

$\S v:\ null\cdot\ b\ =\ null$

$\S v:\ x\cdot\ b\ =\ \textbf{if }(\lambda v:\ x\cdot\ b)\ x\ \textbf{then } x\ \textbf{else } null$

$\S v:\ A,B\cdot\ b\ =\ (\S v:\ A\cdot\ b),\ (\S v:\ B\cdot\ b)$

$\S v:\ A\text{`}B\cdot\ b\ =\ (\S v:\ A\cdot\ b)\ \text{`}\ (\S v:\ B\cdot\ b)$

$\S v:\ (\S v:\ D\cdot\ b)\cdot\ c\ =\ \S v:\ D\cdot\ b\wedge c$

Change of Variable Laws — If f distributes over bunch union and d is fresh

$\forall r.\, fD\cdot\ b\ =\ \forall d:\ D\cdot$ (substitute $f\,d$ for r in b)

$\exists r.\, fD\cdot\ b\ =\ \exists d:\ D\cdot$ (substitute $f\,d$ for r in b)

Identity Laws

$\forall v\cdot\ \top$

$\neg\exists v\cdot\ \bot$

Idempotent Laws — if $D\neq null$

and v does not appear in b

$\forall v:\ D\cdot\ b\ =\ b$

$\exists v:\ D\cdot\ b\ =\ b$

Specialization Law — if $x:\ D$

$\forall v:\ D\cdot\ b\ \Rightarrow\ (\lambda v:\ D\cdot\ b)\ x$

Generalization Law — if $x:\ D$

$(\lambda v:\ D\cdot\ b)\ x\ \Rightarrow\ \exists v:\ D\cdot\ b$

One-Point Laws — if $x:\ D$

and v does not appear in x

$\forall v:\ D\cdot\ v{=}x\Rightarrow b\ =\ (\lambda v:\ D\cdot\ b)\ x$

$\exists v:\ D\cdot\ v{=}x\wedge b\ =\ (\lambda v:\ D\cdot\ b)\ x$

Commutative Laws

$\forall v\cdot\ \forall w\cdot\ b\ =\ \forall w\cdot\ \forall v\cdot\ b$

$\exists v\cdot\ \exists w\cdot\ b\ =\ \exists w\cdot\ \exists v\cdot\ b$

Semicommutative Laws (Skolem)

$\exists v\cdot\ \forall w\cdot\ b\ \Rightarrow\ \forall w\cdot\ \exists v\cdot\ b$

$\forall x\cdot\ \exists y\cdot\ Pxy\ =\ \exists f\cdot\ \forall x\cdot\ Px(fx)$

Absorption Laws — if $x:\ D$

$(\lambda v:\ D\cdot\ b)\ x\wedge\exists v:\ D\cdot\ b\ =\ (\lambda v:\ D\cdot\ b)\ x$

$(\lambda v:\ D\cdot\ b)\ x\vee\forall v:\ D\cdot\ b\ =\ (\lambda v:\ D\cdot\ b)\ x$

$(\lambda v:\ D\cdot\ b)\ x\wedge\forall v:\ D\cdot\ b\ =\ \forall v:\ D\cdot\ b$

$(\lambda v:\ D\cdot\ b)\ x\vee\exists v:\ D\cdot\ b\ =\ \exists v:\ D\cdot\ b$

Distributive Laws — if $D\neq null$

and v does not appear in a

$a\wedge\forall v:\ D\cdot\ b\ =\ \forall v:\ D\cdot\ a\wedge b$

$a\wedge\exists v:\ D\cdot\ b\ =\ \exists v:\ D\cdot\ a\wedge b$

$a\vee\forall v:\ D\cdot\ b\ =\ \forall v:\ D\cdot\ a\vee b$

$a\vee\exists v:\ D\cdot\ b\ =\ \exists v:\ D\cdot\ a\vee b$

$a\Rightarrow\forall v:\ D\cdot\ b\ =\ \forall v:\ D\cdot\ a\Rightarrow b$

$a\Rightarrow\exists v:\ D\cdot\ b\ =\ \exists v:\ D\cdot\ a\Rightarrow b$

$a\Leftarrow\exists v:\ D\cdot\ b\ =\ \forall v:\ D\cdot\ a\Leftarrow b$

$a\Leftarrow\forall v:\ D\cdot\ b\ =\ \exists v:\ D\cdot\ a\Leftarrow b$

Splitting Laws — for any fixed domain

$\forall v\cdot\ a\wedge b\ =\ (\forall v\cdot\ a)\ \wedge\ (\forall v\cdot\ b)$

$\exists v\cdot\ a\wedge b\ \Rightarrow\ (\exists v\cdot\ a)\ \wedge\ (\exists v\cdot\ b)$

$\forall v\cdot\ a\vee b\ \Leftarrow\ (\forall v\cdot\ a)\ \vee\ (\forall v\cdot\ b)$

$\exists v\cdot\ a\vee b\ =\ (\exists v\cdot\ a)\ \vee\ (\exists v\cdot\ b)$

$\forall v\cdot\ a\Rightarrow b\ \Rightarrow\ (\forall v\cdot\ a)\ \Rightarrow\ (\forall v\cdot\ b)$

$\forall v\cdot\ a\Rightarrow b\ \Rightarrow\ (\exists v\cdot\ a)\ \Rightarrow\ (\exists v\cdot\ b)$

$\forall v\cdot\ a{=}b\ \Rightarrow\ (\forall v\cdot\ a)\ =\ (\forall v\cdot\ b)$

$\forall v\cdot\ a{=}b\ \Rightarrow\ (\exists v\cdot\ a)\ =\ (\exists v\cdot\ b)$

Duality Laws (deMorgan)

$\neg\forall v\cdot b \;=\; \exists v\cdot \neg b$

$\neg\exists v\cdot b \;=\; \forall v\cdot \neg b$

$- MAX\, v\cdot n \;=\; MIN\, v\cdot -n$

$- MIN\, v\cdot n \;=\; MAX\, v\cdot -n$

Domain Change Laws

$A:B \;\Longrightarrow\; (\forall v:A\cdot b) \;\Leftarrow\; (\forall v:B\cdot b)$

$A:B \;\Longrightarrow\; (\exists v:A\cdot b) \;\Rightarrow\; (\exists v:B\cdot b)$

$\forall v:A\cdot v:B \Rightarrow p \;=\; \forall v:A\,{}^{\backprime}B\cdot p$

$\exists v:A\cdot v:B \wedge p \;=\; \exists v:A\,{}^{\backprime}B\cdot p$

Solution Laws

$\S v:D\cdot \top \;=\; D$

$(\S v:D\cdot b):\, D$

$\S v:D\cdot \bot \;=\; null$

$(\S v\cdot b):(\S v\cdot c) \;=\; \forall v\cdot b\Rightarrow c$

$(\S v\cdot b),(\S v\cdot c) \;=\; \S v\cdot b\vee c$

$(\S v\cdot b)\,{}^{\backprime}(\S v\cdot c) \;=\; \S v\cdot b\wedge c$

$x:\S p \;=\; x:\Delta p \wedge px$

Extreme Laws — if $D\neq null$

$\forall v:D\cdot \; x \le (MAX\, v:D\cdot x)$

$\exists v:D\cdot \; x = (MAX\, v:D\cdot x)$

$\forall v:D\cdot \; x \ge (MIN\, v:D\cdot x)$

$\exists v:D\cdot \; x = (MIN\, v:D\cdot x)$

Connection Law (Galois)

$n\le m \;=\; \forall k\cdot \; m\le k \Rightarrow n\le k$

——End of Quantifiers

Specifications and Programs

For specifications P, Q, R, and S, and boolean b,

$ok \;=\; x'=x \wedge y'=y \wedge ...$

$x:= e \;=\; x'=e \wedge y'=y \wedge ...$

$P.\, Q \;=\; \exists x'', y'', ...\cdot$ (substitute x'' for x', y'' for y', ... in P)

$\wedge$ (substitute x'' for x, y'' for y, ... in Q)

$P\|Q \;=\; \exists x_P, x_Q, y_P, y_Q, ..., t_P, t_Q\cdot$

(substitute x_P for x', y_P for y', ..., t_P for t' in P)

$\wedge$ (substitute x_Q for x', y_Q for y', ..., t_Q for t' in Q)

$\wedge\; (x_P=x \Rightarrow x'=x_Q) \wedge (x_Q=x \Rightarrow x'=x_P)$

$\wedge\; (y_P=y \Rightarrow y'=y_Q) \wedge (y_Q=y \Rightarrow y'=y_P)$

$\wedge\; ...$

$\wedge\; t' = max\; t_P\; t_Q$

if b **then** P **else** $Q \;=\; b\wedge P\vee\neg b\wedge Q$

var $x:T\cdot P \;=\; \exists x, x':T\cdot P$

while b **do** $P \;=\;$ **if** b **then** $(P.\;$ **while** b **do** $P)$ **else** ok

repeat P **until** $b \;=\; P.\;$ **if** b **then** ok **else** **repeat** P **until** b

$Am\Rightarrow A'n \;\Longleftarrow\;$ **for** $i:= m;..n$ **do** $i:m,..n \wedge Ai \Rightarrow A'(i+1)$

wait until $w \;=\; t:= max\; t\; w$

assert $b \;=\;$ **if** b **then** ok **else** ($print$ "error". $t:= \infty$)

ensure $b \;=\; b\wedge ok$

$x' = (P \text{ result } e) \;=\; P. \; x' = e$

$c? \;=\; r := r+1$

$c \;=\; \mathcal{M}(r-1)$

$c! \, e \;=\; \mathcal{M}w = e \,\wedge\, \mathcal{T}w = t \,\wedge\, (w := w+1)$

$?c \;=\; \mathcal{T}r < t$

$(c?. \, P) \;\mathbb{I}\; (d?. \, Q) \;=\; \quad (?c \,\vee\, \mathcal{T}_c r_c \leq \mathcal{T}_d r_d) \,\wedge\, (c?. \, P)$
$$\vee \;\; (?d \,\vee\, \mathcal{T}_d r_d \leq \mathcal{T}_c r_c) \,\wedge\, (d?. \, Q)$$

$\textbf{chan } c{:} \, T{\cdot} \; P \;\;=\;\; \exists \mathcal{M}_c{:} \, [\infty{*}T]{\cdot} \; \exists \mathcal{T}_c{:} \, [\infty{*}xnat]{\cdot} \; \textbf{var } r_c, \, w_c{:} \, xnat := 0. \; P$

$ok. \, P \;=\; P. \, ok \;=\; P$	identity
$P. \, (Q. \, R) \;=\; (P. \, Q). \, R$	associativity
$\textbf{if } b \textbf{ then } P \textbf{ else } P \;=\; P$	idempotence
$\textbf{if } b \textbf{ then } P \textbf{ else } Q \;=\; \textbf{if } \neg b \textbf{ then } Q \textbf{ else } P$	case reversal
$P \;=\; \textbf{if } b \textbf{ then } b \Rightarrow P \textbf{ else } \neg b \Rightarrow P$	case creation
$P \vee Q. \, R \vee S \;=\; (P. \, R) \vee (P. \, S) \vee (Q. \, R) \vee (Q. \, S)$	distributivity
$(\textbf{if } b \textbf{ then } P \textbf{ else } Q). \, R \;=\; \textbf{if } b \textbf{ then } (P. \, R) \textbf{ else } (Q. \, R)$	distributivity

$ok \,\|\, P \;=\; P \,\|\, ok \;=\; P$	identity
$P \,\|\, Q \;=\; Q \,\|\, P$	symmetry
$P \,\|\, (Q \,\|\, R) \;=\; (P \,\|\, Q) \,\|\, R$	associativity
$P \,\|\, Q \vee R \;=\; (P \,\|\, Q) \vee (P \,\|\, R)$	distributivity
$P \,\|\, \textbf{if } b \textbf{ then } Q \textbf{ else } R \;=\; \textbf{if } b \textbf{ then } (P \,\|\, Q) \textbf{ else } (P \,\|\, R)$	distributivity
$\textbf{if } b \textbf{ then } (P\|Q) \textbf{ else } (R\|S) \;=\; \textbf{if } b \textbf{ then } P \textbf{ else } R \,\|\, \textbf{if } b \textbf{ then } Q \textbf{ else } S$	distributivity
$x := \textbf{if } b \textbf{ then } e \textbf{ else } f \;=\; \textbf{if } b \textbf{ then } x := e \textbf{ else } x := f$	functional-imperative
$\textbf{repeat } P \textbf{ until } b \;=\; P. \; \textbf{while } \neg b \textbf{ do } P$	
$\textbf{while } b \textbf{ do } P \;=\; \textbf{if } b \textbf{ then } \textbf{repeat } P \textbf{ until } \neg b \textbf{ else } ok$	
$\forall \sigma, \sigma'{\cdot} \, (\textbf{if } b \textbf{ then } (P. \; W) \textbf{ else } ok \Leftarrow W) \;\Rightarrow\; \forall \sigma, \sigma'{\cdot} \, (\textbf{while } b \textbf{ do } P \Leftarrow W)$	
$\forall \sigma, \sigma'{\cdot} \, (P. \; \textbf{if } b \textbf{ then } ok \textbf{ else } R \Leftarrow R) \;\Rightarrow\; \forall \sigma, \sigma'{\cdot} \, (\textbf{repeat } P \textbf{ until } b \Leftarrow R)$	

$\rule{11cm}{0.4pt}$ End of Specifications and Programs

Substitution

Let x and y be different state variables, let e and f be expressions of the prestate, and let P be a specification.

$\quad x := e. \; P \;=\; (\text{for } x \text{ substitute } e \text{ in } P)$

$\quad (x := e \,\|\, y := f). \; P \;=\; (\text{for } x \text{ substitute } e \text{ and independently for } y \text{ substitute } f \text{ in } P)$

$\rule{11cm}{0.4pt}$ End of Substitution

Conditions

Let P and Q be any specifications, and let C be a precondition, and let C' be the corresponding postcondition (in other words, C' is the same as C but with primes on all the variables)

$C \wedge (P.\ Q) \ \Longleftarrow \ C \wedge P.\ Q$

$(P.Q) \wedge C' \ \Longleftarrow \ P.\ Q \wedge C'$

$C \Rightarrow (P.Q) \ \Longleftarrow \ C \Rightarrow P.\ Q$

$P.\ C \wedge Q \ \Longleftarrow \ P \wedge C'.\ Q$

$P.\ Q \ \Longleftarrow \ P \wedge C'.\ C \Rightarrow Q$

C is a sufficient precondition for P to be refined by S if and only if $C \Rightarrow P \ \Longleftarrow \ S$.

C' is a sufficient postcondition for P to be refined by S if and only if $C' \Rightarrow P \ \Longleftarrow \ S$.

——End of Conditions

Refinement

Refinement by Steps (Stepwise Refinement) (monotonicity, transitivity)

If $A \ \Longleftarrow \ \textbf{if}\ b\ \textbf{then}\ C\ \textbf{else}\ D$ and $C \Longleftarrow E$ and $D \Longleftarrow F$ are theorems,

then $A \ \Longleftarrow \ \textbf{if}\ b\ \textbf{then}\ E\ \textbf{else}\ F$ is a theorem.

If $A \ \Longleftarrow \ B.C$ and $B \Longleftarrow D$ and $C \Longleftarrow E$ are theorems, then $A \ \Longleftarrow \ D.E$ is a theorem.

If $A \ \Longleftarrow \ B \| C$ and $B \Longleftarrow D$ and $C \Longleftarrow E$ are theorems, then $A \ \Longleftarrow \ D \| E$ is a theorem.

If $A \Longleftarrow B$ and $B \Longleftarrow C$ are theorems, then $A \Longleftarrow C$ is a theorem.

Refinement by Parts (monotonicity, confutation)

If $A \ \Longleftarrow \ \textbf{if}\ b\ \textbf{then}\ C\ \textbf{else}\ D$ and $E \ \Longleftarrow \ \textbf{if}\ b\ \textbf{then}\ F\ \textbf{else}\ G$ are theorems,

then $A \wedge E \ \Longleftarrow \ \textbf{if}\ b\ \textbf{then}\ C \wedge F\ \textbf{else}\ D \wedge G$ is a theorem.

If $A \ \Longleftarrow \ B.C$ and $D \ \Longleftarrow \ E.F$ are theorems, then $A \wedge D \ \Longleftarrow \ B \wedge E.\ C \wedge F$ is a theorem.

If $A \ \Longleftarrow \ B \| C$ and $D \ \Longleftarrow \ E \| F$ are theorems, then $A \wedge D \ \Longleftarrow \ B \wedge E \| C \wedge F$ is a theorem.

If $A \Longleftarrow B$ and $C \Longleftarrow D$ are theorems, then $A \wedge C \ \Longleftarrow \ B \wedge D$ is a theorem.

Refinement by Cases

$P \ \Longleftarrow \ \textbf{if}\ b\ \textbf{then}\ Q\ \textbf{else}\ R$ is a theorem if and only if

$P \ \Longleftarrow \ b \wedge Q$ and $P \ \Longleftarrow \ \neg b \wedge R$ are theorems.

——End of Refinement

Limits

$\exists p \cdot \forall n \cdot n \geq p \Rightarrow x\colon B_n \ \Longrightarrow \ x\colon \lim n \cdot B_n \ \Longrightarrow \ \forall p \cdot \exists n \cdot n \geq p \wedge x\colon B_n$

$\exists p \cdot \forall n \cdot n \geq p \Rightarrow b_n \ \Longrightarrow \ \lim n \cdot b_n \ \Longrightarrow \ \forall p \cdot \exists n \cdot n \geq p \wedge b_n$

——End of Limits

——End of Axioms and Laws

Symbols and Names

abs: $rat{\rightarrow}rat$ $abs\, r\ =\ $ **if** $r{\geq}0$ **then** r **else** $-r$

bool (the booleans) $bool\ =\ \top, \bot$

ceil: $rat{\rightarrow}int$ $r \leq ceil\, r < r{+}1$

char (the characters) $char\ =\ ..., \,{`}a, \,{`}A, ...$

div: $rat{\rightarrow}(\S r{:}\, rat{\cdot}\ r{>}0){\rightarrow}int$ $div\ x\ y\ =\ floor\,(x/y)$

divides: $(nat{+}1){\rightarrow}int{\rightarrow}bool$ $divides\ n\ i\ \ \equiv\ \ i/n{:}\, int$

int (the integers) $int\ =\ nat, -nat$

even: $int{\rightarrow}bool$ $even\ i\ \equiv\ i/2{:}\, int$

                                                $even\ =\ divides\, 2$

floor: $rat{\rightarrow}int$ $floor\, r \leq r < floor\, r + 1$

log (binary logarithm) $log\,(2^x) = x$

                                                $log\,(x{\times}y)\ =\ log\, x + log\, y$

lim (limit)   (see Axioms and Laws)

max: $rat{\rightarrow}rat{\rightarrow}rat$ $max\ x\ y\ =\ $ **if** $x{\geq}y$ **then** x **else** y

                                                $-\,max\, a\, b\ =\ min\,(-a)\,(-b)$

MAX (maximum quantifier)   (see Axioms and Laws)

min: $rat{\rightarrow}rat{\rightarrow}rat$ $min\ x\ y\ =\ $ **if** $x{\leq}y$ **then** x **else** y

                                                $-\,min\, a\, b\ =\ max\,(-a)\,(-b)$

MIN (minimum quantifier)   (see Axioms and Laws)

mod: $rat{\rightarrow}(\S r{:}\, rat{\cdot}\ r{>}0){\rightarrow}rat$ $0 \leq mod\, a\, d < d$

                                                $a\ =\ div\, a\, d \times d\ +\ mod\, a\, d$

nat (the naturals) $0, nat{+}1{:}\, nat$

                                                $0, B{+}1{:}\, B\ \Rightarrow\ nat{:}\, B$

nil (the empty string) $\#nil\ =\ 0$

                                                $nil; S\ =\ S; nil\ =\ S$

                                                $nil \leq S$

null (the empty bunch) $null{:}\, A$

odd: $int{\rightarrow}bool$ $odd\ i\ \ \equiv\ \ \neg\ i/2{:}\, int$

                                                $odd\ =\ \neg even$

ok (the empty program) $ok\ =\ \sigma'{=}\sigma$

                                                $ok.\, P\ =\ P.\, ok\ =\ ok \,\|\, P\ =\ P \,\|\, ok\ =\ P$

rat (the rationals) $rat\ =\ int/(nat{+}1)$

suc: $nat{\rightarrow}nat$ $suc\ n = n{+}1$

xint (the extended integers) $xint\ =\ -\infty, int, \infty$

xnat (the extended naturals) $xnat\ =\ nat, \infty$

xrat (the extended rationals) $xrat\ =\ -\infty, rat, \infty$

                                                $xrat\ =\ int/int$

Symbol	Page	Meaning		Symbol	Page	Meaning
T	3	true		( )	4	parentheses for grouping
⊥	3	false		{ }	17	set brackets
¬	3	not		[ ]	21	list brackets
∧	4	and		2	17	powerset
∨	4	or		¢	14	bunch size, cardinality
⇒	4	implies		$	17	set size, cardinality
$\Longrightarrow$	4	implies		#	18	string size, length
⇐	4	follows from, is implied by		#	21	list size, length
$\Longleftarrow$	4	follows from, is implied by				21, 26	selective union, otherwise
=	4	equals, if and only if		‖	120	indep't (parallel) composition
$=$	4	equals, if and only if		$\mathbb{I}$	135	input composition
⧧	4	differs from, is unequal to		~	17	contents of a set
<	12	less than		*	19	repetition of a string
>	12	greater than		Δ	25	domain of a function
≤	12	less than or equal to		→	21,27	function arrow
≥	12	greater than or equal to		∈	17	element of a set
+	12	plus		⊆	17	subset
⁺	21	list catenation		∪	17	set union
−	12	minus		∩	17	set intersection
×	12	times, multiplication		@	23	index with a pointer
/	12	divided by		λ	24	function, variable introduction
,	14	bunch union		∀	28	for all, universal quantifier
,..	16	union from (incl) to (excl)		∃	28	there exists, existential quantifier
‘	14	bunch intersection		Σ	28	sum of, summation quantifier
;	18	string catenation		Π	28	product of, product quantifier
;..	20	catenation from (incl) to (excl)		§	30	solutions of, solution quantifier
:	14	is in, bunch inclusion		′	37	x' is final value of state var x
:·	90	includes		`	13	`A is a character
::	68	refinement in place		"	22	"hello" is a text or list of chars
:=	38	assignment		a^b	12	exponentiation
.	39	dep't (sequential) composition		a_b	18,131	string indexing
·	24,28,70	variable introduction		$a\,b$	21,25,33	indexing,application,composition
!	132	output		?	132	(postfix) input, (prefix) probe

assert	82		**loop end**	75	
chan	141		**or**	82	
ensure	82		**repeat until**	75, 100	
exit when	75		**result**	83	
for do	79		**var**	70, 86	
frame	71		**wait until**	81	
go to	80		**while do**	74, 100	
if then else	5				

End of Symbols and Names

Precedence

0.   ⊤ ⊥ ( ) { } [ ] **loop end** numbers characters texts names

1.   @ juxtaposition

2.   +prefix −prefix ¢ $ # # * ~ $_2$ Δ → superscript subscript

3.   × / ∩

4.   + − $^+$ ∪

5.   ; ;.. ‘

6.   , ,.. |

7.   = ≠ < > ≤ ≥ : ∴ ∈ ⊆

8.   ¬

9.   ∧

10.   ∨

11.   ⇒ ⇐

12.   := :: ! ? **if then else while do   repeat until   exit when   for do   go to wait until   assert   ensure   or**

13.   λ· ∀· ∃· Σ· Π· §· *lim*· . ‖ Ⅱ **result var· chan· frame·**

14.   **= ⇒ ⇐**

On level 2, superscripting and subscripting serve to bracket all operations within them.

Juxtaposition associates from left to right, so that $a\,b\,c$ means $(a\,b)\,c$. The infix operators @ / − associate from left to right. The infix operators * → associate from right to left. The infix operators × ∩ + $^+$ ∪ ; ‘ , | ∧ ∨ . ‖ Ⅱ are associative (they associate in both directions).

On levels 7, 11, and 14 the operators are continuing. For example, $a = b = c$ neither associates to the left nor associates to the right, but means $a = b \,\wedge\, b = c$. On any one of these levels, a mixture of continuing operators can be used. For example, $a \leq b < c$ means $a \leq b \,\wedge\, b < c$.

On level 12, the precedence does not apply to operands that are surrounded by the operator.

On level 13, the function notation $\lambda v{:}\,D\!\cdot\,b$ surrounds D , so the precedence does not apply to D ; it applies to b . Similarly for ∀· ∃· Σ· Π· §· *lim*· **var· chan·** .

The operators **= ⇒ ⇐** are identical to = ⇒ ⇐ except for precedence.

——End of Precedence

The following operators distribute over bunch union: [ ] @ +prefix −prefix ¬ $ ~ superscript subscript × / ∧ ∩ + − ∨ ∪ ; ;.. ‘ λ *(left operand only)

——End of Reference

Texts and Monographs in Computer Science

(continued from page ii)

Texts and Monographs in Computer Science

Texts and Monographs in Computer Science

Texts and Monographs in Computer Science

(continued)

Study Edition

Edward Cohen
Programming in the 1990s: An Introduction to the Calculation of Programs
1990. XV, 265 pages